THE ESSENTIALS OF C# 4.0

THE ESSENTIALS OF C# 4.0

Arunesh Goyal

Topper, B.Sc. (H) Mathematics
Hitherto, Hon. Director, Institute for Studies in Mathematics
and
Related Sciences in Computers (ISMRSC), Delhi
M.C.A., University of Delhi, DELHI - 110 007

Formerly
Computer Analyst/Consultant, St. Stephen's Hospital, Delhi

KHANNA BOOK PUBLISHING CO. (P) LTD.

Ph.: 011-23244447-48 **E-mail: contact@khannabooks.com**

THE ESSENTIALS OF C# 4.0

Arunesh Goyal

Published by:

Khanna Book Publishing Co. (P) Ltd.

4C/4344, Ansari Road, Darya Ganj, New Delhi-110 002

Phone: 011-23244448 Telefax: 011-23244447

E-mail: contact@khannabooks.com

Website: www.khannabooks.com

Regd. Off: 1694-95, 1st Floor, Nai Sarak, Delhi-110006 (India)

Phone: 011-23283211 Telefax: 011-23256658

Printed in India by:

S.P.S. Printers & Binders, Delhi

To

GOD

The Generator!
The Operator!!
The Destroyer!!!

PREFACE

As is clear from the title, this book intends to make you learn practically the essentials of the C# Version 4.0 programming language. I shall briefly describe the structure and composition of the book in the following paragraphs.

This books deals exclusively and intensively with the C# 4.0 language. The book follows a step-by-step approach towards 'C#' learning. It deals with both the theoretical and practical aspects of the language.

The first chapter includes all that you need to get started with C#. It introduces the .NET Framework as it applies to C# besides the object-oriented paradigm consisting of encapsulation, inheritance, and polymorphism. It also discusses the evolution of C# and as to how closely it is related to C/C++ and Java. It introduces the various syntax rules, data types, and decision control constructs in addition to arrays and the basic gist of strings. The concept of classes, objects, command-line arguments and mathematical functions/methods is also described in short.

The second chapter is on classes, objects, and methods. It introduces the concepts of constructors, destructors, garbage collection, "this", public/private access, call by value/reference, ref and out parameters, params, object initializers, optional and named arguments, recursion, and static besides the Main() method and the command-line arguments taught in the first chapter in more detail.

The next chapter discusses operator overloading, a concept akin to method overloading, and its various nuances elaborately. It also brings forth the operator overloading constraints and the conversion operators, both implicit and explicit.

The fourth chapter of the book seeks to discuss single and multi-dimensional indexers, properties, and the get and set accessors, along with the constraints and restrictions on each one of them, respectively.

The fifth chapter is of vital significance as it forms the backbone of object-oriented languages like C#. It discusses inheritance, virtual methods, method overriding, abstract methods/classes, polymorphism, the universal data type, viz. object, and the concepts of boxing and unboxing vividly.

Interfaces, structures, and enumerations form the part of the next chapter. Herein, explicit interface member implementations, standard interfaces as supported by the .NET Framework, a comparative study between interfaces and abstract classes, the major point of difference between structures and classes, the overwhelming need for structures, that is to say, the why of structures, a real life case example of implementing an enumeration as well as the restrictions imposed on interfaces are brought out succinctly.

Exception handling has become, of late, one of the most important aspects of modern object-oriented languages. This is what is precisely discussed in the seventh chapter of the book. It teaches the art of handling run-time errors gracefully as well as the significance of the two keywords - checked & unchecked.

The final chapter of the book is on Input/Output (without which no language can survive in the world of computers), strings (which were introduced in the first chapter, but are discussed in depth over here), and formatting (by means of which one can make the output look more nice as well as accept input more conveniently).

There are ten case studies in all which are discussed in the foregoing chapters pertaining to wide ranging topics. We hope these will help you to see the practical side of applying C# in the real world and understand the theoretical subject matter of the text much better. Besides, there are about one hundred forty odd solved examples to help you out.

The appendix carries a set of thirty-five typical problems which you will do well to try your hand at in your own interest besides taking up the practical sessions affixed at the end of each chapter. In all, these amount to one hundred fifty practical problems and exercises. We are confident that if you can solve all these problems on your own, you will be on your way to mastering C#.

The glossary and the index section are for your ready reference. The glossary, in particular, has been designed so that you are able to understand much of the computer jargon associated with C# and the .NET environment in a big way.

I don't think anything else needs to be mentioned in this brief synopsis of the book. So, get ready to learn "The Essentials of C# 4.0"!

Arunesh Goyal

ACKNOWLEDGEMENTS

I would, in particular, like to acknowledge the spirited role played by my parents, Smt. Sita & Shri Rabinder Nath Goyal, in the face of adverse onslaught, and tricky circumstances and situations.

I would also like to offer my personal thanks and gratitude to Khanna Book Publishing Co. (P) Ltd., and in particular, to its managing director, Mr. Mukul Seth, for reposing his trust and faith in me in spite of the so many odd provocations I made on him.

Herein, I would also like to laud the role played by each and every one who came into interaction with me during the course of writing this book, nay the whole cosmos, as otherwise this work may perhaps would not have been possible.

But, above all, I would like to put on record and acknowledge my Sad_Guru_Dev, Shri Siddheshwar Baba (Formerly, Sh. B.S. Goel, M.A., Ph.D.; founder of Third Eye Foundation of India) for constantly encouraging me whenever my spirits were down and out. It is, indeed, rightly said:

"Gurura Brahma, Gurura Vishnu, Gurura Devo Maheshwara,
Gurura Sakshat Para_Brahma, Tasmai Shri Guruvey Namah:"!

Arunesh Goyal

AN ANECDOTE

"Success is not being intelligent; it's about how you apply your intelligence!"

A little anecdote shall prove the above point.

There were two friends, one from a rich family and the other one from a poor background. Both of them were intelligent and smart in their own ways. But each of them claimed to be more intelligent than the other guy. Soon, a quarrel ensued between them and they decided to approach a wise old man to decide the issue. Upon listening to their story, the wise man explained to them a technique for making a special recipe and asked both of them to cook it for him next day. "The one who shall prepare a tastier and better meal would be the winner!" he frowned.

Next day, the poor young man came with his cooked recipe at the appointed hour but there was no trace of the rich chap even after five hours. The young fella along with the old wise man then went to the rich friend's house only to find him in the kitchen pacing up and down. "What's the problem?", the wise person enquired. "Oh! You have not taught me properly. See, I have everything ready as told by you for more than eight hours now but the recipe is still not cooked", answered the flabbergasted rich young man.
"I see, why? Have you bothered to use your common sense and light the hearth?", the wise old man remarked. The rich man came to his senses immediately, understanding the cause of his predicament for so long. But, the battle had been lost by now.

Moral of the story: *Use your intelligence to earn money by all means but not at the cost of your name!*

CONTENTS

(At a Glance)

CONTENTS

(In Detail)

CHAPTER 1

GETTING STARTED WITH C#

1.0 INTRODUCTION

Created by Microsoft to support its .NET framework, C# builds on a rich programming heritage. C# (incidentally, C# is pronounced as "C Sharp") directly descends from C & C++. C# is also closely related to another very successful language, viz. Java. Building on the strong foundation that it inherits, C# adds several important innovations that advance the art of programming. Programming languages, throughout the history of computing, have evolved to accomodate changes in the computing environment and C# is no exception. Nothing demonstrates this fact more significantly than the release of its version 4.0. C# 4.0 is the first major revision to C# after its initial release, i.e., version 1.0 and subsequent revisions 2.0 and 3.0. In the intervening period, applications have become far more complex. To counter these changes, C# 4.0 has added a number of new features that provide for writing much more type-safe, reusable, and resilient code. This would become clearer as we go through the book and its chapters one by one.

1.1 EVOLUTION OF C#

C# was created by Anders Hejlsberg at Microsoft in the late 1990's as a part of its overall .NET strategy. Microsoft wanted a new language instead of Java to be developed mainly for two reasons.

Firstly, Java is not fully compatible with the Windows platform. Although Java programs do run on the Windows operating system (here, we, of course, assume that JVM, viz. the Java Virtual Machine has been installed) but, the fact remains that Windows and Java are not closely coupled. Now, considering the fact that Windows is one of the most widely used operating environments, this fact was a serious blow to Java's credentials as a programming language for Windows.

Second, there is the drawback of cross-language interoperability (mixed-language programming). In large distributed systems especially the Internet, such a component, i.e., cross-language interoperability assumes great proportions.

C# was Microsoft's and Hejlsberg's answer to these vital needs.And, its introduction of the concept of generics has revolutionized the computing era. Not only does it greatly expand C#'s expressive power by enabling the creation of type-safe, reusable code but the addition of generics has caused the Collections library to be vastly expanded.

1.2 HOW C# IS RELATED TO C, C++ & JAVA?

We have aready stated that C# is closely related to both C and C++, deriving its syntax from C and the object-oriented features from C++. C# is also very closely related to Java. In fact, the two are akin to close cousins sharing a common ancestry but differing in many significant ways. While, for instance, both support distributed programming and both use intermediate code to achieve safety and portability, the details differ a lot. C# includes delegates, events, properties, and indexers as language elements as well as syntax supporting attributes. Like Java, C# provides for a significant amount of run-time error checking and security. But, unlike Java, C# provides access to pointers. In this way, C# combines the raw power of C++ with the type-safety of Java. A person knowing both C++ and Java would find picking up the concepts of C# quite easy. But, nowhere does it amount to saying that anybody not familiar with C++ and Java would find picking up C# very hard. What is required is a logical creative mind. That's all!

1.3 C# & .NET FRAMEWORK

The .NET environment supports the development and execution of highly distributed component-based applications. C sharp (C#) was developed by Microsoft to enable writing of code for the .NET Framework. C# is closely coupled with the .NET Framework for another reason as well, i.e., the libraries used by C# are defined by the .NET Framework. This framework provides for mixed-language programming (in other words, cross-language interoperability as we have already stated). Related to C#, the .NET Framework (see Figure 1.1) defines two significant entities, viz. CLR (Common Language Runtime) and the .NET Framework class library. While CLR manages the execution of programs (enabling them to be portable, safe, secure and ensuring mixed-language programming as well!), the library provides access to the run-time environment (doing I/O, for instance.).

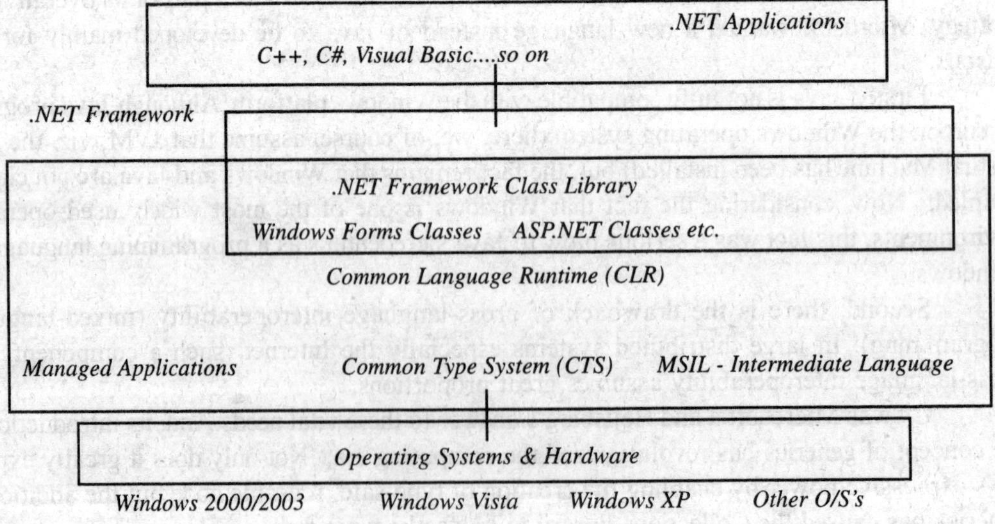

Figure 1.1 C# & .NET Framework

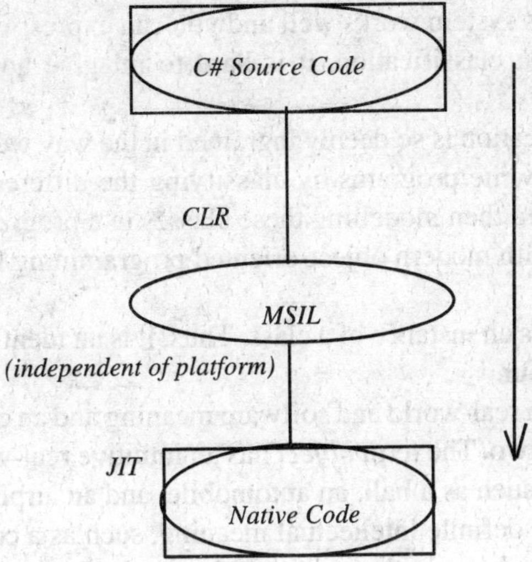

Figure 1.2 Portability of a C# program

We now give you an idea of how the Common Language Runtime works. When you compile a C# program, what you get is Microsoft Intermediate Language (MSIL) and not direct executable code. The concept is somewhat similar to the bytecodes of Java Virtual Machine (JVM). But, the two are not exactly the same. In this context, we recommend our forthcoming work - "The Essentials of JAVA".

MSIL is converted into executable code by JIT (Just-In-Time). When a .NET program is executed, CLR turns the JIT compiler 'ON'. The JIT compiler converts MSIL into native code. In this way, the C# program runs as native code in reality although it was initially converted into MSIL. The direct benefit of this fact is that the program runs almost as fast as it would have had it not been converted into MSIL initially with the additional gain of portability (see Figure 1.2).

1.4 THE OBJECT-ORIENTED PARADIGM UNFOLDED

C#' s object-oriented framework and for that matter any object-based programming language is based on three basic buzzwords, viz., encapsulation, inheritance, and polymorphism. In this context, it would be relevant and useful to define and describe two terms: a class and an object.

Class: A class is a group of data and methods that share some common properties and relationships.

Class is the root word of the term *classification.* When you design a class, you systematically arrange information and behaviour into a meaningful entity. This arranging is an act of classification and is something everybody does - not just programmers. For example, all cars share common behaviour (they can be steered, stopped, accelerated, and so on) and common attributes (they have a steering wheel, an engine, and so on). People use the word *car* to mean objects that share these common behaviours and attributes. As long as everyone agrees on what a word means, this system works well and you can express complex but precise ideas in a concise form. Without classification, it is hard to imagine how people could think or communicate at all!

Given that classification is so deeply ingrained in the way we think and communicate, it makes sense to try and write programs by classifying the different concepts inherent in a problem and its solution and then modelling these classes in a programming language. This is exactly what you can do with modern object-oriented programming languages, such as C#.

Object: An object is an instance of a class. Thus, it is an identifiable entity with certain characteristics and behaviour.

Objects have both a real-world and software meaning and an object model can describe a relationship between the two. The term *object* has an intuitive real-world meaning. There are concrete, tangible objects, such as a ball, an automobile, and an airplane. There are also more abstract objects that have a definite intellectual meaning, such as a committee, a patent, or an insurance contract. Objects have both attributes/characteristics and operations that can be performed on them. For example, a ball has a size, weight, a colour etc. and the ball can be thrown, caught, dropped etc. There can be varying relationships among classes of objects, e.g., an automobile is a special kind of vehicle or an automobile consists of an engine, a chassis, wheels, and other parts.

Objects can also be used in programs as you can set up a software model of a real-world system using a modeling language such as UML (Unified Modeling Language). The model can then be implemented as actual software using a programming language. A software system implemented in this manner is more faithful to the real system, and it can be changed more readily when the real system gets changed. Another advantage of objects in software is that they facilitate reusable software components.

1.4.1 Encapsulation

In order to use an object, it is not mandatory to have access to all of its attributes and methods or to know the details of its internal functions. What is more important is to know how to use the object, howsoever complex, without having to bother about the details of its production. This concept is called *encapsulation* and is an important principle when defining classes. The idea is that a program using a class should not have to worry how the class actually works internally; the program simply creates an instance of a class and calls the methods of that class. As long as those methods do what they say they will do, the program does not care how they are implemented.

A class might have to maintain all sorts of internal state information to perform its various methods. This additional state information and activity is hidden from the program which is using the class. That is exactly why encapsulation is sometimes referred to as information hiding.

Encapsulation actually has two purposes:

(1) To combine methods and data inside a class, that is to say, support classification;

(2) To control the accessibility of the methods and data, that is to say, to control the use of the class.

1.4.2 Inheritance

In C# programming, there is one class of the top of the hierarchy of every C# program, the 'object' class. Thus, all C# classes inherit attributes and methods from this 'object' class.

In common parlance, *inheritance* can have different and conflicting meanings. If someone bequeaths something to you in a will, you are said to inherit it. Again, we say that you inherit half of your genes from your mother and half of your genes from your father. Both of these uses of the word *inheritance* have little to do with inheritance in programming.

Inheritance in programming is all about classification - it is a relationship between classes. For example, when you were at school, you probably learned about mammals and that horses and whales are examples of mammals. Both have every attribute that a mammal does (it breathes air, it suckles its young, it is warm-blooded, and so on), but each also has its own special features (a horse has hooves, a whale has flippers and a fluke). From the object-oriented programming point of view, we can say that *mammals* is the base class having certain features while *horses* and *whales* are derived classes, which "inherit" the standard characteristics from the base class: *mammals*.

Thus, in inheritance, you abstract out common features of your classes and put them in a high level base class. You can add or change features in the specialized derived classes, which "inherit" the standard behaviour from the base class. In this way, inheritance facilitates code reuse and extensibility, and, is a key aspect of the object-oriented programming paradigm.

1.4.3 Polymorphism

Consider the problem of generating monthly statements for different kind of bank accounts. Current and savings accounts differ, with one possibly resulting in a fee and the other in a posting of interest.

A traditional approach would be to maintain a type field in an account structure and to perform processing in a switch statement, with cases for each type. Such use of switch statements is error prone and requires much maintenance when adding a new account type.

An alternative way is to localize the intelligence to generate a statement in each account class, which will support its own *GetStatement* method. Generic monthly statement code can then be written that will handle different types of accounts and will not have to be modified to support an additional account type. Provide a *GetStatement* method in the base class and an override of this method in each derived class. Call *GetStatement* through an object reference to a general *Account* object. Depending upon the actual account class referred to, the appropriate *GetStatement* method will be called.

This ability of the same method call to result in different behaviour depending on the object through which the method is invoked is termed as polymorphism. In fact, 'Poly' means 'many' As we shall see later on, C# paves the way to implement the "one interface, multiple methods" aspect of polymorphism.

Although somewhat advanced, polymorphism can greatly simplify complex systems and is a vital part of the object-oriented paradigm.

1.5 OUR FIRST C# PROGRAM

Now that we have discussed C#' s basic object-oriented nature, it's time to write our first C# program as given below:

```
// Our First C#  Program
/* We can call this:"First.cs";
Author: Arun; Date: 27/03/2011 */
class First
{
        static void Main( )
        {
                System.Console.WriteLine("This is our First C# Program!");
        }
}
```

This program can also be written as:

```
// Our First C#  Program
/* We can call this:"First.cs";
Author: Arun; Date: 27/03/2011 */
using System;
// Notice the change
class First
{
        static void Main( )
        {
                Console.WriteLine("This is our First C# Program!");
        }
}
```

Our first C# program, although quite short, deserves a closer look at some of the key features of any C# program. Let's take a brief look:

i. There are three types of comments allowed in C#. Two of them are exemplified by:
   (a) The single line comment beginning with //:
   ```
   // Our First C# Program
   // Notice the change
   ```
   (b) The multi-line comment begining with /* and ending with */:
   ```
   /* We can call this:"First.cs";
   Author: Arun; Date: 27/03/2011 */
   ```

   Note: The third type of comment is given ahead in section 1.7.3.

ii. Now, have a look at the *line*:

using System;

This line indicates that the program uses the namespace called *System*. This concept is similar to that in C++ and allows one set of names to be separate from the other. Thus, names in one namespace will not conflict with those in another. The program uses the namespace *System* reserved for items associated with the .NET Framework class library, which is the library used by C#.

iii. Again, take a look at the declaration:

```
class First
{
.........................................
.........................................
.........................................
.........................................
.........................................
}
```

This code creates a new class First with the help of the keyword *class* and the identifier *First* with the entire class definition being enclosed within the opening brace *{*" and the closing brace "*}*".

iv. Now, look at the declaration:

```
static void Main( )
{
            .................................................
}
```

This code begins the method *Main( )*.
The keyword *static* allows *Main( )* to be called without having to instantiate a particular instance of the class.This is essential as *Main( )* is involved at program startup.
The keyword *void* indicates that *Main( )* does not return any value. The body of *Main()* is enclosed within the opening brace "*{*" and the closing brace "*}*".

v. Finally, have a look at the code inside *Main()*:

Console.WriteLine("This is our First C# Program!");

This line results in the output:

This is our First C# Program!

followed by a new line.

Note that the above statement ends with a semicolon as do all statements in C#.

1.6 HOW TO COMPILE & RUN A C# PROGRAM

In C#, as in most of the programming languages, the name of the file containing the source code is arbitrary. In our first C# program (Refer Section 1.5), we called our program: *First.cs,* just as a common convention followed by most C# programmers (we could have called it by any name such as *XYZ.cs*, *Example.cs*, and so on). To compile this program, we can use the compiler *csc* at the command line as shown below:

C:\> csc First.cs

This would create the file *First.exe*. Now, we can run the program as follows:

C:\> First

This would result in the output as desired (assuming the .NET Framework is installed on the computer):

This is our First C# Program!

Note 1: In some programming languages, especially Java, the name of the program file is very important. However C# differs in this respect.

Note 2: We can also edit, compile, run, and debug a C# program using the Integrated Development Environment (IDE) supported by Visual Studio.

1.7 SYNTAX RULES

1.7.1 Instructions, Blocks & Expressions

An instruction is a command of any nature ending with a semi-colon (;) e.g.,

```
System.Console.WriteLine("This is our First C# Program!");
```

A group of instructions within the opening brace "{" and the closing brace "}" is called a block e.g.,

```
{
    System.Console.Write("This is our First C# Program!");
    System.Console.WriteLine;
}
// Note that output in both the cases above remains the same.
```

Some instructions have the effect of producing a value. Such instructions are referred to as expressions while the value returned is called the return value of the expression. For instance, consider the following three instructions:

```
int i = (j - k) / (l + m);
int i = 100;
obj.i = 100;
```

1.7.2 Identifiers

An identifier is the name by which a constructor, a variable, method, a class, an interface, a property, a delegate, or an event is referenced. There are certain rules for creating identifier names:

√ The first character must be a letter or an underscore _.

√ After this, the rest of the identifier can be built up of digits, letters, or underscore _. However, two consecutive underscores are prohibited.

√ The identifier can not contain any blanks, tabs, line or paragraph breaks.

√ Reserved keywords can not be used as identifiers (keywords are discussed in section 1.7.6). But, we can precede a keyword with a @ to use it as an identifier, e.g., *@if*.

√ Finally, remember that C# is case-sensitive. Thus, *main()* and *Main()* are different.

Also, there are some conventional rules as well:

√ The identifier should generally reflect that to which it refers.

√ For class/interface/property/delegate/event name, first letter of each word of the identifier should be uppercase.

√ For variable/method name, the identifier should begin with a lowercase letter. If the variable name consists of more than one word, then, the first word should begin with a lowercase letter while rest of the words should begin with uppercase ones.

√ For a constant name, all letters should be uppercase and in case of more than one word, the words should be separated by the underscore _.

Now we take up some examples of identifiers:

```
Num, num, _Num              // Correct
Complex theComplex;         // Correct
int number_Of_Oranges;      // Correct
3Three                      // Incorrect: 3 as first character
if                          // Incorrect: reserved word
num__max                    // Incorrect: two consecutive underscores
```

1.7.3 Comments

We have already discussed two type of comments allowed in C# (refer Section 1.5). C# also allows a third type of comment, i.e. the XML documentation comment beginning with /** and ending with */ e.g.,

```
/** <remarks>
        ......................................
        ......................................
    </remarks> */
```

1.7.4 Literals

A constant repersenting a constant value (that cannot be modified) is referred to as a literal. A literal can be a number (integer or float), a character, a string or a boolean, decimal or hexadecimal.

An integer can be a byte, sbyte, short, ushort, int, unit, long, or ulong . Byte is a 8-bit unsigned integer and sbyte is a 8-bit signed integer. Short is a 16-bit signed integer while ushort is a 16-bit unsigned integer. Int is a 32-bit signed integer while uint is an unsigned 32-bit integer. Long is a 64-bit signed integer while ulong is a 64-bit unsigned integer.

For integer literals, the type of literal is the smallest integer type that will hold it, beginning with int. We can store integer literals stored as long data by affixing 'l' or ' L' at the end of the literal value, as an unsigned integer by appending 'u' or 'U', as an unsigned long integer value by using 'ul' or 'UL', e.g. ,*97 is an int, 97u is a uint* and *97UL is of type ulong.*

A floating point value can be stored as float, or double: the default. We can force a literal to be stored as float by adding the suffix "f" or "F" and as a decimal by adding the suffix "m" or "M", e.g., *7.8f is a float* while *7.8M is a decimal.*

We can also use notations with exponents in the case of floating point literals by adding "e" or "E', followed by an exponent represented by an integer at the end of the literal, e.g., *double i = 7.8E7, double i = 7.8e-8.*

Boolean literals can take the values true or false, e.g.,
bool GOD = true, bool MATTER = false.

Character literals are represented by a single character between single quotation marks, e.g., *'a', 'B'* etc.

A hexadecimal literal must begin with a 0x, e.g., *the decimal number 14 is written as 0xE in hexadecimal notation.*

We will soon talk about string literals also.

But, first, we need to introduce the escape sequences. C#, like other programming languages, allows the use of special character escape sequences (Table 1.1).

Table 1.1 Character Escape Sequences

Escape Sequence	Meaning
\\	*Backslash*
\0	*Null*
\'	*Single Quotation Mark*
\"	*Double Quotation Mark*
\b	*Backspace*
\r	*Carriage return*
\t	*Horizontal Tab*
\v	*Vertical Tab*
\f	*Form Feed*
\n	*New Line (line feed)*
\a	*Alert (bell)*

String literals are represented by characters between double quotes, e.g., "blue". Additionally, you can also have a *verbatim string literal*, which begins with an @ followed by the quoted string. The contents of the quoted string are accepted as such and can span two or more lines so that you can include tabs, newlines etc. But, in general, you don't need to use the escape sequences. The only exception is that to obtain a double quote ("), you must include two double quotes in a row ("").

Let us now take up a case study to practically illustrate the various escape sequences as well as the different string literals introduced in this section.

String Literals & Escape Sequences - A CASE STUDY

In this case study, we shall demonstrate the various escape sequences, especially, \n, \t, and \" as well as the different string literals, especially, verbatim string literals by taking up a practical example program by way of *Example 1*.

Example 1

```
/* Demonstrates escape sequences in strings */
/* Demonstrates verbatim string literals */

/* Author: Arunesh; Date: 27/03/2011 */

using System;

class Demo_EscSeq_VerbStrLit
{
        static void Main( )
        {
                Console.WriteLine("First Line \n Second Line");
                \\ use \n

                Console.Writeline();

                Console.WriteLine("First \t Second \t Third");
                \\ use \t

                Console.Writeline();

                Console.WriteLine("\"What?\", he said.");
                \\ use \"

                Console.WriteLine();

                Console.WriteLine(@"Verbatim
                                String Literal
                                        spanning several lines.
                        ");
```

```
            Console.Writeline();

            Console.WriteLine(@"Tabbed output:
            1       2       3
            4       5       6
            ");

            Console.Writeline();

            Console.WriteLine(@"I always ask, ""Do you like C#?""");
            \\ use ""

        }
}
```

Output:

First Line
Second Line

First　　　　*Second*　　　　　　　*Third*

"What?", he said.

Verbatim
　　String Literal
　　　　spanning several lines.

Tabbed output:
1　　2　　3
4　　5　　6

I always ask, "Do you like C#?"

1.7.5 Data Types

C# is a strongly typed language. Thus, all operations are type-checked by the compiler for type compatability and illegal operations are not allowed. For instance, you cannot assign floating point values to integers as in C/C++.

In C#, there are three kinds of types:

(1) Value types;
(2) Reference types; and,
(3) Pointer types.

We now discuss these one by one in the following three subsections.

Note: A new data type known as *dynamic*, which causes type checking to be postponed until run-time, has been added by C# 4.0. It is an exception to C#'s normal compile-time type checking.

Table 1.2 C# Value Types

Type	Description
bool	*represents true/false values*
byte	*8-bit unsigned integer*
char	*character*
decimal	*numeric type for financial calculations*
double	*double-precision floating point*
float	*single-precision floating point*
int	*integer*
long	*long integer*
sbyte	*8-bit signed integer*
short	*short integer*
uint	*an unsigned integer*
ulong	*an unsigned long integer*
ushort	*an unsigned short integer*

1.7.5.1 Value Types

Value types directly contain their data. Each variable of a value type has its own copy of the data. Value types are typically allocated on the *stack* and are automatically destroyed when the variable goes out of scope. Values types include the thirteen simple/primitive types enumerated alphabetically in Table 1.2.

Out of the thirteen simple types, the *decimal* data type in C# is something new that is not built into C/C++. The *decimal* data type uses 96 bits and can precisely represent any decimal number up to 28 significant digits. This is especially handy and useful in financial calculations.

Again, in C/C++, the character width is typically 8 bits and uses the ASCII character set. But, in C#, as in Java, characters are akways 16 bits wide and are represented by the Unicode character set.

In addition to the thirteen primitive types, C# has three more value types, viz. structures, enumerations, and nullable types. We shall take up structures and enumerations in chapter 6 (discussion of nullable types is beyond the scope of this book).

1.7.5.2 Reference Types

Reference types do not contain data directly but only refer to data. Variables of reference types store references to data, called *objects*. Two different variables can reference the same object. Reference types are allocated on the *managed heap* and eventually get destroyed through a process known as *garbage collection* (see chapter 2).

Reference types include *strings*, *objects*, class types, array types, interfaces, and delegates. We shall be discussing all of these (except delegates) in due course.

1.7.5.3 Pointer Types

Pointer types are only used in *unsafe code* and this discussion is beyond the scope of this book.

Let us now take up a <u>case study</u> pertaining to the different data types (value types, especially the simple/primitive types) introduced in this section.

Simple/Primitive Types - A CASE STUDY

In this case study, we shall consider four examples (*Example 2 - Example 5*) to practically illustrate the various simple/primitive types taken up in this section.

Example 2

```
/* Number of seconds in a year */
/* Author: Arunesh; Date: 27/03/2011 */

using System;

class Demo_Byte_Short_Int_Long
{
    static void Main( )
    {
        long year_seconds;
        int days_year = 365;
        short hours_day = 24;
        byte seconds_hour = 3600;

        year_seconds = days_year * hours_day * seconds_hour;

        Console.WriteLine("There are " + year_seconds + " seconds in a
                                                        year.");

    }
}
```

Output:

There are 31536000 seconds in a year.

Example 3

```
/* Compute the area of a circle with a given radius */
/* Author: Arunesh; Date: 27/03/2011 */

using System;

class Demo_Float_Double
{
```

```
    static void Main( )
    {
        float r, pi = 3.14;
        double a;
        r = 5.25;
        a = pi * r * r;

        Console.WriteLine("Area of circle with radius " +  r + " units is"
                                        + a + " sq. units.);
    }
}
```

Output:

Area of circle with radius 5.25 units is 86.54625 sq. units.

Example 4

```
/* Compute Future Value of an Investment */
/* Author: Arunesh; Date: 27/03/2011 */

using System;

class Demo_Decimal
{
    static void Main( )
    {
        decimal investment = 1000.0m;
        decimal interest = 0.07m;
        int years = 10;

        Console.WriteLine("Investment = Rs." + investment);
        Console.WriteLine("Rate of  interest = " + interest);
        Console.WriteLine("For " + years + " years");

        for (int z = 0; z < years; z++)
        // for loops are discussed later in this chapter
            investment = investment + (investment * interest);

        Console.WriteLine("Future Value = Rs." + investment);
    }
}
```

Output:

Investment = Rs.1000
Rate of interest = 0.07
For 10 years
Future Value = Rs.1967.1513572895653224900000

/* In *Example 4*, note the use of the suffix 'm' to the decimal constants; also note that the *Future Value* is accurate to several decimal places; we shall learn in chapter 8 how to format such results more appealingly, attractively, and effectively.
*/

Example 5

```
/* Boolean variables */
/* Author: Arunesh; Date: 27/03/2011 */

using System;

class Demo_Boolean
{
        static void Main( )
        {
                bool bvar = true;
                if (bvar)
                        Console.WriteLine("Value of bvar is" +  bvar);

                Console.Writeline();

                bvar = ( 1 > 2);
                if (bvar = false)
                        Console.WriteLine("Value of bvar is now " +  bvar);
        }
}
```

Output:

Value of bvar is True

Value of bvar is now False

1.7.6 Keywords

A keyword is a *reserved word* that is used for a specific purpose. There are 80 keywords in C# enumerated as follows in alphabetical order:

abstract Used to declare a class and when certain methods of that class are declared.
as A binary operator type that casts the left operand type specified by the left operand.
base A variable similar to *this* except that it accesses a base class implementation of a member.
bool A logical data type that can be *true/false*.
break Used to exit a loop early.
byte A one-byte unsigned integral data type.
case Used to test a condition in the switch construct.
catch Used in exception handling along with *try*.
char A two-byte Unicode character data type.
checked A statement/operator enforcing arithmetic bounds checking on an expresion/ statement block.
class Used to declare a *class*.
const Used to declare a constant.
continue Used to prohibit a loop from running when a condition is fulfilled.
decimal A 16-bit precise decimal data type.
default Used in the *switch... case* construct as the *default case*.
delegate A type for defining a method signature.
do Used in a *do .... while* loop.
double A 64-bit floating point data type.
else Used with *if* statement.
enum A value type defining a group of named numeric constants.
event A member modifier for a delegate field/property.
explicit An operator defining an explicit expression.
extern A method modifier indicating that the method is implemented with unmanaged code.
false One of the values for *bool* data type.
finally Used with *try ... catch* block.
fixed A statement used to pin up a reference type so that the garbage collector shall not move it during pointer arithmetic operations.
float A 32-bit floating point data type.
for Used in the *for* loop to repeat a set of instructions.
foreach A variation of the for loop to iterate over collections etc.
get An accessor that returns the values of a property.
goto A jump statement that jumps to a label within the same method and scope.
if Used to test whether a condition is fulfilled.
implicit An operator defining an implicit expression.
in The operator used in the *foreach* loop.
int A 32-bit signed integral data type.
interface Used when an *interface class* is declared.
internal An access modifier indicating that the type/type modifier is accessible only to other types in the same assembly.
is A relational operator evaluating to true if the left operand's type matches, is derived from, or implements the type specified by the right operand.
lock A statement acquiring a lock on a reference-type object in order to operate multiple threads in cooperation.
long A 64-bit signed integal data type.

namespace	A set of types mapping to a common region called its namespace.
new	Used to instantiate a class.
null	Used to indicate a value that does not exist.
object	The type all other types derive from.
operator	A method modifier that overloads operators.
out	A parameter modifier specifying that the parameter is passed by reference and must be assigned by the method being called.
override	A method modifier specifying that a method of a class overrides a virtual method of the class.
params	A parameter modifier specifying that the last parameter of a method can accept multiple parameters of the same type.
private	Used to define a class, a variable or a *private* method.
protected	Used to define a class, a variable or a *protected* method.
public	Used to define a class, a variable or a *public* method
readonly	A field modifier specifying that a field can only be assigned once, either in its declaration or in type constructor's declaration.
ref	A parameter modifier specifying that the parameter is passed by reference and is assigned before being passed to the method.
return	Used to *return* a value or transfer control.
sbyte	A 8-bit signed integral data type.
sealed	A class modifier that specifies that the class cannot be inherited.
set	An accessor that sets the value of a property.
short	A 16-bit signed integral data type.
sizeof	An operator that returns the size (in bytes) of a struct.
stackalloc	An operator that returns a pointer to the specified number of value types allocated on a stack.
static	Used to define a class, a variable or a *static* method.
string	A predefined reference type that represents an immutable sequence of Unicode characters.
struct	A value type combining data and functionality in a single unit.
switch	Used in the *switch* ... *case* contruct.
this	Refers to the current object.
throw	Used in exception handling
true	One of the values for *bool* data type.
try	Used in the *try*... *catch* block for exception handling.
typeof	An operator that returns the type of an object.
uint	A 32-bit unsigned integral data type.
ulong	A 64-bit unsigned integral data type.
unchecked	A statement/operator that prevents arithmetic bounds checking on an expresion/ statement block.
unsafe	A method modifier/statement that permits pointer arithmetic to be performed within a particular block.
ushort	A 16-bit unsigned integral data type.
using	Specifies that types in a particular namespace can be referred to without requiring their fully qualified type names.
value	The name of the implicit variable set by the set accessor of a property.
virtual	A class-method modifier indicating that a method can be overridden by a derived class.
void	Used to indicate no return value.
volatile	Modifier to authorize an attribute of an object to be modified independently of a C# program.
while	Used in the *do* ... *while* loop and the *while*... loop.

1.7.7 Operators

C# classifies the operators into four categories - arithmetic, relational, logical, and bitwise (Tables 1.3 - 1.6).

Table 1.3 Arithmetic Operators

Arithmetic Operator	Result
+	*Addition*
-	*Subtraction (also unary minus)*
*	*Multiplication*
/	*Division*
%	*Modulus (remainder of division)*
++	*Increment*
--	*Decrement*

Note 1: The operator '+' is also used for concatenating character strings.

Note 2: Division by 0 and the modulus of a division by 0 generate a run-time exception error.

Note 3: The increment and decrement operators can either be prefixed or postfixed, e.g.

```
x --;   // Subtract 1 from the value of x after evaluating x
-- x;   // Subtract 1 from the value of x before evaluating x
```

Table 1.4 Relational Operators

Relational Operator	Result
==	*Equal to*
!=	*Not Equal to*
>	*Greater than*
>=	*Greater than or Equal to*
<	*Less than*
<=	*Less than or Equal to*

Table 1.5 Logical Operators

Logical Operator	Result
!	*Logical NOT*
&	*Logical AND*
|	*Logical OR*
^	*Exclusive OR (XOR)*
&&	*Short-Circuit Logical AND*
||	*Short-Circuit Logical OR*

In Table 1.5, we have two types of logical AND operators: & and the Short-Circuit &&. When the operator & is used, C# evaluates the value of the expressions on either side of the operator. But, if && is used, C# evaluates the value of the expression on the left hand side(LHS) of the operator. If it is false, the right hand side (RHS) expression is not evaluated and the result of the operation is false. Similar is the case with | and || operators. If the expression on the LHS of || is true, the RHS is not evaluated and the result of the operation is true.

Table 1.6 Bitwise Operators

Bitwise Operator	Result
~	*Bitwise Unary NOT (1's complement)*
&	*Bitwise AND*
|	*Bitwise OR*
^	*Bitwise Exclusive OR (Bitwise XOR)*
>>	*Shift Right*
<<	*Shift Left*

C# also includes a special *ternary* (three-way) operator that can replace certain types of *if-then-else* statements (see section 1.8 also for *if* statements as well as this special *ternary* operator). This is denoted by ?: and has the general form:

expression1 ? expression2 : expression3;

where, expression1 is any expression evaluating to a boolean value. If expression1 is true, expression2 is evaluated; otherwise expression3 is evaluated. The result of the operator is the final expression evaluated e.g.

result = denominator == 0 ? denominator : numerator / denominator;

Thus, if the denominator happens to be 0, the result of the division is 0; otherwise the result is the dividend of the division operation.

We also have the parantheses ( ) that can alter the precedence of the operations, the square brackets [ ] for array indexing, and the dot operator . to dereference objects.

Besies all these operators, C# also has assignment operators as given in Table 1.7.

Table 1.7 Assignment Operators

Assignment Operator	Result
=	*Assignment*
+=	*Addition Assignment*
-=	*Subtraction Assignment*
*=	*Multiplication Assignment*
/=	*Division Assignment*
%=	*Modulus Assignment*
&=	*AND Assignment*
|=	*OR Assignment*
^=	*Exclusive OR Assignment*
>>=	*Shift Right Assignment*
<<=	*Shift Left Assignment*

Table 1.8 details the complete precedence of C# operators right from the highest to the lowest. Note that op is any operator that can be used along with the assignment operator = as shown in Table 1.7.

Table 1.8 Operator Precedence

<table>
<tr><td colspan="10">From Highest</td></tr>
<tr><td>( )</td><td>[ ]</td><td>.</td><td>++</td><td>--</td><td>checked</td><td>new</td><td>-></td><td>typeof</td><td>unchecked</td></tr>
<tr><td></td><td></td><td></td><td>(postfix)</td><td>(postfix)</td><td></td><td></td><td></td><td></td><td></td></tr>
<tr><td>!</td><td>~</td><td>(cast)</td><td>+</td><td>-</td><td>++</td><td>--</td><td>sizeof</td><td>&</td><td></td></tr>
<tr><td></td><td></td><td></td><td>(unary)</td><td>(unary)</td><td>(prefix)</td><td>(prefix)</td><td></td><td>(address of)</td><td></td></tr>
<tr><td>*</td><td>/</td><td>%</td><td></td><td></td><td></td><td></td><td></td><td></td><td></td></tr>
<tr><td>+</td><td>-</td><td></td><td></td><td></td><td></td><td></td><td></td><td></td><td></td></tr>
<tr><td><<</td><td>>></td><td></td><td></td><td></td><td></td><td></td><td></td><td></td><td></td></tr>
<tr><td><</td><td>></td><td><=</td><td>>=</td><td>is</td><td>as</td><td></td><td></td><td></td><td></td></tr>
<tr><td>==</td><td>!=</td><td></td><td></td><td></td><td></td><td></td><td></td><td></td><td></td></tr>
<tr><td>&</td><td></td><td></td><td></td><td></td><td></td><td></td><td></td><td></td><td></td></tr>
<tr><td>^</td><td></td><td></td><td></td><td></td><td></td><td></td><td></td><td></td><td></td></tr>
<tr><td>|</td><td></td><td></td><td></td><td></td><td></td><td></td><td></td><td></td><td></td></tr>
<tr><td>&&</td><td></td><td></td><td></td><td></td><td></td><td></td><td></td><td></td><td></td></tr>
<tr><td>||</td><td></td><td></td><td></td><td></td><td></td><td></td><td></td><td></td><td></td></tr>
<tr><td>??</td><td></td><td></td><td></td><td></td><td></td><td></td><td></td><td></td><td></td></tr>
<tr><td>?:</td><td></td><td></td><td></td><td></td><td></td><td></td><td></td><td></td><td></td></tr>
<tr><td>=</td><td>op=</td><td>=></td><td></td><td></td><td></td><td></td><td></td><td></td><td></td></tr>
<tr><td colspan="10">To Lowest</td></tr>
</table>

Also, note that Table 1.8 presents an exhaustive and complete list of operators currently available in C# 4.0. And, while we have already covered most of these operators, we are going to discuss some others such as *new, checked, unchecked,* etc. in subsequent chapters, and leave the others such as => *(which is used in Lambda Expressions)*, out of our discussion.

1.7.8 Variables And their Scope & Lifetime

The basic unit of storage in a C# program is the variable. It is a combination of an identifier, a data type and an optional initializer with the most general form:

<data type> identifier [= value][, identifier [= value ....];

In all the examples so far, we have used only constants as initializers. However, C# permits variables to be initialized dynamically, using any expression that is valid at the point where the variable is declared.

The following program (*Example 6*) is a case in point.

Example 6

```
/* Dynamic Initialization of Variables */
/* Author: Arunesh; Date: 27/03/2011 */

using System;
class Demo_Dynamic_Initialization
{
        static void Main( )
        {
                int i1 = 3, i2 = 4;

                int i3 = Math.Sqrt((i1 * i1) + (i2 * i2));
                // i3 dynamically initialized

                Console.WriteLine(" Hypotenuse of triangle with sides " + i1  + "and "
                                + i2 " is " + i3);

        }

}
```

Output:

Hypotenuse of triangle with sides 3 and 4 is 5.0

1.7.8.1 Implicitly Typed Variables

In C#, it is mandatory for a variable to be declared before using it. Under normal conditions, the declaration includes the type of the variable followed by its name. Beginning with C# 3.0, however, this mandatory declaration of the type of the variable was taken off and it became possible to leave it to the compiler to decide the type of a local variable depending upon the value used to initialize the variable. This is termed as *implicitly typed variable*, which is declared using the keyword *var*, and it has to be initialized, e.g.,

var z = 3.75;

/* Since *z* is initialized with a floating point literal (whose type is *double* by default), the type of *z* is *double*. Suppose, we had used:

var z = 3.75f;

then, type of *z* would have been *float*.

*/

Example 7 demonstrates implicitly typed variables.

Example 7

```
/* Implicitly Typed Variables */
/* Author: Arunesh; Date: 27/03/2011 */

using System;
class Demo_Implicitly_Typed_Variables
{
        static void Main( )
        {
                var i1 = 3.0,
                var i2 = 4.0;
                // i1 and i2 are implicitly typed variables
                // they are of type double as they are initialized to double values

                var i3 = Math.Sqrt((i1 * i1) + (i2 * i2));
                // i3 is also implicitly typed variable
                // its type is also double since return type of Sqrt() is double

                Console.WriteLine(" Hypotenuse of triangle with sides " + i1   + "and "
                                        + i2 " is " + i3);

                // i3 = 1.1M;
                /* Note that once the type of an implicitly typed variable has been fixed, it
cannot be changed throughout its lifetime; that's why the above line has been commented out
as otherwise it would result in a compile-time error; i3 is implicitly typed and a double; so, we
cannot now change it to a decimal type. */
        }
}
```

Output:

Hypotenuse of triangle with sides 3.0 and 4.0 is 5.0

In general, you should avoid using *implicitly typed variables* unless and until special circumstances warrant their use. *Implicitly typed variables* were designed and introduced to address some special issues, the most important of which is the *Language-Integrated Query (LINQ)*, that is not described in this book.

Finally, only one *implicitly typed variable* can be defined in one declaration, e.g.,

var i1 = 3.0, i4 = 4.0;

is wrong and will cause a compilation error.

1.7.8.2 Variable Scope

All the variable that have been used so far were declared at the beginning of the *Main()* method. But, variables can be declared within any block in C# (a block begins with an opening curly brace '{' and ends with a closing curly brace '}'). Each time a new block is created, a new scope is also created. A scope determines what variables are visible to other parts of the concerned program. It also determines the lifetime of those variables. In general, variables declared within a scope are not accessible to code outside that scope. In fact, the variables within a scope are local to that scope and whence, protected from unauthorized access/modification. These scope rules form the very basis for encapsulation.

Further, scopes may be nested with the outer scope enclosing the inner scope. This implies that variables/objects declared in the outer scope shall remain visible/accessible to code within the inner scope. However, the reverse is false, that is to say, variables/objects declared in the inner scope shall remain hidden to code outside it.

We now take up an example (*Example 8*) to see the effect of nested scopes.

Example 8

```
/* Nested Variable Scope */
/* Author: Arunesh; Date: 27/03/2011 */

using System;
class Variable_Scope
{
        static void Main( )
        {
                int i;
                // known to all code within Main()

                i = 1;

                if (i == 1)
                {
                        int j = 2;
                        // known only to this block

                        Console.WriteLine(" i = " + i + " j = " + j);
                        // i & j are both known here

                        i = j /2;
                }
                j = 3;
                // Error! j not known here

                Console.WriteLine(" i = " + i);
                // i is still known here
        }
}
```

One of C#'s scope rules may surprise you, especially if you come from a C/C++ background. Even though blocks can be nested, variables in the inner scope cannot bear the same name as the ones in the enclosing scope. In C/C++, there is no such restriction. However, the designers of C# opined that such "name hiding" could well lead to programming errors and whence, disallowed it.

As a case in point, take the following example (*Example 9*).

<u>Example 9</u>

```
/* Tries to give the same name to variables in inner and outer scopes */
/* Author: Arunesh; Date: 27/03/2011 */

using System;
class Variable_Error
{
    static void Main( )
    {
        int i;

        for (i = 0; i < 3; i++)
        //for loops are discussed later in this chapter
        {
            Console.Writeline("value of i = " + i);

            int i = 0;
            // Error! i is already declared in Main()

            Console.Writeline("new value of i = " + i);
            // will not print

        }
    }
}
```

/* The C# program in *Example 9* is illegal and shall result in compile-time error!

*/

1.7.8.3 Variable Lifetime

As we shall learn in the following chapter, the lifetime of a variable/object is confined to its scope. This, in fact, implies that a variable shall not hold its value once it goes out of scope. In other words, variables/objects are created when they enter their scope, and destroyed when they leave their scope. Thus, if a variable declaration includes an initializer, then that variable shall be reinitialized each time it enters its block.

As a case in point, take the following example (*Example 10*).

<u>Example 10</u>

```
/* Lifetime of a vartiable */
/* Author: Arunesh; Date: 27/03/2011 */

using System;
class Variable_Lifetime
{
        static void Main( )
        {
                int i;

                for (i = 0; i < 3; i++)
                // for loops are discussed later in this chapter
                {
                        int j = 100;
                        // j is initialized to 100 each time the for block is entered

                        Console.Writeline("value of j = " + j);
                        // always outputs j = 100

                        j = -1;
                        Console.Writeline("new value of j = " + j);
                }
        }
}
```

<u>Output</u>:

```
value of j = 100
new value of j = -1
value of j = 100
new value of j = -1
value of j = 100
new value of j = -1
```

/* As we can see, *j* is reinitialized to 100 each time the inner '*for*' loop is entered; although it is subsequenly assined the value -1, this value is lost.

*/

1.7.9 Type Conversion & Casting

When one type of data is changed to another type of variable, an *implicit* widening type conversion will take place if the following two conditions are met:

(1) The two types are compatible; and,
(2) The destination type has a range which is greater than the source type.

For instance, *long* to *double* and *byte* to *int* are widening conversions. However, the reverse is not true, that is to say, there is no *implicit* conversion from *double* to *long* or from *int* to *byte* as they are not widening conversions.

Besides, there are no *implicit* conversions between *decimal* and *float* or *double*, or from numeric types to *char* or *bool*. Moreover, *char* and *bool* are incompatible, and whence, there is no *implicit* conversion between the two.

Thus, *implicit* type conversions apply only to widening conversions between compatible types. For all other cases, you must use a *cast*. A *cast* is an *explicit* type conversion with the most general form:

(cast) expression

where, *cast* is the specified data type to which you wish to convert the specified *expression.*

For example, given

float f1, f2;

if you want the expression *f1 / f2* to be of type *int,* you can say:

(int) (f1 / f2)

In this case, although *f1* and *f2* are of type *float,* the *cast* converts the result of the expression *(f1 / f2)* to *int.* The parentheses around *f1 / f2* are essential as otherwise, the *cast* to *int* will apply only to *f1* and not to the quotient. The *cast* is needed here since there is no *implicit* convesion from *float* to *int.*

If a *cast* involves a narrowing conversion, informatioin might be lost. For example, if a floating point value is *cast* to to an integer type, the fractional component will be lost due to truncation. Thus, if the value *3.34* is assigned to an integer, the resulting value will be simply *3* and *0.34* w ill be lost.

1.8 DECISION/PROGRAM CONTROL STRUCTURES/STATEMENTS

A programming language uses control structures to pave the way for the advancement and branching of the flow of execution based on changes to the state of the program. C#'s program control statements can be put in three distinct categories: conditional/selection, repetitive/iterative, and jump. We shall discuss one by one all of these in the following three subsections.

1.8.1 Conditional Statements

1.8.1.1 if

if puts a condition on the execution of an instruction. The test of the *<condition>* must return a boolean, i.e. true/false value.

Syntax 1

```
if (<condition>) <instruction>;
```

For example,

```
if (X > Y) System.Console.WriteLine(“X is Greater than Y”);
```

Syntax 2

```
if (<condition>) <instruction 1>;
else
 <instruction 2>;
```

For example,

```
if (X > Y) System.Console.WriteLine(“X is Greater than Y”);
else
System.Console.WriteLine(“X is Less than or Equal to Y”);
```

Syntax 3

```
if (<condition>)
{
        <instruction sequence>;
}
```

For example,

```
if (X > Y)
{
        System.Console.WriteLine(“X is Greater than Y”);
        System.Console.WriteLine(“Y is Less than X”);
}
```

Syntax 4

```
if (<condition>)
{
        <instruction sequence 1>;
}
else
{
<instruction sequence 2>;
}
```

For example,

```
if (X > Y)
{
        System.Console.WriteLine("X is Greater than Y");
        System.Console.WriteLine("Y is Less than X");
}
else
{
        System.Console.WriteLine("X is Less than or Equal to Y");
        System.Console.WriteLine("Y is Greater than or Equal to X");
}
```

It is also possible to interlink the conditions by means of the *if-else if - else* ladder.

Syntax 5

```
if (<condition 1>)
{
        <instruction sequence 1>;
}
else if (<condition 2>)
{
        <instruction sequence 2>;
}
else if (<condition 3>
{
        <instruction sequence 3>;
}
else if (X < Y)
{
..................................................... //    conditions 4,
.................................................... //                5,
.................................................... //                6 etc.
else            // none of the above conditions 1,2 3, 4, 5, 6 etc. is fulfilled
{
        <instruction sequence 7>;
}
```

For example,

```
if (X > Y)
{
        System.Console.WriteLine("X is Greater than Y");
        System.Console.WriteLine("Y is Less than X");
}
else if (X < Y)
{
        System.Console.WriteLine("X is Less than Y");
        System.Console.WriteLine("Y is Greater than X");
}
else
System.Console.WriteLine("X is Equal to Y");
```

1.8.1.2 exp_1 ? exp_2 : exp_3;

As already discussed in section 1.7.7, C# has the above expression (special *ternary* operator) also.

Here, if *exp_1* is true, *exp_2* is evaluated else *exp_3* is evaluated.

This is equivalent to:

```
if (exp_1)
        exp_2;
else
        exp_3;
```

For instance, consider the following example:

```
if (ball == "red")
        ball = "blue";
else
        ball = "white";
```

This is equivalent to the expression:

```
ball = (ball == "red" ? "blue" : "white");
```

1.8.1.3 switch

Rather than stringing together a series of *if-elseif-elseif .... -else* tests and statements, it sometimes makes more sense to use the *switch* statement that enables the running of a specified sequence of instructions depending on the value of a specified expression.

Syntax

```
switch (<test_expression>)
{
        case <value 1> : <instruction sequence 1>;
                         break;
        case <value 2> : <instruction sequence 2>;
                         break;
        case <value 3> : <instruction sequence 3>;
                         break;
        ..............................................................//      value 4,
        ..............................................................//      value 5,
        ..............................................................//      value 6,
        ..............................................................//          ,
        ..............................................................//          ,
        ..............................................................//        etc.
        default : <instruction sequence>;
}
```

As soon as a matching value is found, the corresponding instruction sequence is carried out and the following values are not checked. The *default* label can be used to execute an instruction sequence when there are no matches for the *test_expression*. The *break* statement is necessary to isolate each case. Howevwer, two or more cases may have the same instruction sequence. If a case value matches the *test_expression*, its corresponding instructions are executed and the *break* provides an early exit from the *switch* construct.

The *test_expression* must be of type *byte, short, int,* or *char,* or *string,* or of an *enumeration type*, and each of the values specified in the case statements must be of a type compatible with the *test_expression*. Also, each case value must be a unique literal (i.e., it must be a constant, not a variable). Moreover, duplicate case values are not allowed.

Let us now take up a case study as a practical demonstration of the *switch* construct.

switch statement - A CASE STUDY

In this case study, we shall çonsider an example program (*Example 11*) using the *switch* construct, and then debate on its possible output.

Example 11

```
/* Author: Arunesh; Date: 27/03/2011 */
using System;
class Demo_Switch
{
    static void Main( )
    {
        int mon = 6;
        string sea;
        switch(mon)
        {
            case 12:
            case 1:
            case 2:
                    sea = “Winter”;
                    break;
            case 3:
            case 4:
            case 5:
                    sea = “Spring”;
                    break;
            case 6:
            case 7:
            case 8:
                    sea = “Summer”;
                    break;
            case 9:
            case 10:
            case 11:
                    sea = “Autumn”;
                    break;
            default:
                    sea = “Invalid”;
        }
```

```
            Console.WriteLine("June is in the " + sea + " season.");
        }
}
```

/* Clearly, depending upon the value of the variable *mon*, there are five possible outcomes of the program.

These are enumerated as follows:

(1) *June is in the Winter season.*
{ for case values: 12, 1, and 2. }

(2) *June is in the Spring season.*
{ for case values: 3, 4, and 5. }

(3) *June is in the Summer season.*
{ for case values: 6, 7, and 8. }

(4) *June is in the Autumn season.*
{ for case values: 9, 10, and 11. }

(5) *June is in the Invalid season.*
{ for all other case values,
which is the default option. }

In our case, since the matching value of mon is 6, the correct result is the third outcome, that is to say, the output of the program is as follows.

Output:

June is in the Summer season.

*/

1.8.2 Iterative Constructs

1.8.2.1 while

Runs an *instruction sequence* while the *condition* is verified. The *condition* is tested before the loop is run. If, in the first test itself, the *condition* happens to be false, the loop shall never be run.

Syntax

```
while (<condition>)
{
        <instruction sequence>;
}
```

For example,

```
// a never ending infinite loop
while (true)
{
        System.Console.WriteLine("Infinite Loop");
}
```

1.8.2.2 do...while

In this case, the *condition* is after the loop. Thus, the *instruction sequence* is executed at least once and then is repeated as long as the *condition* is fulfilled, i.e., true.

Syntax

```
do
{
        <instruction sequence>;
}
while (<condition>);
```

For example,

```
// the loop runs as long as the variable v is not equal to 5
int v = 0;
do
{
        v++;
        System.Console.WriteLine("v:    ", + v);
}
while (v ! = 5);
```

Output:

```
        v:      1
        v:      2
        v:      3
        v:      4
        v:      5
```

1.8.2.3 for

This loop enables the execution of an *instruction sequence* a certain number of times repetitively as long as a *condition* is fulfilled, i.e., true.

Syntax

```
for (<counter = start>; <test counter>; <increment/decrement counter>)
{
        <instruction sequence>;
}
```

where,

<counter = start>: local initialization of the variable counter.

<test counter>: condition. If condition is true, the loop is executed.

<increment/decrement counter>: modifies counter in order to make the condition false after a certain number of passages throgh the loop. Otherwise, it becomes an infinite loop.

As a case in point, take *Example 12*.

Example 12

```
/* Testing for Primes: Simple Demonstration of the for loop */
/* Author: Arunesh; Date: 27/03/2011 */
using System;
class Demo_For
{
        static void Main( )
        {
                int n;
                bool  b = true;
                n = 14;
                for (int i = 2; i <= n/2; i++)
                {
                        if ((n % i )== 0)
                        {
                                b = false;
                                break;
                                // break statement is discussed in the next section
                        }
                }
                if (b)
                        Console.WriteLine(n + " is Prime.");
                else
                        Console.WriteLine("n + " is Not Prime.");
        }
}
```

Output:

14 is Not Prime.

Note that the following *for* loop:

for(; ;);

is an *infinite* loop.

Also, note that like all other programming languages, C# allows nested loops (one loop inside another).Here, the loops could be any combination of *while, do ... while* or *for* loops.

1.8.2.4 foreach

This loop cycles through the elements in a collection. Refer the section on arrays (section 1.9 to be precise) for more details.

1.8.3 Jump Statements

1.8.3.1 break

The *break* statement has two important uses. Firstly, we have already seen that it terminates a case statement in a *switch* construct. Second, it can be used to exit a loop (if a *break* statement is encountered inside a loop, the loop is terminated and program control resumes at the next statement following the loop) as we saw in *Example 12 (Testing for Primes.Simple Demonstration of the for loop).*

Now, we take up an example (*Example 13*) to see how the *break* statement can be used to exit from nested loops.

Example 13

```
/* break to exit from nested loops */
/* Author: Arunesh; Date: 27/03/2011 */
using System;
class Demo_Break
{
        static void Main( )
        {
                        for (int l = 0; l < 10; l++)

                        {
                                for (int m = 0; m < 50; m++)
                                {
                                        if (m == 5) break;        // exit both loops
                                        Console.Write(m + "    ");
                                }
                                Console.WriteLine("This shall NOT Execute!");
                        }
                        Console.WriteLine("Block one COMPLETE!");
        }
}
```

Output:

```
0    1    2    3    4    Block one COMPLETE!
```

1.8.3.2 continue

Sometimes we may wish to force an early iteration of a loop. This, in effect, is a *goto* past the body of the loop to the loop's end. In *while* and *do ... while* loops, a *continue* statement causes the control to be transferred to the *condition* of the loops but in a *for* loop, control first goes to the *iteration,* i.e. *increment/decrement* portion and then to the *condition/test* part of the loop. For all these three loops, any intermediate code is bypassed.

Consider *Example 14* as a case in point.

Example 14

```
/* continue to force an early iteration of the while loop */
/* Author: Arunesh; Date: 27/03/2011 */
using System;
class Demo_Continue
{
    static void Main( )
    {
        i = 0;

        while (i <= 5)
        {
            Console.Write(i + "        ");

            i = i + 1;

            if ((i % 2) == 0)
                continue;
            /* if i is even,
                go to beginning condition of loop */

            Console.WriteLine();
        }
    }
}
```

Output:

```
0    1
2    3
4    5
```

1.8.3.3 *return*

A complete discussion of this statement cannot be taken up until we have discussed the concept of methods in a later chapter. For now, we take a preliminary look at it.

At any time in a method, the *return* statement might be used to cause execution to branch back to the caller of the method. In other words, the *return* statement terminates the method in which it is executed immediately.

Consider *Example 15* as a case in point.

Example 15

```
/* Using the return statement */
/* Author: Arunesh; Date: 27/03/2011 */
using System;
class Demo_Return
{
        static void Main( )
        {
                bool b = true;

                Console.WriteLine("Before Returning!");

                if (b)
                        return;
                // back to caller

                Console.WriteLine("This shall NOT print!");
        }
}
```

Output:

Before Returning!

/* Note that the *if(b)* statement is necessary because if it is not there, the C# compiler would flash an "unreachable code" error as it would know that the last *WriteLine()* statement would never be executed, in effect, and is thus unreachable.

The *if* statement has been used as a way to to eliminate this compiler error (it is done to trick the compiler) and demonstrate the *return* statement here.

*/

1.8.3.4 goto

This is C#'s unconditional jump statement, i.e., the program flow goes to the label specified by *goto*. This statement should be avoided as far as possible as sometimes, it can become difficult to understand the flow of control and consequently unwanted/unexpected results.

But certain situations may warrant the use of *goto*, to exit from a deeply nested routine. Take, for instance, *Example 16*.

Example 16

```
/* Using the goto statement */
/* Author: Arunesh; Date: 27/03/2011 */
using System;
class Demo_Goto
{
        static void Main( )
        {
                int l , m, n;
                Console.WriteLine("l \t m \t n");
                for (l = 1; l < 15; l++)
                        for(m = 1; m < 15; m++)
                                for(n = 1; n < 15; n++)
                                {
                                        Console.WriteLine(l + "\t" + m + "\t" + n);
                                        if (n == 10)
                                                goto halt;
                                }
                halt:   Console.WriteLine("PROGRAM HALTED!");
        }
}
```

Output:

```
l    m    n
1    1    1
1    1    2
1    1    3
1    1    4
1    1    5
1    1    6
1    1    7
1    1    8
1    1    9
1    1    10
PROGRAM HALTED!
```

Note: The *goto* statement can also be used in a *switch* construct instead of the *break* statement. But, it should be used carefully as otherwise, one might lose the flow of control leading to undesirable outcomes.

1.8.3.5 exception handling

In addition to the *jump* statements discussed above, C# has another way by means of which the flow of execution of the program can be altered, viz., by means of *exception handling*. It is the means by which runtime errors can be trapped and handled. It is implemented by means of the keywords: *try, catch, throw,* and *finally*.

This *exception handling* mechanism allows the program to make a nonlocal branch, in effect .We shall take up this topic in detail in a separate chapter later on, in fact, chapter 7, to be precise.

1.9 ARRAYS

An array is a variable that contains a list of elements of the same type of simple or compound data such as a class. Each element is stored in its own cell that makes it easier to access the different elements of the array. An array variable can contain any sort of information: numeric (integers, floating-pont etc.), character strings (*string*), or any object. It is also possible to create a multi-dimensional array that is an array of arrays.

To use an array in C#, we declare the defined type of the variable, create the array object, and finally store the desired information iun the array. To declare an array variable, we use the following form:

<Type> [ ] <Name>;

where, *<Type>* represents the data type to be stored in the array and *<Name>* is the name of the array variable, e.g.

```
int [ ] i_arr;       //array of integer called i_arr
float [5] f_arr; //array of five floating-point variables f_arr[0], f_arr[1], ......,
                    f_arr[4]
complex [ ] compp;      // array of complex objects called compp
long [2,  3] l_arr;     /* 2 by 3 two-dimensional array with elements:
                        l_arr[0, 0], l_arr[0, 1], ..........., l_arr[1, 2] */
short [ , , ] s_arr;    // three-dimensional array of shorts called s_arr
```

Once an array variable is declared, we must fix its size and allocate it memory space. As arrays are C# *objects*, we should either use the *new* operator (we shall learn more about *new* and *objects* in the next chapter) to create a new instance in an array or directly initialize the contents of the array using accolade operators, viz., { }. We can use either of the two methods as given below:

```
<Type> [ ] <Name> = new  <Type> [nElements];or
<Type>  [  ] <Name> = {element1, element 2, ..............................., elementN};
```

where, *nElements* is the size of the array i.e., the number of cells and *N* is a whole number, e.g.

```
int [ , ] coordinates = new int [2, 3];
int  [ , ] coordinates = { {7, 8, 9}, {-1, -2, -3}};
```

Note: If we try to access, say, the sixth element of a five-element array, the *IndexOutOfRangeException* is raised during run-time (as already mentioned, *exception handling* has been treated as a separate chapter, in fact, chapter 7, to be more precise). Moreover, arrays are implemented as *objects*. So, to know the size of an array, we use the property *Length* (*properties* have been taken up as a separate topic in chapter 4), e.g.,

```
int [] y = new int [5];
int x = y.Length;
// x = 5;
```

Now, we take up a case study pertaining to arrays.

Arrays - A CASE STUDY

In this case study, we shall consider four examples (*Example 17 - Example 20*) referring to the various nuances and aspects of arrays. We shall also be briefly taking up *jagged* arrays, *implicitly typed* arrays, and the *foreach* loop, which is a variation of the *for* loop discussed already. We shall also illustrate the *foreach* loop with the help of an example program (*Example 21*) in the case study.

Example 17

```
/* Initializing a one-dimensional array */
/* Author: Arunesh; Date: 27/03/2011 */
using System;
class Init_1DimArray
{
    static void Main( )
    {
        int [ ] days_month = {31, 28, 31, 30, 31, 30, 31, 31, 30, 31, 30, 31};

        Console.WriteLine("April has " + days_month[3] + "days.");
    }
}
```

Output:

April has 30 days.

Example 18

```
/* Initializing a two-dimensional array */
/* Author: Arunesh; Date: 27/03/2011 */
using System;
```

```
class Init_2DimArray
{
        static void Main( )
        {
                int [ , ] d2_arr = new int [2, 3];
                int i, j, k  = 0;

                for ( i = 0; i < 2; i++)
                        for (j = 0; j < 3; j++)
                        {
                                d2_arr[i, j] = k;

                                Console.Write(d2_arr[i, j] + "        ");

                                k = k + 1;
                        }
                Console.WriteLine();
        }
}
```

Output:

0   1   2   3   4   5

Example 19

```
/* Manually allocating differing  second dimensions*/
/* Author: Arunesh; Date: 27/03/2011 */
using System;
class Array_Manual_Alloc
{
        static void Main( )
        {
                int [ , ] d2_arr = new int [3, ];

                d2_arr[0] = new int [1];
                d2_arr[1] = new int [2];
                d2_arr[2] = new int [3];

                int i, j, k  = 0;
```

```
            for ( i = 0; i < 3; i++)
                for (j = 0; j < (i + 1); j++)
                {
                    d2_arr[i, j] = k;
                    k = k + 1;
                }
            for ( i = 0; i < 3; i++)
            {
                for (j = 0; j < (i + 1); j++)
                    Console.Write(d2_arr[i, j] + "        ");
                Console.WritelLine();
            }
        }
}
```

Output:

```
        0
        1       2
        3       4       5
```

Example 20

```
/* Demonstration of the property Length*/
/* Author: Arunesh; Date: 27/03/2011 */
using System;
class Array_Length
{
        static void Main( )
        {
                int [ ] d11_arr = new int [5];

                int [ ] d12_arr = {2, 4, 6, 8};

                Console.WriteLine("Length of  d11_arr is " + d11_arr.Length);
                Console.Writeline();
                Console.WriteLine("Length of d12_arr is " + d12_arr.Length);
        }
}
```

Output:

Length of d11_arr is 5

Length of d12_arr is 4

Jagged Arrays

A *jagged array* is an array of arrays in which the length of each array can differ. A two-dimensional jagged array can be declared in the general form:

type[ ] [ ] array_name = new type [size] [ ];

where, *size* indicates the number of rows in the array. For instance,

```
int[ ] [ ] jagged = new int [3] [ ];
jagged[0] = new int [7];
jagged[1] = new int [6];
jagged[2] = new int [8];
```

Implicitly Typed Arrays

As already stated in this chapter, we can declare *implicitly typed variables* by using the keyword *var*. Using the same technique, it is also possible to declare *implicitly typed arrays*.

An *implicitly typed array* is declared by using the keyword *var*, but it is not followed by [ ]. Moreover, the array must be initialized at the time of declaration because the data type of its members shall define the element type of the array. And, all initializers must be of same or compatible type, e.g.,

```
var nums = new[ ] {6, 7, 8, 9, 10, 11};
// type of array nums is array of int and it has six elements
/* note that new [ ] has to be used even though the array is
        being initialized; it is not optional over here. */
var nums = new [ , ] {{6.6, 7.7}, {8.8, 9.9}, {10.10, 11.11}};
// nums is a 2-dimensional array of double;
// it has dimensions 2x3
```

You can also declare *implicitly typed jagged arrays*, e.g.,

```
var nums = [ ] {
            new [ ] {9, 10, 11},
            new [ ] {1.0m, 2.0m},
            new [ ] {3.3, 4.4, 5.5, 6.6, 7.7, 8.8}
           };
```

/* notice the use of *new [ ]* in two ways; it creates an array of arrays, and then, creates each individual array based on the number and type of members; all members in each individual array have to be and must be of same or compatible type. */

foreach Loop

As already mentioned, the *foreach* loop is a variation of the *for l*oop, which has been discussed already. The most general form of the *foreach* loop is:

foreach (type var_name in collection)
statement;

As per our promise, we shall now illustrate the *foreach* loop with the help of the following example program (*Example 21*).

Example 21

```
/* Demonstration of foreach loop */
/* Author: Arunesh; Date: 27/03/2011 */
using System;
class Demo_Foreach
{
        static void Main( )
        {
                int s = 0;
                int [ ] d = new int [5];

                for (int k = 0; k < 5; k++)
                        d[k] = k;

                foreach ( int x in d)
                {
                        s + = x;
                        Console.WriteLine("Value = " + x);
                }

                Console.writeLine("Sum = " + s);
}
```

Output:

Value = 0
Value = 1
Value = 2
Value = 3
Value = 4
Sum = 10

1.10 STRINGS: A BRIEF INTRODUCTION

In C#, string is a built-in data type. When we create a string literal, we are actually creating a string object. We can create string objects in two ways, either by assigning a reference to a string literal e.g.,

string s = *"Test";*

or, from a char array as shown below:

char [ ] c_arr = {'T', 'e', 's', 't'};
string s = new string(c_arr);

We can have <u>arrays of strings</u> e.g.,

string [ ] s_arr = {"This", 'is", "a", "test."};

Then, *s_arr* [0] = *"This";*
s_arr[1] = "is",
s_arr[2] = "a";
s_arr[3] = "test.";

Another thing to understand about strings is that objects of type *string* are <u>immutable</u> i.e., once a *string* object is created, its contents cannot be altered. This may look like a serious drawback but it is not on two accounts. First, if we need to change a string, we can always create a new string with the desired modifications. Second, unused string objects are automatically *garbage-collected* (we shall be discussing *garbage collection* in the next chapter). So, you need not worry or bother about discarded strings.

The *string* class contains several methods, some of which are given in Table 1.9.

Note that String is the only-integer type that can be used in the <u>switch</u> construct. For *string* objects, C# provides the operator '+' to concatenate two strings.To test two strings for equality, we can use the == operator or the != operator besides the *Equals()* method given in Table 1.9.

To obtain the value of an individual character of a string, you simply use an *index*. For example:

string str = "Testing";
Console.Wite(str[0]);
// This displays *"T"*, the first character of *"Testing"*
// Like arrays, string indexes begin at *0*

/* Also, note that you cannot assign a new value to a character in a string using an i*ndex*. An i*ndex* can only be used to obtain the value of a character in a string. This is because, as we have already stated, strings are <u>immutable</u>.

*/

Table 1.9 Some commonly used String Methods

Method	Meaning
static int Compare(string strA, strB, StringComparison comparisonType)	*Returns less than 0 if strA is less than strB; greater than 0 if strA is greater than strB; and 0 if the strings are equal; comparisonType specifies how the comparison is conducted*
bool Equals(string value, StringComparison comparisonType)	*Returns true if the invoking string is the same as specified by value; comparisonType specifies how the comparison is conducted*
int IndexOf(char value)	*Searches the invoking string fo the first occurrence of the character specified by valuer (an ordinal search is used); returns the index of first match; -1 on failure*
int IndexOf(string value, StringComparison comparisonType)	*Searches the invoking string for the first occurrence of the substring specified by value (an ordinal search is used); returns the index of first match; -1 on failure; comparisonType specifies how the comparison is conducted*
int LastIndexOf(char value)	*Searches the invoking string for the last occurrence of the character specified by valuer (an ordinal search is used); returns the index of first match; -1 on failure*
int LastIndexOf(string value, StringComparison comparisonType)	*Searches the invoking string for the last occurrence of the substring specified by value (an ordinal search is used); returns the index of first match; -1 on failure; comparisonType specifies how the comparison is conducted*
string ToLower()	*Returns a lowercase version of invoking string*
string ToUpper()	*Returns a uppercase version of invoking string*

We now take up a case study pertaining to the various facets, nuances, and aspects of strings.

In this case study, we shall be mainly dealing with the important features and concepts of strings in a practical manner, that is to say, by means of some practical case examples.

We hope you would enjoy the sheer practical experience and the sheer thrill of it, if one were to put it that way!

So, go on; read, absorb and understand!!

Strings - A CASE STUDY

In this case study, we take up three examples (*Example 22 - Example 24*) to demonstrate the various concepts of strings covered in this section.

Example 22

```
/* Demonstration of  string arrays*/
/* Author: Arunesh; Date: 27/03/2011 */
using System;
class Demo1_String
{
        static void Main( )
        {
                string [ ] sobj = { “ONE 1”, “TWO  2”, “THREE 3”};

                for (int k = 0; k < sobj.Length; k++)
                        Console.WriteLine(“sobj[ + k + “]: ” + sobj[k]);
        }
}
```

Output:

sobj[0]: ONE 1
sobj[1]: TWO 2
sobj[2]: THREE 3

Example 23

```
/* Controlling a switch statement with strings*/
/* Author: Arunesh; Date: 27/03/2011 */
using System;
class Demo2_String
{
        static void Main( )
        {
                string [ ] sobj = { “ONE 1”, “TWO  2”, “THREE 3”};

                foreach (string s in sobj)
                {
                        switch(s)
                        {
                                case “ONE1”:        Console.WriteLine(“one”);
                                                    break;
```

```
                case "TWO2":        Console.WriteLine("two");
                                    break;

                case "THREE3":      Console.WriteLine(Three");
                                    break;
            }
        }
    }
}
```

Output:

one
two
three

Example 24

```
/* Demonstration of  string methods and other string concepts*/
/* Author: Arunesh; Date: 27/03/2011 */
using System;
class Demo3_String
{
    static void Main( )
    {
        string sobj1 = "ONE1";
        string sobj2 = "TWO2";
        string sobj3 = sobj1 + "+" + sobj2;
        string sobj4 =TWO2"

        Console.WriteLine(sobj4);

        if (sobj4 != sobj2)
            Console.WriteLine(" NOT Equal");
        else
            Console.WriteLine("Equal");

        Console.Write("Length of sobj1:    ");
        Console.WriteLine(sobj1.Length);
```

```
            sobj2 = sobj2.ToLower();
            Console.WriteLine(sobj2);

            int indx = sobj3.IndexOf('O');
            Console.Write("Index of first occurence of O in sobj3:   ");
            Console.WriteLine(indx);

            indx = sobj3.LastIndexOf('O');
            Console.Write("Index of last occurence of O in sobj3:    ");
            Console.WriteLine(indx);
        }
}
```

Output:

ONE1+TWO2
Equal
Length of sobj1:   4
two2
Index of first occurrence of O in sobj3:   0
Index of last occurrence of O in sobj3:   7

1.11 AN APPLICATION WITH MULTIPLE (TWO) CLASSES

As in Java and C++, w can have an application with multiple *classes*.
Consider *Example 25* that uses two *classes* - C1 and C2, as a case in point.
We shall be dealing with *classes* in detail in the next chapter. The point here is to give you a preliminary idea about *classes* and how they are used in C#.

<u>*Example 25*</u>

```
/* A program with two classes */
/* Author: Arunesh; Date: 27/03/2011 */
using System;
class C1
{
        float radius;

        void get(float x)
        {
                radius = x;
        }
}
class C2
{
        static void Main( )
        {

                float area;

                Circle Circle1 = new Circle();
                /*  we shall take up new in the next chapter;
                for now, understand that it creates an object
                Circle1 */

                Circle1.get(5);
                // assigns value 5 to radius

                area = 3.14 * Circle1.radius * Circle1.radius;

                Console.WriteLine("area of Circle = " + area + " sq. units.");
        }
}
```

<u>Output</u>:

```
        area of circle = 78.5 sq. units.
```

1.12 USE OF COMMAND-LINE ARGUMENTS

Once again, as in Java and C/C++, we can use command-line arguments in C# as well (This is illustrated by the following example, *Example 26,* to be precise). Further, you may note that the concept of command-line arguments is discussed more elaborately in the next chapter.

Example 26

```
/* Demonstrates CommandLineArguments */
/* Author: Arun; Date: 27/03/2011 */
using System;
class Demo_Command-LineArguments
{
        static void Main(string [] args)
        // notice the Java -like change in the parametrers to Main( )
        {
                int ctr, k = 0;
                string str;
                ctr = args.length;

                if (ctr == 0)
                        break;

                Console.WriteLine("C#  is")

                while (k < ctr)
                {
                        str = args[k];

                        Console.WriteLine("args[" + k + "]: \t" + str + "." );
                        // notice the use of the escape sequence tab \t
                }

                Console.WriteLine("Number. of Command-Line arguments:\t" + ctr);
        }
}
```

A sample run:

C:> *Demo_Command-LineArguments* PORTABLE MULTITHREADED DYNAMIC
C# is
args[0]: **PORTABLE.**
args[1]: **MULTITHREADED.**
args[2]: **DYNAMIC.**
Number of Command-Line Arguments: **3**
(assuming that the program is called *Demo_Command-LineArguments*)

1.13 USE OF MATHEMATICAL FUNCTIONS/METHODS

Real-life problems frequently employ mathematical functions/methods such as *sin, cos, sqrt, log* etc.

C# supports all these functions/methods through the *Math* class in the *System* namespace.

The following example program (*Example 27)* invokes the *Sqrt()* method in the *Math* class of the *System* namespace so as to find the *square root* of the double precision floating point value *625.0*.

<u>*Example 27*</u>

```
/* Using Mathematical Functions */
/* Author: Arunesh; Date: 27/03/2011 */

using System;
class Square_Root
{
        static void Main( )
        {
                double i1, i2 = 625.0;

                i1 = Math.Sqrt(i2);

                System.Console.WriteLine("Square root of " + i2 + " is " + i1 + ".");
        }
}
```

<u>Output</u>:

Square root of 625 .0 is 25.0.

/* You may note that the *Sqrt()* method in the *Math* class of the *System* namespace returns a value of type *double* as well as takes an argument of type *double*.

It is precisely for this reason that we have declared the variables *i1* and *i2* to be of type *double*.In this particular case, the magnitude of the numbers invloved is not too great. Otherwise, had they been declared to be single precision *float* values instead, a *narrowing conversion* could have caused loss of vital data.

You may also note that we have already discussed the concepts of *narrowing* and *widening conversions* already in this chapter.
*/

PRACTICAL SESSION

#1 Distinguish between:
(a) An object and a class; and
(b) Inheritance and polymorphism.

#2 (a) List three major differences between C# and Java.
(b) List two major similarities between C# and Java

#3 Is C# a portable language? Support your answer with appropriate reason(s).

#4 Can we use a keyword in C# as a variable name? Why or why not? Elaborate.

#5 (a) How do we compile and run a C# program?
(b) Can we use command line arguments in C#? If yes, give a suitable example.

#6 What is a verbatim string literal? Elucidiate with suitable example(s).

#7 What are the simple data types used in C#? List with appropriate examples.

#8 (a) Explain the use of the keyword *var*.
(b) What is an implicitlty typed array?
(c) What is a jagged array? Explain with a suitable example.

#9 What do you understand by encapsulation? How is it relevant to C#? Elucidate.

#10 In what ways are arrays of strings different from those of value types?

#11 A recent research study suggests that a person's ideal weight is related to his/her height (in inches) according to the following equations:

*Female = 3.5 * height - 108*
*Male = 4.0 * height - 128*

Write a complete program that makes the user enter a starting and ending height, calculates the ideal weights for males and females, and finally stores the results in an array(s).

#12 (a) How do we type cast a data type in C#?
(b) What kind of type conversion is supported by C#?

#13 Indicate the valid and invalid variable names amongst the following giving reason(s) for your answer:

char *x+y* *_v* *var* *min__val* *finalmarks* *sum_total*

#14 Write a program to convert a given temperature in degrees celsius to fahrenheit.
{ Tip: Use the formula $F = 1.8\,C + 32.$}

#15 Point out the errors, if any, in the following codes:

i.
```
Class main
{
    static void Main()
    {
        int l = 100;
    }
}
```

ii.
```
class Scope
{
    static void Main()
    {
        int l = 100;
    }
    int l = 1;
}
```

#16 The present value of a future asset is determined by the number of years into the future at which the asset will bev received and the current market rate of interest. For instance, if I proimise to pay you Rs.100 ayear from now and the current interest rate is 5%, the present value of the asset is Rs.95.23. Stated differently, placing Rs.95.23 in the bank today at 5% interest would yield you Rs. 100 a year from now. The equation is:

$p = (a * 1) / (1 + i)^y$, where,

p is the present value,
a is the future amount,
i is the interest rate, and
y is the number of years into the future the asset is deferred.

How would you code this formula and why?
{Tip: Try to use *decimal* data type. }

#17 Point out the errors, if any, in each of the following C# statements:

i. `x = ++y * 10--;`
ii. `z = sqrt(16);`
iii. `a/ = b*c;`
iv. `u = /t;`
v. `i = j = 6.9, -8.7;`

#18 Determine the value of each of the following logical expressions given that:
x = 4; y = -6; z = 6;

i *x == y && z > x*
ii. *x > z || x < y*
iii. *x < z && z > x*
iv. *y > 0 || y < 0*
v. *x > 3 && z < 7 && y > -7*

#19 Distinguish between:

i. A *while* loop and a *do...while* loop.
ii. *break* and *continue.*

#20 Point out the error(s), if any, in the following program:

```
class Constants
{
    static void Main( )
    {
        const int k;
        int m = 99;
        k = 5;
        const int n = k * 50;
        System.Console.WreiteLine(k + m);
    }
}
```

#21 State True(T) or False(F):

i. One *if* can have more than one *else* clause.
ii. On encountrering a *continue* statement, the program continues as it is.
iii. A series of *if...else* statements can always be replaced by the *switch* construct.
iv. We can have duplicate case values in a *switch* statement.
v. On encountering a *break* statement, the program execution is terminated.

#22 Consider the following code fragment:

```
x = 4;
y = 4;
if (k > 0)
    x = x + 1;
    y = y - 1;
```

What shall be the values of x and y if:

i. *k = 2;*
ii. *k = 0;*

#23 Under what conditions you will prefer to use the ternary conditional operator *?:* over the *if....else* statements?

#24 Suppose a movie theatre charges half price for children aged 12 or under and adults aged 65 or older.
Write an *if* statemnent that accounts for this pricing policy.

#25 Assumning that a monetary asset grows by x percent each year, calculate the worth of the asset after n years. (use simple interest)

#26 Suppose a small pizaa sells for Rs.8, a medium one a rupee more, and a large pizza for a rupee more than the medium one. Assume that the variable *size* stores the custromer's selection and write the code to determine the final price.
{Tip: Use the *switch* construct.}

#27 "C# is the language of the future"! Comment, elucidate and elaborate.
{Tip: Compare C# with Java in this context! }

#28 Given that one inch equals 2.53 cm, write a loop that produces a listing showing the conversion into centimeters for lengths from one inch through two feet, with the interval between any two successive lengths being one inch.

#29 Given any whole number, write a program that computes and prints its factorial.
{ Tip: For a whole number *n, factorial n = n! = n * (n-1) * (n-2) * .... * 1.* }

#30 Using *for* loops, write a program to print the following pattern:

```
$    $    $    $    $
     $    $    $    $
          $    $    $
               $    $
                    $
```

#31 (a) Explain giving suitable examples the concept of:
i. *goto* statement;
ii. *return* statement.
(b) Distinguish betwen *goto* and *return* statements.

#32 Have the user enter a value using *command-line arguments* and display a message informing the user whether the integer number entered by him was even or odd *(0 is neither even nor odd).*

#33 Compare the *for* and *foreach* loops in terms of their functions, citing appropriate example(s), wherever necessary..

#34 Check the following code for compilation errors, if any, and rectify them:

```
using System;
class Value
{
    static void Main()
    {
        int value = 3;
        switch(value)
        {
            case 0:
                Console.WriteLine("Value = " + 0 + ".");
                break;
            case 1:
                Console.WriteLine("Value = " + 1 + ".");
                break;
            case 2:
                Console.WriteLine("Value = " + 2 + ".");
                break;
            case 3:
            case 3:
                Console.WriteLine("Value = " + 3 + ".");
                break;
            case 4:
                Console.WriteLine("Value = " + 4 + ".");
                break;
            case 5:
                Console.WriteLine("Value = " + 5 + ".");
                break;
            default:
                Console.WriteLine("Value < 0 || > 5.");
        }
    }
}
```

#35 Identify the error(s), if any, in the following code fragments:

(a)
```
if (code == true)
        System.Console.WriteLine("Passed");
else
        System.Console.WriteLine("failed");
```

(b)
```
if (code == 1)
        x = y + z;
else
        x = 0;
```

#36 Debug the following programs:

(a)
```
class Array_First
{
    static void Main()
    {
        int i_Arr [];
        for (int m = 0; m < i_Arr.length; m++)
        {
            i_Arr[x] = m;
            System.Console.Write(i_Arr[m] + "      ");
        }
        System.Console.WriteLine();
    }
}
```

(b)
```
class Array_Second
{
    static void Main()
    {
        String s_Arr [] =
            { "Robust", "Dynamic", "Portable",
            "Multithreaded"} ;
        for (int n = 0; n < s_Arr.length(); n++)
            System.Console.Write(s_Arr[n] + " ...   ");
        System.Console.WriteLine();
    }
}
```

#37 Check the following code for errors, if any, and rectify them:

```
class Check
{
    static void Main()
    {
        int i = 1000;
        if (i = 100)
            System.Console.WriteLine("Check = Right.");
        else    System.Console.WriteLine("Check = Wrong.");
    }
}
```

#38 Write a program with multiple (two) classes to calculate the area of a square with side 3 units.

#39 Pick out the errors, if any, in the following code fragment:

```
int m;
int x[ ] = int[5];
int[.]y = int[6];
for (m = 1; m <= 5; ++m)
        x[m] = y[m] = m;
x = y = new int[10];
for (m = 0; m < 5; ++m)
        System.Console.WriteLine(x[m]);
```

#40 Write a program to output the question: "Can you elaborate on how C# is the sharpest language in vogue today?".

CHAPTER 2

CLASSES, OBJECTS, AND METHODS

2.0 INTRODUCTION

This chapter elucidates classes, objects and methods. It elaborates the keyword *new*, constructors, destructors, the concept of "Garbage Collection", and the keyword *this*. It also explains in plain terms the *public* and *private* access to the members of a class. It goes on to discuss method overloading, call by value/reference, the *ref* and *out* parameters, the "params" keyword/ modifier, passing and returning of objects/arrays, *optional* and *named* arguments, the concept of "object initializers", the various forms of *Main()*, recursion, and the use of the keyword *static*.

The entire object-oriented concept of C# revolves around the "class". We already know that an object is an instance of a class. We have been using the most elementary form of a class in the first chapter mainly to encapsulate the *Main()* method. A class is the basis for object-oriented programming in C# (indeed, for that matter, for any computer language that uses object-oriented programming such as C++, Java etc.) because we need to encapsulate within the class any concept that we may wish to implement. And, class is the basic unit of encapsulation in C#. A class defines the form of an object. It defines both the data and the code, which will operate on that data. Since object is an instance of a class, the class specifies how to build or construct objects.

The concept of class is, thus, critical to C# and can be used to create/generate objects of its type. At this juncture, we must make one point absolutely clear. Inspite of all its importance, a class is but a logical abstraction. And, no physical representation of a class exists in memory unless and until an object of that class has been created/generated.

As already stated, a class puts data and the code operating upon it together into one programming unit. In other words, it combines data and members that operate upon this data into a single unit. This is what is meant by encapsulation, which as already explained in the previous chapter, is one of the central themes of object-oriented languages like C#.

The way a class combines its data and member methods, which operate upon this data, into a single entity will become clearer in the light of the following discussion in which we shall be elaborating and elucidating the most general form of a class in programming terms.

2.1 DEFINING A CLASS

To define a class, we need to declare its exact form, nature, and contents by specifying the data it contains along with the code that operates on this data. We need to tell you here that *data members* or *fields* declared inside a class could be instance variables / static variables (we shall discuss *static* towards the end of this chapter) while the *code* or *function members* are written in the form of methods, constructors, destructors, operators, indexers, properties, and events; the first three, namely, methods, constructors and destructors, we shall be discussing in this chapter itself while the rest of them (except events), we shall be taking up for discussion in subsequent chapters later on.

Thus, instance variables, or simply variables, and methods (similar to *functions* in C/ C++) are the members of a simple class, which can be defined using the keyword 'class'(a keyword, as we have learnt in the previous chapter, is a reserved word) in the following manner:

```
class   class-name
{
        // the following are all instance variables
        access_specifier type variable1;
        access_specifier type variable2;
        ..................................
        ..................................
        access_specifier type variableM;

        // the following are all methods
        access_specifier return_type method1(parameters)
        {
                // method1_body
        }
        access_specifier return_type method2(parameters)
        {
                // method2_body
        }
        ..................................
        ..................................
        access_specifier return_type methodN (parameters)
        {
                // methodN_body
        }
}
```

where, *class-name* is the user-defined identifier/name of the class while *access specifier* can be any of the three keywords, viz. *public*, *private*, or *protected*. We must note that in the absence of such a specifier, class members are private, by default, and are accessible only by other members of the class. The public class members, on the other hand, are accessible throughout the scope of their declaration. The protected keyword/access specifier has a role only in case of inheritance (refer Chapter 5 for a detailed account of inheritance).

2.2 GENERATING OBJECTS / ADDING METHODS

We know that an object is an instance of a class. We can use the keyword *new* to declare/create/generate an object by using the corresponding class-name as per the following most general format:

class-name object-name = new class-name();

where, *object-name* is the name of the object being defined/declared and *class-name* is the name of the corresponding class. For example,

Book EssentialsOfCsharp = new Book();
/ EssentialsOfCsharp is an instance of the class "Book".*
*Thus, EssentialsOfCsharp is an object of type "Book". */*

Now, consider the following declration:

Book book = new Book();

We can also split this up into two parts as:

Book book; // declaring a reference to an object
book = new Book(); // allocating a Room object

The first part declares *book* as a reference to an object of type *Book*. When, this gets executed, *book* has the value 'null' indicative of the fact that it does not point to an actual object as yet. If we try to use *book* at this time, we shall get a compilation error.

The second part allocates an actual object and causes a reference to it to *book*. When this gets executed, we can use *book* as an actual *Book* object. In real terms, however, *book* has simply the naming address of the actual *Book* object.

The following figure (Figure 2.1) is illustrative of what we have stated about the entity *book* thus far.

S.No.	*Part*	*Effect*
1.	*Book book;*	*null* ⟵ *book*
2.	*book = new Book();*	*Book Object* ⟵ *book*

Figure 2.1 Declaration of an Object of type Book

A word about the *new* operator. The *new* operator dynamically allocates memory for an object. Its most general form is:

class_var = new class_name();

where, *class_var* is the variable of the class type being created while *class_name* is the name of the instance of the class being created. What is important to understand is that *new* allocates memory for an object during run-time. If it is unable to allocate memory due to some reson such as insufficient memory space etc., a run-time exception occurs (incidentally, exception handling is being dealt with in a later chapter separately, in fact, chapter 7, as mentioned previously as well).

The *class_name* followed by parentheses introduces the constructors for that class. We shall be learning about constructors in detail in section 2.3. For now, it is sufficient to say that a constructor specifies what occurs when an object of a class is created. Constructors have many uses and form an important part of all classes. In the real world, most classes explicitly define their own constructors. If no constructor is defined, C#, by itself, supplies a default constructor, which initializes all the member variables to their default values (for most value types, the default value is 0; for *bool*, the default is *false*; and, for reference types, the default is null).

Now, consider the following code fragment:

```
Book book1 = new Book();
Book book2 = book1;
```

You might be tempted to think that *book1* and *book2* are two separate and distinct objects. You might also imagine that *book2* is being assigned to a copy of the object being referred to by *book1*.

Far from it! Both *book1* and *book2*, instead, refer to the same object so that any change to the object through *book2* shall affect the object to which *book1* is referring. This is illustrated in the form of the following diagram (Figure 2.2):

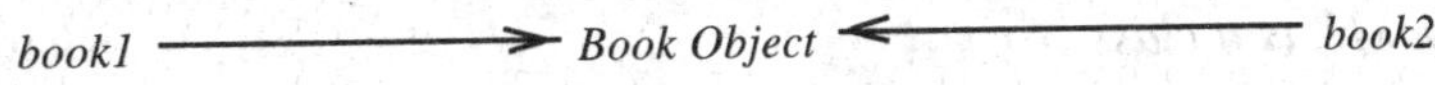

Figure 2.2 Both book1 & book2 Refer to the Book object

We would like to mention one more point here. Both *book1* and *book2* refer to the same object but have no other link to each other, e.g., consider the following code fragment:

```
Book book1 = new Book();
Book book2 = book1;
//......some..................................
//......other..................................
//......code..................................
book1 = null;
```

Thus, *book1* has been unhooked from the original object and set to '*null*' without affecting the original object or *book2*. In other words, *book2* still points to the original object *Book*.

The most general form of a method is:

access_specifier ret_data_type method_name(partameter_list)
{
// method_body
}

where, *ret_data_type* is the type of the data returned by the method (in the absence of *ret_data_type*, *void* must be mentioned instead), *method_name* is the name of the method while *parameter_list* is the list of parameters / arguments separated by commas(in the absence of any parameters, the *parameter_list* shall be empty). Also, *access specifier* can be any of the three keywords, viz. *public*, *private*, or *protected.* We must note that in the absence of such a specifier, the method is private, by default, and accessible only to other members of the class. The public methods, on the other hand, are accessible throughout the scope of their declaration (we shall declare most of the methods as public in this chapter so that they can be called by any other code in the program). As stated earlier in this chapter as well, the protected specifier has a role only in case of inheritance for which you may like to refer Chapter 5.

Methods having a return *data_type* other than *void* return a value to the calling routine in the following way:

return value;

where, *value* is the value that is returned by the method.

You can call a member of a class with the help of the dot (.) operator. Consider the following example (*Example* 28).

<u>*Example 28*</u>

```
/* Illustrates classes, objects, and methods */
/*Author: Arunesh; Date: 27/03/2011 */
using System;
class Book1
// "Book1" is a class
{
        private  int no_of_copies;

        public void display()
        // "display()" is a method
        {
                Console.WriteLine("Number of copies sold = " +  no_of_copies);
        }
}
class Books
{
        static void Main()
        {
                Book1 EssentialsOfCsharp = new Book1();
                // generate object EssentialsOf Csharp of  type Book1
```

```
            EssentialsOfCsharp.no_of_copies = 700000;

            EssentialsOfCsharp.display();
            // notice the dot operator
      }
}
```

Output of the above example (*Example 28*)? It is as follows:

Number of copies sold = 700000

A mild alteration of *Example 28* is the following example (*Example 29*) which shall serve to illustrate parameterized methods.

Example 29

```
/* Illustrates Parametrized Methods */
/*Author: Arunesh; Date: 27/03/2011 */
using System;
class Book2
// "Book2" is a class
{
      int no_of_copies;
      // private by default

      public void init(int n)
      // notice the parameter n passed to method init()
      {
            no_of_copies = n;
      }

      public void display()
      // "display()" is a method
      {
            Console.WriteLine("Number of copies sold = " + no_of_copies);
      }
}
class Books
{
      static void Main()
      {
                  Book2 EssentialsOfJAVA = new Book2();
                  EssentialsOfJAVA.init(700000);
                  EssentialsOfJAVA.display();
      }
}
```

Output of *Example 29*? It does not change but is the same as that of the previous one, that is to say:

Number of copies sold = 700000
// can you think, why?

2.3 CONSTRUCTORS

Typically, a constructor is used to give initial values to the instance variables defined by the class or to carry out other startup operations needed to create a fully formed object. The most general form of a constructor is:

```
access_specifier class_name(arg_list)]
{
        // code for constructor
}
```

where, the *access_specifier* is usually public since constructors are generally called from outside their class, *class_name* is the name of the particular class and the *arg_list* can either be empty or it can have one or more parameters.

In C#, value types are initialized to zero and reference types to null by the default constructor. We can also define our own constructors and in this case, they override the default constructor.. This constructor is a special method that is a member of the class with the same name as that of the the class and with no return type. But, a constructor can have an *acess_specifier* which is, in general, public, as stated above as well.

To understand the concept of constructors practically, consider the following program that creates the class stack (*Example 30*).

Example 30

```
/* Illustration of Constructor */
/* Author: Arunesh; Date: 27/03/2011 */
using System;
class stc
{
        public int stk[25];
        public int sz;

        public stc
        // Constructor Method
        {
                sz = 0;
                Console.Writeline("Stack Created.");
                /* This is just to illustrate the constructor. In actual practice, a
                constructor performs only initializations etc. */
        }
```

```
        public void  push (int k)
        {
                if (sz == 25)
                {
                        Console.Writeline("Stack FULL.");

                return;
                }
                stk[sz] = k;
                sz++;
        }

        public int  pop()
        {
                if (sz == 0)
                {
                        Console.Writeline("Stack EMPTY.");
                        return 0;
                }
                sz--;
                return stk[sz];
        }
}
class stc_demo
{
        static void Main()
        {
                stc s = new stc();
                // stc Object Created

                s.push(1);
                s.push(2);

                Console.Writeline(s.pop());
                Console.Writeline(s.pop());
        }
}
```

Output:

```
        Stack Created.
        2
        1
```

2.3.1 Parametrized Constructors

It is possible to pass parameters/arguments to constructors. These parameters are passed just as in the case of any other method and help in initializing an object when it is created. *Example 31* is a case in point.

Example 31

```
/* Illustration of a Parametrized Constructor */
/* Author: Arunesh; Date: 27/03/2011 */
using System;
class mycl
{
        public int i, j;

        public mycl(int x, int y)
        {
                i = x;
                j = y;
                // Parameters x, y used to initialize i, j
        }

        public void display()
        {
                Console.Writeline("\n" + i + "\t" + j);
        }
}

class mycl_demo
{
        static void Main()
        {
                mycl obj = new mycl(7, 8);

                obj.display();
        }
}
```

Output:

```
        7       8
```

2.3.2 Using 'new'

In section 2.2, we have already introduced 'new'. In general, the 'new' operator relates to classes and has the most general form:

new class_name(arg_list)

where, *class_name* is the name of the class being instantiated. The *class_name* followed by parentheses invokes the constructor for that class. In case a class does not declare its own constructor, 'new' uses the default constructor given by C#. Thus, 'new' can be used to create an object of any class type.

As a point of interest, it is permissible to use 'new' with the value types, e.g.,

int n = new int();

This calls the default constructor for type *int*, which initializes n to zero. in general, invoking 'new' for a value type invokes the default constructor for that value type. However, it does not allocate memory dynamically as for reference types. To be frank, it is not advisable to use 'new' with the value types.

2.4 GARBAGE COLLECTION & DESTRUCTORS

We have also seen how objects are dynamically allocated from a pool of free memory by using the *new* operator. In case of insufficient memory, the *new* operator fails and a run-time exception occurs (Exception Handling is discussed in chapter 7). For this reason, we need to reclaim the free memory from unused objects. In languages like C++, the *delete* operator is employed to achieve this but in C#, a more sophisticated technique is used, viz., *garbage collection.* The *garbage collection* system employed by C# works automatically without any programmer intervention. It reclaims memory when no references to an object exist and this recycled memory can then be used for subsequent allocation. But, there is a caveat. It is impossible to say when exactly *garbage collection* shall occur. It will not take place simply because one or more objects exist that are no longer in use. For example, unlike C++, it is not called when a variable containg a reference to an object goes out of scope.

It is possible to define a method that will be called prior to an object's final destruction by the garbage collector. This method is referred to as the *destructor* . It is declared exactly like the constructor except that it is preceded by the ~ (tilde) character. Note that it has no return type, no access specifier, and takes no arguments.To add a destructor to a class, simply include it as a member. It is called whenever an object of its class is about to be recycled. The code for a destructor specifies the actions to be carried out before an object is destroyed., which can be used in some extremely special circumstances to ensure that the object is destroyed cleanly, e.g., you might use a destructor so that a system resource used by an object is released.Thus, it should be clear that destructors are called before *garbage collection.* There is no precise way to know when a particular destructor shall be called or it shall be called at all as it is possible for for the program to terminate before *garbage collection* occurs.

However, it must be pointed out that destructors are not normally required but are described here briefly for the sake of completeness. The most general form of a destructor is:

```
~class_name()
{
        // code for destructor
}
```

where, *class_name* is the name of the concerned class.

2.5 "this" KEYWORD

When a method is called, it is implicitly passed an argument that is a reference to the invoking object and this reference is called *"this"*. As an example, consider the following (*Example 32*):

Example 32

```
/* Illustration of 'this' Keyword */
/* Author: Arunesh; Date: 27/03/2011 */
using System;
class square
{
        public int i;
        public square(int x = 0)
        // Note the default value
        {
                this.i = x;
        }

        public int area()
        {
                return (this.i * this.i);
                // Note the Parentheses! Can do without them. But, they increase the clarity!
        }
}
class this_demo
{
        static void Main()
        {
                square s1 = new square(4);
                square s2 = new square();
                Console.Writeline( "Area of s1 = " + s1.area());
                Console.Writeline("Area of s2 = " + s2.area());
        }
}
```

Output:

```
Area of s1 = 16
Area of s2 =  0
        // Can you figure out, why zero?
```

Generally, no C# programmer would use *this* as shown in the above example because nothing much is achieved/gained but its use becomes desirable in certain special cases and precisely for this reason, we needed to introduce you to *this*.

2.6 PUBLIC/PRIVATE ACCESS

(Note: Protected access is discussed in chapter 5 on inheritance.)

When a member of a class is public, it can be accessed throughout the program by any of its code. On the other hand, use of the private specifier restricts its use only to other members of the particular class in question.

There are certain general guidelines for making members of a class public or private. Members of a class that are used only within that class must be made private. Data that should be within a specified range must be made private with access to them provided through public methods that can perform such range checks. If by changing a member, we happen to cause a change beyond that member, access to this particular member must be controlled and such a member should be made private. Members that can create trouble if not properly used must be made private and access to them must be controlled through public methods that can prevent such improper use of those members. Methods that get and set the values of private data must be made public if there is no reason to declare them as private. Finally, if there is no reason for instance variables to be private, they should be declared as public. To illustrate the contents of this section, we take the help of *Example 33*.

Example 33

```
/* Illustrates Public/Private Access */.
/* Author: Arunesh; Date: 27/03/2011 */
using System;
class Cl
{
        public int a;      // public access
        private int b;     // explicitly private
        int c;             // private by default

        public void set_b(int j)
        {
                b = j;
        }
        public int get_b()
        {
                return b;
        }
        public void set_c(int k)
        {
                c = k;
        }
```

```
        public int get_c()
        {
                return c;
        }
}

/* It is okay for public members of the class to access
its private members in the above methods */

class Public_Private
{
        static void Main()
        {
                Cl obj = new Cl();

                // obj.b = 7; obj.c = 8;           // WRONG!
                /* b and c being private members of the class cannot be accessed
                in the above fashion.
                The correct way is given below. */

                obj.set_b(7);
                obj.set_c(8);
                // Can you tell why?

                Console.Writeline();

                Console.Writeline(obj.get_b() + "/t" + obj.get_c());

                obj.a = 10;
                /* Nothing Wrong with the above statement!
                a is public; can be accessed directly. */
        }
}
```

<u>Output</u>:

```
        7       8
```

2.7 PASSING REFERENCES TO METHODS

So far, we have been passing value types such as *int*, *double* etc. as parameters to methods.But, it is both common and correct to pass a reference type as a parameter to a method as can be seen in the following program (*Example 34*).

Example 34

```
/* Illustrates Passing of Objects/Reference Types as parameters to methods */.
/* Author: Arunesh; Date: 27/03/2011 */
using System;
class secure
{
        double a, b;
        secure(double x, double y)
        {
                a = x;
                b = y;
        }
        integer equality(secure s)
        {
                if (s.a == a && s.b == b)
                        return 1;
                else
                        return 0;
        }
}
class ObjectPassing
{
        static void Main()
        {
                secure s1 = new secure(10.5, -10.5);
                secure s2 = new secure(-10.5, 10.5);
                secure s3 = new secure(10.5, -10.5);

                Console.WriteLine("s1 equals s2:\t" + s1.equality(s2));
                // object s2 passed as parameter to equality() method

                Console.WriteLine("s3 equals s1:\t" + s3.equality(s1));
                // object s1 passed as parameter to equality() method

                Console.WriteLine("s2 equals s3:\t" + s2.equality(s3));
                // object s3 passed as parameter to equality() method
        }
}
```

Output:

s1 equals s2: 0
s3 equals s1: 1
s2 equals s3: 0

/* A word about the output. Here, we are treating '1' as boolean value "True", and '0' as boolean value "False". The *equality()* method inside class *secure* compares two objects and returns the integral results.
*/

2.8 PASSING ARGUMENTS/PARAMETERS (CALL BY VALUE/REFERENCE)

Essentially, there are two ways by means of which an argument/parameter can be passed to a subrotine/function/method in any computer language. The first method copies the *value* of an argument into the formal parameter of the subroutine and whence, changes made to the formal parameter of the subroutine have no effect on the original argument. This technique of passing an argument is referred to as "Call by Value".

In the second approach, instead of the value of the argument, a reference to the argument is passed to the formal parameter of the subroutine. The subroutine uses this reference to access the actual argument specified in the call and whence, changes made to the formal parameter of the subroutine are reflected in the original argument used to call the subroutine as well. Quite appropriately, this technique of passing an argument is termed as "Call by Reference".

In C#, value types such as int, double etc. are passed by value while objects are implicitly passed by reference. We shall take up appropriate examples illustrating both these methods in the following two subsections.

2.8.1 "Call by Value"

In C#, value types such as int, double etc. are passed by value (*Example 35*).

Example 35

```
/* Illustrating "Call by Value" */
/* Author: Arunesh; Date: 27/03/2011 */
using System;
class A
{
        void m(int y, int z)
        {
                y /= 4;
                z *= 4;
        }
}
```

```
class Call_by_Value
{
        static void Main()
        {
                A a = new A();

                int i = 20;
                int j = 5;

                Console.WriteLine("Before Calling");

                Console.WriteLine("i = \t", + i);
                Console.WriteLine("j = \t", + j);

                Console.Writeline();

                a.m(i, j);

                Console.WriteLine("After Calling");

                Console.WriteLine("i = \t", + i);
                Console.WriteLine("j = \t", + j);
        }
}
```

Output:

```
        Before Calling
        i =     20
        j =     5

        After Calling
        i =     20
        j =     5
```

/* We can easily see that in the preceding example (*Example 35*), the operations occurring inside method *m* have had no effect on the values of *i* and *j* used in the call, that is to say, their values did not change to 5 and 20, respectively, after the call.
*/

2.8.2 "Call by Reference"

In C#, objects/reference types are implicitly passed by reference (*Example 36*).

<u>*Example 36*</u>

```
/* Illustrating "Call by Reference" */
/* Author: Arunesh; Date: 27/03/2011 */
using System;
class A
{
        int i;
        int j;

        A (int i, int j)
        {
                this.i = i;
                this.j = j;
        }
        void m(A aa)
        {
                aa.i /= 4;
                aa.j *= 4;
        }
}
class Call_by_Reference
{
        static void Main()
        {
                A a = new A(20, 5);

                Console.WriteLine("Before Calling");

                Console.WriteLine("a.i = \t", + a.i);
                Console.WriteLine("a.j = \t", + a.j);

                Console.Writeline();

                a.m(a);

                Console.WriteLine("After Calling");

                Console.WriteLine("a.i = \t", + a.i);
                Console.WriteLine("a.j = \t", + a.j);
        }
}
```

Output:

Before Calling
a.i = 20
a.j = 5

After Calling
a.i = 5
a.j = 20

/* Thus, it can be easily seen that in the above case (*Example 36*), the operations occurring inside method *m* have had an effect on the object *a* used as the argument.
*/

2.9 USING THE ref AND out PARAMETERS

We know that value types are implicitly passed by value to a method. But you might want to pass a value type by reference. There are, in general, two reasons for this. First, to allow a method to alter the contents of its arguments, e.g., to swap/exchange the values of two integral arguments. Second, to allow a method to return more than one value, e.g., to return the integral and fractional components of a floating-point number. The use of *ref* and *out* modifiers solves these two problems, respectively, as we shall see in the following two subsections.

2.9.1 Using ref Parameter

The *ref* paramter modifies creates a "Call by Reference" instead of a "Call by Value".
Let us consider *Example 37* as a simple case in point.
Carefully, notice the use and placement of *ref*.

Example 37

```
/* Illustrating Using ref to Pass a Value Type by Reference */
/* Author: Arunesh; Date: 27/03/2011 */
using System;
class RefA
{
        public void Cube(ref int k)
        // this method modifies its argument;
        // carefully, note the ue of ref
        {
                k = k * k * k;

        }
}
```

```
class RefParameter
{
        static void Main()
        {
                RefA obj = new RefA();

                Console.WriteLine("Before Calling");
                int n = 5;
                Console.WriteLine('n =\t" + n);

                Console.Writeline();

                obj.Cube(ref n);
                // carefully, note the use of ref

                Console.WriteLine("After Calling");
                Console.WriteLine('n =\t" + n);
        }
}
```

Output:

```
        Before Calling
        n =     5

        After Calling
        n =     125
```

/* The output confirms the fact that the value of the argument, *n*, was indeed changed by the method *Cube()*
*/

You must understand something important about *ref*, that is, an argument passed by *ref* must have a value before calling. The reason for this is: the method that receives an argument passed by *ref* assumes that the parameter indeed refers to a valid value. This, in turn, implies that using *ref*, you cannot use a method to initialize an argument.

Next, we take up a program (*Example 38*) containing a method *Exchange()* which swaps the values of its two integral arguments.

Example 38

```
/* Illustrating Using ref to swap Value Types*/
/* Author: Arunesh; Date: 27/03/2011 */
using System;
class RefB
{
        public void Exchange(ref int l, ref int m)
        // this method modifies its argument;
        // carefully, note the ue of ref
        {
                int temp;
                temp = l;
                l = m;
                m = temp;
        }
}
class RefSwap
{
        static void Main()
        {
                RefB obj = new RefB();

                Console.WriteLine("Before Calling");
                int j = 5, k = 10;
                Console.WriteLine('j = \t" + n + "\t k = \t" + k);

                Console.Writeline();

                obj.Exchange(ref  j, ref k);
                // carefully, note the use of ref

                Console.WriteLine("After Calling");
                Console.WriteLine('j=\t" + j + "\t k = \t" + k);
        }
}
```

Output:

```
        Before Calling
        j =     5       k =     10

        After Calling
        j =     10      k =     5
```

/* As the output shows, the values of the two integral value type arguments *j* and *k*, have indeed been swapped by the method *Exchange()* in this case by the use of *ref* parameter modifier.

*/

2.9.2 Using out Parameter

The *out* parameter is very similar to the *ref* paramter except that it can be used to only pass a value out of a method and it is not useful to initialize a variable being used as an *out* parameter before calling the concerned particular method. Further, inside the method, an *out* parameter is assumed to be unassigned (having no initial value); this, in turn, implies that the method must assign the *out* parameter a value before its termination, i.e., after calling the method, the parameter shall contain a value. Consider *Example 39* as a simple case in point.

Example 39

```
/* Illustrating Using out */
/* Author: Arunesh; Date: 27/03/2011 */
using System;
class UsingOut
{
        public int Decompose(double f, out double fraction)
        // this method decomposes a floating-point number
        // into its integral & fractiuonal parts
        {
                int w_no;

                w_no = (int) f;
                // note the use of cast

                fraction = f - w_no;
                // passing fractional part of f back via fraction

                return w_no;
                // return integral part of f
        }
}
class OutParameter
{
        static void Main()
        {
                UsingOut obj = new Usingout();
                int k;
                double frac;
```

```
        k = obj.Decompose(2.101, out frac);
        // carefully, note the use of out

        Console.WriteLine("Integral part of 1.201 =\t" + k);
        Console.WriteLine("Fractional part of 1.201 =\t" + frac);
    }
}
```

Output:

```
    Integral part of 1.201 =        1
    Fractional part of 1.201 =      0.201
```

As the above output shows, by using the *out* parameter, it is indeed possible for one method bto return more than one values. In this particular case, the *Decompose()* method returns two values: the integral part of *f* as its return value and the fractional part of *f* via the *out* parameter *fraction.*

Note: We can have more than one *out* parameter. In fact, a method can return as many values as necessary via *out* parameters.

2.9.3 Using ref and out on References

Using *ref* and *out* parameter is not confined to value types only. They can be used on references as well, that is to say, when a refeence is passed. In such an event, the reference, itself, is passed by reference. This, in turn, allows a method to modify or change what object the reference is referring to, e.g., swapping two references by using *ref.*

2.10 CAN WE HAVE A VARIABLE NUMBER OF ARGUMENTS?

The answer is "YES".

We can do so by using the *params* modifier/keyword.

Let us now take up a case study pertaining to the use of the *params* keyword/modifier. The case study will allow us to practically understand its use so that we can have a variable number of arguments/parameters.

The *params* Keyword - A CASE STUDY

Suppose, we wish to find the maximum value from a set of integers (we do not know how many integers!). We can do so as shown in *Example 40.*

Example 40

```
/* Illustrating the params modifier/keyword
used for Variable number of Arguments */
/* Author: Arunesh; Date: 27/03/2011 */
using System;
class Max
{
	public int maxVal(params int[ ] numbers)
	// notice the use of params
	{
		int n;

		if (numbers.Length == 0)
		{
			Console.WriteLine("Invalid Arguments");
			return 0;
		}

		n = numbers[0];

		for (int k = 0; k < numbers.Length; k++)
			if (numbers[k] > n)
				n = numbers[k];
		return n;
	}
}
class Params_Demo
{
	static void Main()
	{
		Max obj = new Max();
		int max;

		int a = 7; b = 8;
```

```
            // call with 2 values
            max = obj.maxVal(a, b);
            ConsoleWriteLine("Maximum: /t" + max);
            Console.WriteLine();

            // call with 5 values
            max = obj.maxVal(10, 25, 45, 15, 20);
            ConsoleWriteLine("Maximum: /t" + max);
            Console.WriteLine();

            int [ ] args = {90, 60,30, 40, 150, 180, 110, 170};

            // call with an integral array
            max = obj.maxVal(args);
            ConsoleWriteLine("Maximum: /t" + max);
            Console.WriteLine();
        }
}
```

Output:

Maximum: 8

Maximum: 45

Maximum: 180

Note: We can also use regular parameters along with the *params* keyword. For instance,

```
public int maxVal(string s, params int [ ] numbers)
{
        s = "Maximum: /t";
        ................................
        ................................
        ................................
}
```

However, in all such cases, the *params* keyword must be the last one in the parameter list, and, in no case, there can be more than one *params* modifier.

2.11 RETURNING OBJECTS/ARRAYS

A method can return any type of data including class types and arrays. (Remember, in C#, arrays are treated as objects. This differs from C++ where arrays are invalid as return types.) *Example 41* includes a method *proportion()* that creates a square (an object) that is essentially the same as the invoking square but propotionately larger/smaller by a given factor.

<u>Example 41</u>

```
/* Illustrates a method returning an object */
/* Author: Arunesh; Date: 27/03/2011 */
using System;
class square
{
        double side;

        public square(double s)
        {
                side = s;
        }

        public void show()
        {
                Console.WriteLine("side: /t"+ side);
        }

        public int area()
        {
                Console.WriteLine( "area: /t" + (side * side));
                Console.WriteLine();
        }

        public square proportion(double f)
        {
                return new square(side * f);
        }
}
class Object_Demo
{
        static void Main()
        {
                square s1 = new square(25.0);

                s1.show();
                s1.area();
```

```
        square s2 = s1.proportion(0.2)
        // create a square 5 times smaller than s1

        s2.show();
        s2.area();
    }
}
```

Output:

```
    side:   25.0
    area:   625.0

    side:   5.0
    area:   25.0
```

In C#, arrays are implemented as objects. Therefore, a method can also return an array, unlike C++. We would like to make one more point here. Just as in C++, nesting of member methods is permitted in C# as well. Now, what exactly is meant by nesting of member methods? The following program (*Example 42*) is illustrative of both the above mentioned phenomena, viz. returning an array and nesting of member methods.

Example 42

```
/* Returning an array & Nesting of member methods */
/* Author: Arunesh; Date: 27/03/2011 */
using System;
class lst
{
    public int [ ] args;

    public int [ ] numb create_lst(int [ ] args)
    {
        for (i = 0; i < args.Length; ++i)
            numb[i] += args.Length;

        return(numb);
        // Notice that an array is being returned
    }

    public void dispout(int [ ] args)
    {
        for (i = 0; i < args.Length; ++i)
            Console.Write(args[i] + "/t");
        Console.WriteLine();
    }
```

```
        public void modify(int [ ] args)
        {
                for (i = 0; i < args.Length; ++i)
                        args[i] *= -1;
                dispout();
                /*  Notice the called member method. This is
                                        what is meant by nesting of member methods. */
        }
}

class ReturnArray_NestingMethods
{
        static void Main()
        {
                lst nest = new lst();

                int [ ] numbes;

                numbers = nest.create_lst(10, 20, 30, 40);

                Console.Write("Given List:/t");
                dispout(numbers);

                Console.WriteLine();

                Console.Write("Modified List:/t");
                modify(numbers);
        }
}
```

Output:

```
        Given List:     14      24      34      44

        Modified List:  -14     -24     -34     -44
```

2.12 METHOD OVERLOADING

This is one of the ways C# implements polymorphism. In general, to overload a method, we simply declare different versions of it, i.e. methods with the same name but different parameter declarations. At this point, it must be pointed out that it is not sufficient for overloaded methods to differ just in their return types. Rather, they must differ in the number or types of their parameters.Consider *Example 43* as a case in point.

<u>*Example 43*</u>

```
/* Illustrating Method Overloading */
/* Author: Arunesh; Date: 27/03/2011 */
using System;
class Over
{
        public void method_demo()
        {
                Console.WriteLine("NO Arguments"):
        }

        public void method_demo(int i)
        {
                Console.WriteLine("ONE Integer Argument"):
        }

        public void method_demo(int i, int j)
        {
                Console.WriteLine("TWO Integer Arguments"):
        }
}

class Overload_Demo
{
        static void Main()
        {
                Over obj = new Over();

                // Now, we shall call the three overloaded methods one by one.

                obj.method_demo();
                Console.Writeline();

                obj.method_demo(4);
                Console.Writeline();
```

```
            obj.method_demo(7, 8);
      }
}
```

Output:

NO Arguments

ONE Integer Argument

TWO Integer Arguments

2.12.1 Overloaded Constructors

We have already discussed method overloading. Constructors can also be overloaded. Doing so allows us to create objects in many different ways (*Example 44*).

Example 44

```
/* Illustration of an Overloaded Constructor */
/* Author: Arunesh; Date: 27/03/2011 */
using System;
class cl
{
      public int x;

      public cl()
      {
            x = 0;
            Console.WriteLine(x);
      }

      public cl(int i)
      {
            x = i;
            Console.WriteLine(x);
      }

      public cl (int i, int j)
      {
            x = i + j;
            Console.Writeline("\n" + i + "\t" + j + "/t" + x);
      }

      // Note the overloaded constructor cl() in three different ways.
}
```

```
class cl_overloaded
{
        static void Main()
        {
                cl  c1 = new cl();
                Console.Writeline();

                cl c2 = new cl(99);
                Console.Writeline();

                cl c3 = new cl(7, 8);
        }
}
```

Output:

```
        0

        99

        7       8       15
```

2.12.2 Calling an Overloaded Constructor via "this"

While working with overloaded constructors, it is, at times, useful to call one constructor through another using the following form of the "this" keyword:

```
constructor_name(arg_list1) : this(arg_list2)
{
        // body of constructor that can be empty
}
```

The overloaded constructor that matches the argument list specified by *arg_list2* gets executed first followed by the statements, if any, in the original constructor.

2.13 OBJECT INITIALIZERS

Object initializers provide an alternative way to explicitly calling a class' constructor. They provide an alternative way to create an object and initialize its fields and/or properties (properties are discussed at length in chapter 4). The most general form of object initialization syntax is:

new class_name {name1 = expr1, name2 = expr2, ..., nameN = exprN}

where, *name1, name2, ..., nameN,* specify the names of the fields/properties which are accessible members of the class specified by *class_name, N* being a whole number. Type compatibility between the initializing expressions and the fields/properties is, of course, a must.The following simple program (*Example 45*) is illustrative of the concept of *object initializers*.

Example 45

```
/* Illustration of  Object Initializers */
/* Author: Arunesh; Date: 27/03/2011 */
using System;
class cl
{
        public int x;
        public string s;
        public double d;
}
class cl_obj_init
{
        static void Main()
        {
                cl  c = new cl {x = 99, s = "game", d = 999.999};

                // construct a cl object c by use of object initializers
                Console.WriteLine(c.x);
                Console.Writeline();

                Console.WriteLine(c.s);
                Console.Writeline();

                Console.WrriteLine(c.d);
        }
}
```

Output:

```
        99

        game

        999.999
```

/* As the <u>output</u> shows, the values of *c.x, c.s,* and *c.d h*ave been initilaized to *99, "game"*, and *999.999*, respectively. Notice the fact that neither does class *cl* define any explicit constructors nor has the normal constructor syntax been used. Another important point to understand is that the order of the object initializers doesn't matter. Thus, the <u>output</u> would have been the same even if we had initialized *c* as:

cl c = new cl {d = 999.999, x = 99, s = "game"};
*/

However, in general, you would not be using *object initializers* with named classes (such as *cl* in *Example 45*). Mostly, you would be using the normal constructor call syntax in such cases. Indeed, *object initializers* are mostly to be used with anonymous types generated by a LINQ expression (incidentally, anonymous types and LINQ have been left out of discussion in this book).

2.14 OPTIONAL ARGUMENTS

Optional arguments is a new feature added by C# 4.0 that allows specifying a default value for a method's parameter. The default value shall be used if the argument corresponding to the parameter is not supplied when calling the concerned method. The most general form of optional arguments syntax is:

static void method_name(type1 param1, type2 param2, ..., opt_arg1 = const1, opt_arg2 = const2, ...)
{
// body of method method_name
}

where, *const1, const2, ...* are constant expressions secifying the default values of the respective *optional arguments*

.It should be clear from this syntax that all *optional arguments* must appear to the right of those that are required. For instance, the following method declaration is illegal/invalid:

static void Demo(int i = 10, string s) { // body of method Demo }
// Erroneous! s must be declared before i

Again, once you have started to declare *optional arguments*, you cannot declare a required parameter. For instance, the following method declaration is also illegal/invalid:

static void Demo(double d, int i = 10, string s) { // body of method Demo }
/ Incorrect again! Since d is optional, i should come before d or s should also be optional */*

The following simple program (*Example 46*) is a correct illustration of the concept of *optional arguments*.

Example 46

```
/* Illustration of  Optional arguments */
/* Author: Arunesh; Date: 27/03/2011 */
using System;
class cl
{         static void method_opt_arg(double a, double b = 2.0, double c = 3.0)
          {
                    Console.WriteLine("Values of a, b, c are:");
                    Consloe.WriteLine(a);
                    Console.writeLine(b);
                    Console.writeLine(c);
                    Console.WriteLine();
          }
          static void Main()
          {
                    method_opt_arg(100.0, 200.0, 300.0);
                    // explicitly pass all arguments

                    method_opt_arg(100.0, 200.0,);
                    // letting c default

                    method_opt_arg(100.0);
                    // letting both b & c default
          }
}
```

Output:

```
Values of a, b, c are:
100.0
200.0
300.0

Values of a, b, c are:
100.0
200.0
3.0

Values of a, b, c are:
100.0
2.0
3.0
```

/* As the output shows, the default values of the *optional arguments b*, and *c* are used when they are not supplied in the call to *method_opt_arg()*.
*/

Note: Apart from methods, *optional arguments* can also be used with constructors, indexers, and delegates. (While indexers have been described in chapter 4, delegates have been left out of discussion in the present book.)

2.14.1 Optional arguments Compared to Overloading

In certain situations, *optional arguments* provide a better way than method overloading. This can be easily understood by taking the case of *method_opt_arg()* in *Example 46*. If we had used method overloading instead of *optional arguments*, we would have needed to specify three different versions of this method to achieve the same result, as enumerated below:

i *method_opt_arg(double a)* { // body of method_opt_arg }

ii *method_opt_arg(double a, double b)* { // body of method_opt_arg providing the value of *b*}

iii *method_opt_arg(double a, double b, double c)* { // body of method_opt_arg providing the value of *b, c*}

Although the use of this method overloading approach is indeed not wrong, using *optional arguments* is certainly a better alternative in this particular case. However, it must be remembered that in some cases, method overloading might not be implementable using *optional arguments*.

2.14.2 Optional Arguments vs. "params" Modifier

At first glance, there seems to be a degree of overlapping between methods that use the "params" modifier and those that take *optional arguments*. However, there are some basic and fundamental differences between the two:

- A method that takes *optional arguments* still has a fixed parameter list, and you cannot pass an arbitrary list of arguments.
- A method that uses the "params" modifier has, in effect, a completely arbitrary list of parameters, and none of them can have default values.
- In general, you use the "params" modifier for methods that take any number ofparameters (inclusive of none), while you use *optional arguments* only when it is not convenient to force a caller to provide an argument for every parameter.

2.14.3 Can Optional Arguments Lead to Ambiguity?

The use of *optional arguments* can result in ambiguous situations, especially in cases where a method taking *optional arguments* is overloaded. In such cases, the compiler gets confused and unable to determine which version of the overloaded method to call when the *optional arguments* are not supplied. For instance, consider the following two versions of *method_opt_arg():*

```
I       static void method_opt_arg(double a, double b = 2.0, double c = 3.0)
        {
                Console.WriteLine("Values of a, b, c are:");
                Consloe.WriteLine(a);
                Console.WriteLine(b);
                Console.WriteLine(c);
                Console.WriteLine();
        }
II      static void method_opt_arg(double a, int b = 2, int c = 3)
        {
                Console.WriteLine("Values of a, b, c are:");
                Consloe.WriteLine(a);
                Console.WriteLine(b);
                Console.WriteLine(c);
                Console.WriteLine();
        }
```

/ Carefully, note that the only difference between the above two overloads of method_opt_arg() is that in case I, the type of b, c is double, while in case II, the type of b, c is int, where b, c are the optional parameters in both the cases. */*

Now, given these two versions/cases, the following call to *method_opt_arg()* is ambiguous:

```
method_opt_arg(100.0);
// Compiler error: Ambiguous!
```

/ The call is ambiguous since the complier comes unstuck as it is at a complete loss to know whether to use version I in which b, c are of type double or to use vesion II in which b, c are of type int. */*

The above situation is indicative of the fact that you may be required to avoid using *optional arguments* in cases where their use can lead to such ambiguity!

WE now take up a *practical* case study pertaining to *optional arguments.*

Optional Arguments - A CASE STUDY

In this section, we take up a case study of the concept of *optional arguments* with the help of the following practical example (*Example 47*). The program contains a method named *Print()* which prints on the console (monitor/screen) a string either entirely or partially depending upon the use of its *optional arguments*.

Example 47

```
/* Optional arguments - a Practical case*/
/* Author: Arunesh; Date: 27/03/2011 */
using System;
class cl
{       static void Print(string s, int begin = 0; int end = -1)
        // print s partially or entirely
        {
                int n;

                if (end == -1)
                        end = s.Length;
                        // notice the use of the property Length in a string array
                if (end > s.Length | begin < 0 | begin > end)
                        return;
                        // checking for out-of-bounds conditions
                for (n = begin; n < end; n++)
                        Console.Write(s[n]);
                        // print each character of s from begin to end one by one
                Console.WriteLine();
        }
        static void Main()
        {
                s = "My favourite game is Cricket! What about yours?";
                // initialize s, the required argument

                Print(s);
                // optional arguments: begin = 0 (default); end = -1 (default)

                Print(s, 30);
                // optional arguments: begin = 30; end = -1 (deault)
```

```
        Print(s, 21, 28);
        // optional arguments: begin = 21; end = 28
    }
}
```

Output:

My favourite game is Cricket! What about yours?
What about yours?
Cricket!

A careful glance at the *Print()* method shows that the string to be printed, viz. *s*, is its first argument which is a required one. The second and third arguments, viz., *begin* and *end*, are *optional arguments* which indicate the beginning and ending indexes of the string *s* to be printed.

If *end* is not passed a value, it defaults to *-1*, which suggests that the ending inex is the termination point of *s*. If *begin* is not passed a value, it defaults to *0*, which suggests that the beginning index is the starting point of *s*.

Whence, if neither of the two *optional arguments* are supplied a value, that is to say, they are not present in the call to *Print(), s* is displayed entirely/ completely. Otherwise, the suggested part of *s* is printed.

This, in turn, implies that if *Print()* is called with only one argument, that is, *s*, then *s* is printed entirely. If *Print()* is called with two arguments, that is, *s* and *begin*, then the characters of *s* starting with *begin* through the termination point of *s* are printed. Finally, if all the three arguments, viz., *s*, *begin*, and *end*, are specified, then the part of *s* starting at *begin* and terminating at *end* is printed.

This case study reveals the essential benefit that the use of *optional arguments* has to offer. You need to pass only those arguments that are quintessential and default values need not be explicitly specified/passed!

2.15 NAMED ARGUMENTS

Named arguments is a new feature added by C# 4.0 that allows specifying the name of the parameter to which an argument applies. With this approach, the order of the arguments does not matter. Normally, the order of the arguments must correspond to the order of the parameters declared by the method, that is to say, the parameter to which an argument is assigned is defined by its position in the argument list. *Named arguments* remove this constraint. This concept is a bit like *object initializers* discussed earlier but the syntax is not the same. The most general form of the *named arguments* syntax is:

param_name: val

where, *param_name* is a valid parameter name for the concerned method and *val* is the *value (constant)* being passed to the parameter *param_name.*

The following simple program (*Example 48*) is illustrative of the concept of *named arguments*. It contains a method called *Display_Max()* which determines and displays the maximum of its two parameters.

<u>*Example 48*</u>

```
/* Illustration of Named arguments */
/* Author: Arunesh; Date: 27/03/2011 */
using System;
class cl
{
        staic voidDisplay_Max(int m, int n)
        {
                int max = m >= n ? m : n;
                Console.WriteLine("Maximum of " + m + " and " + n " =\t" + max);
        }

        static void Main()
        {
                // call Display_Max() in various ways
                Display_Max(31, 45);
                // call using positional arguments

                Display_Max(m: 31, n: 45);
                // call using named arguments

                Display_Max(n: 45, m: 31);
                // order is not important with named arguments

                Display_Max(31, n: 45);
                // call using both a positional argument and a named argument
```

```
        // Display_Max(m:31, 45);
        /* Error: all positional arguments must come before any named arguments;
        whence, the above line has been commented out! */
    }
}
```

Output:

Maximum of 31 and 45 = 45
Maximum of 31 and 45 = 45
Maximum of 31 and 45 = 45
Maximum of 31 and 45 = 45

/* As the output shows, all the ways of calling the method *Display_Max()* result in the same outcome.
*/

Note 1: *Named arguments* can also be used along with *optional arguments*. For instance, taking the *Print()* method in section 2.14.4, some of the ways in which it can be called using *named arguments* are elaborated as follows:

```
Print(end: 28, s: "My favourite game is Cricket! What about yours?", begin: 21);
// declare all arguments by name

Print(end: 28, s: "My favourite game is Cricket! What about yours?");
// specifying s and end by name, and letting begin default

Print("My favourite game is Cricket! What about yours?", end: 28);
// specifying s by position, end by name, and letting begin default
```

Note 2: Apart from methods, *named arguments* can also be used with constructors, indexers, and delegates. (As already stated, while indexers have been described in chapter 4, delegates have been left out of discussion in the present book.)

2.16 THE *Main()* METHOD (Revisited)

So far, we have been using one form of *Main()*. But, it must be pointed out that it has various overloaded forms. Some of these forms can be made to return a value while others can receive arguments. We discuss each one of these in the following two subsections.

2.16.1 Returning Values from *Main()*

The following form of *Main()* can be used to return a value to the calling process or the operating system:

static int Main() *// note the use of int instead of void*

This return value suggests whether the program has terminated smoothly or abnormally. A return value of '*0*' conventionally reveals normal termination while all other values are suggestive of some type of error occurrence.

2.16.2 Passing Arguments to *Main()* (Command-line Arguments)

We have already introduced the concept of *command-line arguments* briefly in the previous chapter (*Example 26*). Here, we elaborate this concept further in detail.

The data/information directly after the name of the program on the command line when it is run is termed as *command-line arguments*. The concerned C# program passes on these arguments to the *Main()* method. One of the following two forms of *Main()* must be put to use to receive these arguments:

static void Main(string[] args)
static int Main(string[] args)

The first form returns *void* and has already been used in *Example 26* (chapter 1) as stated already. The second form returns *int* (and can be made use of to return an integral value as discussed already in the previous section). For both of these two forms, the length of the *args* array is equal to the number of *command-line arguments*, which could well be zero. Moreover, the *command-line arguments* are stored as strings in the *string* array *args* passed to *Main()*.

As mentioned before, we have already made use of the first form in one of the previous examples in the preceding chapter. So, we shall illustrate the second form in the <u>case study</u> described next.

Command-line Arguments - A CASE STUDY

To practically understand the way that the command-line arguments can be put to use, take the following program (*Example 49*). It makes use of coded writing to encrypt/decrypt messages. The message to be encrypted/decrypted is specified on the command line. The code is reasonable (neither too easy nor too difficult). To encrypt a word, each letter is incremented by 25 so that 'A' becomes 'Z', 'B' becomes 'a', and so on. To decrypt, each letter is decremented by 25.

Example 49

```
/* Command-LineArguments - a Practical case */
/* Author: Arun; Date: 27/03/2011 */
using System;
class Code
{
        static int Main(string [] args)
        // notice the reurn type int
        {
                int ctr, j, k;
                string s;

                ctr = args.Length;
                string single_space_str = " ";

                if (ctr != 0)
                        s = args[0];
                        // initialize s with first argument

                if (ctr < 2)
                // checking if args present
                {
                        Console.WriteLine("Usage:encrypt/decrypt Word1
                                                        [Word2 Word3..]");
                        return 1;
                        // returning 1 to indicate failed attempt
                }
```

```
        else if (s != "encrypt" & s != "decrypt")
        // if args present, checking if
        // first argument is encrypt or decrypt
        {
                Console.WriteLine("First argument has to be encrypt or
                                                              decrypt");
                return 1;
                // returning 1 to indicate failed attempt
        }
        else
        // encrypt/decrypt message
        {
                for (j = 1; j < ctr; j++)
                {
                        for (k = 0; k < args[j].Length; k++)
                        {
                                if (s = "encrypt")
                                        Console.Write((char) (args[j][k] + 25));
                                else
                                        Console.Write((char) (args[j][k] - 25));
                        }
                        Console.Write(single_space_str);
                        // leave single space before next word
                }
                Console.WriteLine();
                // leave a newline before next message on the command line

                return 0;
                // returning 0 to indicate normal termination


        }
    }
}
```

/* To use the program, specify either the "encrypt" or "decrypt" command followed by the message/phrase you want to encode or decode. Assuming that the program is called *Code*, two sample runs follow.
*/

Sample runs:

C:> *Code* encrypt ONE TWO
nmd svn

C:> *Code* decrypt nmd svn
ONE TWO

There are three important things to particularly note in the program (*Example 49*).

First thing to note is that the program checks if the *command-line arguments* are actually present before proceeding. This is extremely essential and failure to check this can result in program malfunctionung.

Second, since the first argument has to be "encrypt" or "decrypt", this is also checked by the program before executing.

Finally, the third point to note is how the program returns a termination code. If the proper command line is not in place, the program returns 1 suggestive of abnormal termination. Otherwise, when the program terminates well and good, 0 is returned by it to the operating system.

2.17 RECURSION

Recursion is a special type of method invocation in which a method calls itself. C# allows this phenomenon. A typical example of *recursion* is the computation of the factorial of a whole number, say *w*, given by:

*w! = w * (w - 1) * (w - 2) * .... *2 * 1*, e.g.,

*factorial of 3 = 3! = 3 * 2 * 1 = 6.*

The following program (*Example 50*) shows how to go about finding factorials using a *recursive* method.

<u>Example 50</u>

```
/* Illustrates the concept of Recursion */
/* Author: Arunesh; Date: 27/03/2011 */
using System;
class lst
{
        public int create_lst(int i)
        // recursive method
        {
                int r;
                if (i == 1)
                        return 1;

                r = create_lst(i - 1) * i;
                // Factorial

                return r;
        }
}
class Recursion
{
        static void Main()
        {
                lst nest = new lst();

                Console.WriteLine("Factorials of 3, 4, and 5 are given below respectively.");
                Console.Writeline(nest.create_lst(3));
                Console.Writeline(nest.create_lst(4));
                Console.Writeline(nest.create_lst(5));
        }
}
```

<u>Output</u>:

```
        Factorials of 3, 4, and 5 are given below respectively.
        6
        24
        120
```

2.18 DEALING WITH STATIC

We can have static methods and variables in a class and even static classes. Also discussed in this section are static constructors.

2.18.1 Static Members In a Class

Static members in a class are used when we need to use them independently of any object of that class. A class member, in general, must be accessed through an object of that class but we can create a member that can be used by itself without reference to a specific instance. Such a member is created by preceding its declaration by the keyword static as shown in *Example 51*.

Example 51

```
/* Illustrates static member, that is, variables and methods, in a class */
/* Author: Arunesh; Date: 27/03/2011 */
using System;
class Stat
{
        public static int i = 80;
        // a static variable
        public static int Mult3()
        // a static method
        {
                return (i * 3);
        }
}
class Static_Demo
{
        static void Main()
        {
                Console.WriteLine("Initial value of static variable i: /t" + Stat.i);
                Stat.i = 100;
                Console.WriteLine("Now, value of static variable i: /t" + Stat.i);
                int result = Stat.Mult3();
                Console.WriteLine("Result after applying static method Mult3(): /t"
                                        + result);
        }
}
```

Output:

```
        Initial value of static variable i:              80
        Now, value of static variable i:                 100
        Result after applying static method Mult3():     300
```

Note: There are several restrictions that apply to static methods. First, a static method cannot have a 'this' reference. Next, a static method can directly only call other static methods. Finally, a static method can directly access only static data.

2.18.2 Static Classes

C# has the added ability to create static classes (*Example* 52).

Example 52

```
/* Static_Class_Demo.cs
/* Author: Arunesh; Date: 27/03/2011 */
using System;
static class NumberStatic
// a static class
{
        static public bool isOdd(double n)
        {
                return ((n % 2) == 0 ? false : true);
        }

        static public isEven(double n)
        {
                return (!(isOdd(n));
        }
}
// Note that all the methods in the above static class are static

class Static_Class_Demo
{
        static void Main()
        {
                if (NumberStatic.isOdd(7))
                        Console.WriteLine(" 7 is Odd ");
                if (NumberStatic.isEven(8))
                        Console.WriteLine("8 is Even ");
        }
}
```

Output:

```
        7 is Odd
        8 is Even
```

Note: There are two restrictions that apply to static classes. First, no object of a static calss can be created. And, secondly, a static class can have only static members.

2.18.3 Static Constructors

We have already seen static methods earlier. In the same way we can have static constructors. A static constructor, in general, is used to initialize attributes that apply to a class rather than an instance. It can be used to initialize components of a class before having created any objects of that class. For instance, consider *Example 53*.

Example 53

```
/* Illustration of a Static Constructor */
/* Author: Arunesh; Date: 27/03/2011*/
using System;
class cl
{
        public int i;
        public static int j;

        public cl()
        // INSTANCE CONSTRUCTOR
        {
                i = 11;
                Console.WriteLine("Instance Constructor: /t" + i);
        }
        static cl()
        // STATIC CONSTRUCTOR
        {
                j = 111;
                Console.WriteLine("Static Constructor: /t)" + j);
        }
}
class Static_Constructor
{
        static void Main()
        {
                cl obj = new cl();
                Console.WriteLine("obj.i: /t" + obj.i);
                Console.WriteLine("cl.j: /t" + cl.j);
        }
}
```

Output:

```
        Instance Constructor:   11
        Static Constructor:     111
        obj.i:                  11
        cl.j:                   111
```

PRACTICAL SESSION

#1 What do you understand by a *class* in C#? How is a *class* declared? Elaborate and explain in detail.

#2 (a) Suppose you are adding the following data items as members to a class:
i. A person's Last Name
ii. A Zip Code
iii. The days of the week
How would you write them in the class?

(b) Suppose you want to add a general method to the *clsDates* class that returns the number of days in a given month.
How would you write the code?

(c) Give a good example where you would use the *public* access specifier to define the class data members.

#3 Point out the error(s), if any, in the following class declaration:

```
class abc
{
        int z;
        public int get_abc()
        {
                return z;
        }
        void set_abc(int a)
        {
                z = a;
        }
}
```

#4 In C#, can objects be passed as parameters?
If not, why not?
If yes, how? Elaborate and explain in detail.

#5 Explain the difference and distinguish between a value type variable and a reference variable.
{Tip: Consider "*Call by Value*" vs. "*Call by Reference*"! }

#6 State True (T) or False (F):

(i) A constructor method is a default method.
(ii) Constructors do not return any value.
(iii) Arguments to a constructor can be passed at the time of creation of the object.

#7 Fill in the blanks:

(i) Every useful program requires some data elements to be _______________ before they are put into use.
(ii) A _______________ method initializes the members of an object at the time of its _______________ automatically.
(iii) A constructor with one or more arguments is called the __________ constructor.
(iv) The name of the constructor is the same as that of its __________ name.
(v) A destructor is an _____________ of a constructor with a ____________ as prefix.

#8 State True (T) or False (F):

(i) It is necessary to declare a class before any object of its type can be declared.
(ii) The access to any *private* member of a class is not allowed to any outside function.
(iii) All declarations in a class are *private*, by default.
(iv) An individual object within an array of objects may be accessed by means of the *dot* operator.

#9 Fill in the blanks:

(i) The keywords - *private* and *public* - are called ___________ specifiers.
(ii) The functions declared and defined within a class are, by default, are _______ functions.
(iii) A class combines data and functions into a single unit. This activity is known as _________________________.
(iv) *Static* variables are used to maintain ___________ values in the entire class.

#10 (a) What is a constructor? Explain its utility citing suitable example(s).

(b) Define:
 (i) Default constructor
 (ii) Parametrized constructor

#11 What do you mean by the term "destructor"?
In what way(s) is the destructor similar to and different from a constructor?

#12 Explain the concept of garbage collection in C#?
Is there a similar provision in C++?

#13 What is the role of *static* member variables and methods in C#.
Explain citing suitable example(s) to support your answer.

#14 What shall be the <u>output</u> of the following program code:

```
using System;
class Jim
{
        public void print(double d)
        {
                Console.WriteLine("double");
        }
        public void print(int i)
        {
                Console.WriteLine("int");
        }
        public void print(string s)
        {
                Console.WriteLine("s");
        }
}

class Jimmy
{
        static void Main()
        {
                Jim Baker;
                char Chr = 'C';
                int Mum = 99;
                floatF = 3.142;
                char Str[ ] = "string";
                Baker.print(Chr);
                Baker.print(F);
                Baker.print(Mum);
                Baker.print(Str);
        }
}
```

#15 Write a C++ program to implement a class Student having following members:

<u>Data Members</u>

(a) Name of the Student

(b) Marks in three main subjects: Physics, Chemistry & Mathematics

<u>Method Members</u>

(a) To assign initial values

(b) To compute total, average, and percentage marks

(c) To display the data (both given and computed.)

#16 Study the following code and answer the queries that follow:

```
using System;
class Read
{
        public Read()
        // Method 1
        {
                Console.Writeline("Open the Book.");
        }
        public void Reads()
        // Method 2
        {
                Console.Writeline("Actual Reading.");
        }
        ~Read()
        // Method 3
        {
                Console.Writeline("Close the Book.");
        }
};
```

What are Methods 1, 2, 3 known as and when do they get involved/invoked/called? Explain and elaborate in brief.

#17 Choose the correct alternative(s):

(a) The member methods must be declared before the class declaration.

(b) There cannot be a variable declaration in the class.

(c) The keyword <u>class</u> is optional.

(d) All of the above are correct.

(e) None of the above is correct.

#18 Pick the correct alternative in each of the following multiple choice problems:

(i)
```
// s is a user-defined class
s1 = new(s);
s2 = new (s);
```
(a) Contents of s1 and s2 will be eaxactly same.
(b) Contents of s1 and s2 will be different.
(c) s1 and s2 point to the same memory location.
(d) None of the above.

(ii) (a) Class is always a value type.
(b) Class is always a reference type.
(c) Class is a value type as well as a reference type.
(d) None of the above.

(iii) (a) Data members of a class are public by default.
(b) Data members of a class are private by default.
(c) Data members of a class are protected by default.
(d) None of the above.

(iv) (a) Static members of a class never receive the 'this' reference.
(b) Instance members of a class always receive the 'this' reference.
(c) While calling an instance member method, we don't need to pass the 'this' reference explicitly.
(d) All of the above.
(e) None of the above.

#19 Pick the correct alternative in each of the following multiple choice problems:

(i) During the lifetime of an object, how many times can we call a constructor?
(a) Any number of times.
(b) Any number of times before the object is deleted.
(c) Only once.
(d) None of the above.

(ii) (a) If a zero-argument constructor is not provided, the compiler provides a default zero-argument constructor.
(b) If a zero-argument constructor is provided, the compiler still provides a default zero-argument constructor.
(c) If a one-argument constructor is provided, the compiler still provides a default zero-argument constructor.
(d) None of the above.

(iii) (a) There is one garbage collector for each program runnung in memory.
(b) An object is destroyed by the garbage collector when only one reference refers to it.
(c) There is one common garbage collector for all programs running in memory.
(d) None of the above.

#20 How are static constructors useful?
Support your answer with suitable reason(s) and example(s).

CHAPTER 3

OPERATOR OVERLOADING

3.0 INTRODUCTION

One of the most powerful features of C# is its ability to overload operators akin to method overloading. C# allows for redefining the meaning of an operator with respect to the class being created. This feature of C# is referred to as *operator overloading*. An important point to be noted is that when an operator is overloaded, none of its original meanings are lost but the type of objects that it can be applied to gets expanded, that is to say, a new operator with respect to the specific concerned class, is incorporated. The effects and consequences of the operator are entirely under control and may vary from one class to the other. For instance, a class that executes a stack might use the + operator to push objects onto the stack, while a class that executes a linked list might use the same operator, viz., +, to incorporate an object to the linked list, and so on and so forth. A major benefit of *operator overloading* is that it allows for seamless integration of a new class type into the programming zone/domain. This feature is often referred to as *type extensibility* which is a vital aspect of OOP languages such as C#, C++, and so on. In the next section, we shall actually see how to overload unary and binary operators relative to a new class type.

3.1 OPERATOR OVERLOADING - THE FUNDAMENTALS

We overload an operator by using the operator keyword to define an *operator method* that describes the action of this operator with respect to its class. Next, we elaborate the general forms of *operator methods* to overload the unary and binary operators respectively.

```
// How to overload an unary operator - generalized form of operator method
public static return_type operator op(parameter_type operand)
{
        /* operations */
}
// How to overload a binary operator - generalized form of operator method
public static return_type operator op(parameter_type1 operand1, parameter_type2 operand2)
{
        /* operations */
}
```

where, *op* stands for the operator we are overloading such as +, -, *, / etc. Also, as previously stated, the word operator before *op* is a keyword. The *return_type* declares the type of value returned by the *operator method* (note that the method must be both *public* as well as *static)*. Even though the *return_type* can be any type you wish, it is more often than not, the same type as the class for which the method is being defined. This helps in using the overloaded operator in expressions. In case of unary operators, the *operand* must be of the same type as the class for which the operator is being overloaded. In case of binary operators, at least one of the two operands, viz., *operand1* and *operand 2*, must be of the same type as the class for which the operator is being overloaded. These two conditions, in turn, imply that you cannot overload any C# operator for classes/objects that have not been created by you, e.g., you cannot overload/redefine the C# operator + for *int*, *double*, or *string*. One final point to be remembered is that operator parameters cannot use the *ref* and *out* modifiers.

Let us illustrate whatever we have said so far with the following program (*Example 54*) that overloads binary +, binary -, unary -, unary ++, and unary -- for the class of complex numbers.

Example 54

```
/* Illustration of Operator Overloading */
/* Author: Arunesh; Date: 23/03/2011 */
using System;
class complex
{
    int a, b;                    // a + ib form
    public complex()
    { a = b = 0;}

    public complex(int i, int j)
    { a = i; b = j; }

    public void display()
    {
        Console.WriteLine(a + " i" + b);
        Console.WriteLine();
    }

    /* Overloading binary + for complex*/

    public static complex operator +(complex op1, complex op2)
    {
        complex result = new complex();
        result.a = op1.a + op2a;
        result.b = op1.b + op2.b;

        return result;
    }
```

```
/* Overloading binary - for complex*/

public static complex operator -(complex op1, complex op2)
{
        complex result = new complex();
        result.a = op1.a -  op2.a;
        result.b = op1.b -  op2.b;

        return result;
}

/* Overloading unary - for complex*/

public static complex operator -(complex op)
{
        complex result = new complex();
        result.a = -op.a;
        result.b = -op.b;

        return result;
}

/* Overloading  unary ++ for complex */

public static complex operator ++(complex op)
{
        complex result = new complex();
        result.a =  op.a + 1;
        result.b =  op.b + 1;

        return result;    // return incremented result
}

/* Overloading unary -- for complex */

public static complex operator --(complex op)
{
        complex result = new complex();
        result.a =  op.a - 1;
        result.b =  op.b - 1;

        return result;    // return decremented result
}
}
```

```
class Operator_Overloading1
{
        static void Main()
        {
                complex obj1 = new complex(5, 15);
                complex obj2 =  new complex(3, 30);
                complex obj3 = new complex();

                Console.Write("obj1 = ");
                obj1.display();
                Console.Write("obj2 = ");
                obj2.display();

                obj3 = obj1 + obj2;       // add obj1 and obj2
                Console.Write("obj3 = obj1 + obj2 = ");
                obj3.display();

                obj3 = obj1 + obj2 + obj3;       // add obj1, obj2 and obj3
                Console.Write("obj3 = obj1 + obj2 + obj3 = ");
                obj3.display();

                obj3 = obj1 - obj2;       // subtract obj2 from obj1
                Console.Write("obj3 = obj1 - obj2 = ");
                obj3.display();

                obj3 = -obj1;   // assign -obj1 to obj3
                Console.Write("obj3 = -obj1 = ");
                obj3.display();

                obj3 = obj1++;            // post-increment obj1
                Console.Write("obj3 = obj1++ = ");
                obj3.display();
                Console.Write("obj1 = ");
                obj1.display();

                obj3 = --obj1;            // pre-decrement obj1
                Console.Write("obj3 = --obj1 = ");
                obj3.display();
                Console.Write("obj1 = ");
                obj1.display();
        }
}
```

Output:

obj1 = 5 + i15

obj2 = 3 + i30

obj3 = obj1 + obj2 = 8 + i45

obj3 = obj1 + obj2 + obj3 = 16 + i90

obj3 = obj1 - obj2 = 2 -i15

obj3 = -obj1 = -5 -i15

obj3 = obj1++ = 5 + i15

obj1 = 6 + i16

obj3 = --obj1 = 5 + i15

obj1 = 5 + i15

/* When two operands of type complex are added together, the + operation does not change the contents of either operand. Instead, the result is returned is a new object of type complex. This is consistent with the usual meaning of the + operation. Imagine *13* and *14* added together. The + operation does not change either *13* or *14* but returns the result as *27*, a new value.

Again, the fact that the + operator returns an object of type complex allows the + operator to be used in compond expressions, such as *obj1 + obj2 + obj3*. In this case, first *obj2* is added to *obj1* and then the result, an object of type complex again, is added to *obj3*. Had the + operator returned a value of any other type, such compound expressions could not have been made to work.

Once again, when the coordinates (the real and imaginary parts) of the two complex numbers are added together, the addition takes place by means of respective integer additions. This happens because the coordinates themselves are integer values and the fact that the + operator is overloaded for the class of complex numbers has no effect on its original meaning as applied to integer quantities.

Finally, consider the operartor *-()*. It works similar to the operator *+()* but for the fact, that in this case, the order of the parameters matters. You may note that addition is commutative but subtraction is not so that *x - y* is not the same as *y - x*. In the case of binary operators, the first operator to an operator method shall contain the operand on the left while the second parameter shall contain the operand on the right. While carrying out the overloading of such noncommutative operators as -, it is important to remember which operand is the left and which one is on the right. */

3.2 OPERATOR OVERLOADING CONSTRAINTS

We need to point out certain restrictions and constraints to operator overloading enumerated as follows:

(A) The precedence and associativity of an operator cannot be altered.

(B) The number of operators required by an operand cannot be altered.

(C) New operator symols cannot be invented, e.g., you cannot create a new operator symbol ** for raising one number `to the power of another number. Instead, you would have to create a method for this.

(D) The meaning of an operator when applied to C# built-in types cannot be altered, e.g., the expression *2 + 3* has a certain predefined meaning and this cannot be overridden. Indeed, if you were allowed to do this, things would get too complicated!

(E) Certain operators such as the dot (.) operator which indicates access to a class member cannot be overloaded as shown in Table 3.1.

Table 3.1 List of Operators that cannot be Overloaded

<table>
<tr><td colspan="4">assignment operators =, +=, -= etc. .</td></tr>
<tr><td>&&</td><td>| |</td><td>[ ]</td><td>()</td></tr>
<tr><td>new</td><td>is</td><td>sizeof</td><td>typeof</td></tr>
<tr><td>?</td><td>-></td><td>.</td><td>as</td></tr>
<tr><td>??</td><td>=></td><td>default</td><td>checked</td></tr>
<tr><td colspan="4">unchecked</td></tr>
</table>

(F) Certain operators must be overloaded as a pair as shown in Table 3.2.

Table 3.2 List of Operators that must be Overloaded as a Pair

Relational operators:
== *and* !=
< *and* >
<= *and* >=

Boolean operators:
true and false

Further, overloading the == and != operators requires overriding of *Object.Equals()* and *Object.GetHashCode()*. (These methods and the mechanism/technique of overriding are described at length in chapter 5.)

3.3 OPERATOR OVERLOADING INVOLVING C# BUILT-IN TYPES

For any particular class and an operator, the *operator method* can, itself, be overloaded. But, you might ask - "What's the need for this?" One of the simple reasons is that we might need to carry out operations between a class type and other data types, such as built-in types, e.g., we have seen in *Example 54* how to add two *complex numbers* but we may need to add a built-in type, such as *int* to a *complex number*, or the othe way round, that is, a *complex number* to an *int*. We might mention here that such operations are indeed not only possible but are permissible as well since we have already explained that while overloading a binary operator, only one of the operands needs to be of the same type as its class; the other one can be any other data type. Here is a version of *complex* in *Example 55* that has three overloaded + methods.

Example 55

```
// Illustration of Operator Overloading for:
//  complex + complex; complex + int;  and, int + complex
/* Author: Arunesh; Date: 23/03/2011 */
using System;
class complex
{
        int a, b;                               // a + ib form

        public complex()
        { a = b = 0;}

        public complex(int i, int j)
        { a = i; b = j; }

        public void display()
        {
                        Console.WriteLine(a + "  i" + b);
                        Console.WriteLine();
        }

        /* Overloading binary + for complex + complex*/

        public static complex operator +(complex op1, complex op2)
        {
                complex result = new complex();
                result.a = op1.a +  op2.a;
                result.b = op1.b +  op2.b;

                return result;
        }
```

```
    /* Overloading binary + for complex + int*/

    public static complex operator +(complex op1, int op2)
    {
                complex result = new complex();
                result.a = op1.a +  op2;
                result.b = op1.b +  0;
                        // note the adition of 0 to the imaginary part of op1
                        // this is because int op2 as complex is: op2 + i0

                return result;
    }

    /* Overloading binary + for int + complex */

    public static complex operator +(int op1, complex op2)
    {
                complex result = new complex();
                result.a = op2.a +  op1;
                result.b = op2.b +  0;
                        // note the adition of 0 to the imaginary part of op2
                        // this is because int op1 as complex is: op1 + i0

                return result;
    }
}
class Operator_Overloading2
{
     static void Main()
     {
           complex obj1 = new complex(5, 15);
           int N = 3;
           complex obj2 = new complex();

           Console.Write("obj1 = ");
           obj1.display();
           Console.WriteLine("N = " + N);
           Console.WriteLine();

           obj2 = obj1 +  N;
           Console.Write("obj2 = obj1 + N = ");
           obj2.display();
```

```
        obj2 = N + obj2;
        Console.Write("obj2 = N + obj2 = ");
        obj2.display();
    }
}
```

<u>Output</u>:

```
    objl = 5 + il5

    N = 3

    obj2 = objl + N = 8 + il8

    obj2 = N + obj2 = 11 + i21

            // The above output is self-explanatory! Isn't it?
            // Indeed, WE think you can comprehend it quite easily.
            // In fact, WE are rather sure you would prove Us right!
```

3.4 OVERLOADING RELATIONAL OPERATORS

The relational operators such as <, or >= can also be overloaded and the process is quite uncomplicated. In general, overloaded relational operators return *true* or *false* in consonance with their normal usage and allows them to be used in conditional expressions; returning any other value would, in effect, restrict their utility and operation to a great extent. Here is a version of *complex* in *Example 56* that overloads the < and > operators. (We have already mentioned certain restrictions related to relational operators in section 3.2 including the one that < and > must be overloaded as a pair, that is to say, < or > cannot be overloaded individually as such.) *Example 56* compares complex numbers based on their magnitudes. One complex number is less than the other if its magnitude is less than the magnitude of the other. Similarly, one complex number is greater than the other if its magnitude is greater than that of the other. If neither of the two operators (< and >) returns true, then the complex numbers are equal in magnitude.

<u>Example 56</u>

```
/* Overloading Relational Operators < and > */
/* Author: Arunesh; Date: 23/03/2011 */
using System;
class complex
{
    int a, b;                       // a + ib form

    public complex()
    { a = b = 0;}
```

```
        public complex(int i, int j)
        { a = i; b = j; }

        public void display()
        {
                Console.WriteLine(a + " i" + b);
        }

        /* Overloading relational operator < for complex */

        public static bool operator <(complex op1, complex op2)
        {
                        if (Math.sqrt(op1.a * op1.a +  op1.b * op1.b) <
                                Math.sqrt (op2.a * op2.a + op2.b * op2.b))
                                return true;
                        else
                                return false;
        }

        /* Overloading relational operator > for complex */

        public static bool operator <(complex op1, complex op2)
        {
                        if (Math.sqrt(op1.a * op1.a +  op1.b * op1.b) >
                                Math.sqrt (op2.a * op2.a + op2.b * op2.b))
                                return true;
                        else
                                return false;
        }
}
class Operator_Overloading3
{
        static void Main()
        {
                complex obj1 = new complex(5, 10);
                complex obj2 =  new complex(10, 30);
                complex obj3 = new complex(1, 3);
                complex obj4 = new complex(10, 5)

                Console.Write("obj1 = ");
                obj1.display();
```

```
            Console.Write("obj2 = ");
            obj2.display();
            Console.Write("obj3 = ");
            obj3.display();
            Console.Write("obj4 = ");
            obj4.display();
            Console.WriteLine();

            if (obj1 < obj2)
                    Console.WriteLine("obj1 < obj2 is true");
            else if (obj1 > obj2)
                    Console.WriteLine("obj1 > obj2 is true");
            else
                    Console.WriteLine("obj1 and obj2 are equal in magnitude");
            Console.WriteLine();

            if (obj1 < obj3)
                    Console.WriteLine("obj1 > obj3 is true");
            else if (obj1 > obj3)
                    Console.WriteLine("obj1 < obj3 is true");
            else
                    Console.WriteLine("obj1 and obj2 are equal in magnitude");
            Console.WriteLine();

            if (obj1 < obj4)
                    Console.WriteLine("obj1 < obj4 is true");
            else if (obj1 > obj4)
                    Console.WriteLine("obj1 > obj4 is true");
            else
                    Console.WriteLine("obj1 and obj4 are equal in magnitude");
        }
}
```

Output:

```
        obj1 = 5 + i10
        obj2 = 10 +i30
        obj3 = 1 + i3
        obj4 = 10 + i5

        obj1  < obj2 is true

        obj1 > obj3 is true

        obj1 and obj4 are equal in magnitude
```

3.5 OVERLOADING TRUE & FALSE

The two keywords, *true* and *false*, can be used as unary operators as well for the purpose of overlaoading. We have already stated in section 3.2 that these two unary boolean operators must be overloaded as a pair and cannot be overloaded individually as such. The most general form as to how to overload these two operators is:

```
// How to overload the unary operator true - generalized form of operator method
public static bool operator true(parameter_type operand)
{
        /* return true or false */
}
// How to overload the unary operator false - generalized form of operator method
public static bool operator false(parameter_type operand)
{
        /* return true or false */
}
```

Thus, both return a *bool* result. Once true and false are overloaded as a pair for a specific class, the objects of that class can be used to control/execute the *if, while, do-while* and *for* constructs as well as in a *ternary ? :* expression.

For the class *complex*, the operators true and false can be overloaded in the following manner (*Example 57*: here, we shall be assuming that a complex number is true if at least one of its coordinates (real and imaginary parts) is non-zero. If both the real and imaginary parts are zero, then, the complex number is false.)

<u>*Example 57*</u>

```
/* Overloading true and false for complex*/
/* Author: Arunesh; Date: 23/03/2011 */
using System;
class complex
{
        int a, b;                              // a + ib form

        public complex()
        { a = b = 0;}

        public complex(int i, int j)
        { a = i; b = j; }

        public void display()
        {
                Console.WriteLine(a + " i" + b);
        }
```

```
/* Overloading unary operator true for complex */

public static bool operator true(complex op)
{
        if ((op.a != 0) \\ (op.b != 0))
                return true;
                        // at least one of the real and imaginary parts is non-zero
        else
                return false;
}

/* Overloading unary operator false for complex */

public static bool operator false(complex op)
{
        if ((op.a == 0) && (op.b == 0))
                return true;
                        // both the real and imaginary parts are zero
        else
                return false;
}

/* Overloading unary ++ for complex */

public static complex operator ++(complex op)
{
        complex result = new complex();
        result.a =  op.a + 1;
        result.b =  op.b + 1;
        return result;
}

/* Overloading unary -- for complex */

public static complex operator --(complex op)
{
        complex result = new complex();
        result.a =  op.a - 1;
        result.b =  op.b - 1;
        return result;
}
}
```

```
class TrueFalse_Overloading
{
        static void Main()
        {
                complex obj1 = new complex(3, 0);
                complex obj2 =  new complex(0, 3);
                complex obj3 = new complex(0, 0);
                complex obj4 = new complex(3, 3);

                Console.Write("obj1 = ");
                obj1.display();
                Console.Write("obj2 = ");
                obj2.display();
                Console.Write("obj3 = ");
                obj3.display();
                Console.Write("obj4 = ");
                obj4.display();

                Console.WriteLine();

                if (obj1)
                        Console.WriteLine("obj1 is true");
                else
                        Console.WriteLine("obj1 is false);

                if (obj2)
                        Console.WriteLine("ob2 is true");
                else
                        Console.WriteLine("obj2 is false);

                if (obj3)
                        Console.WriteLine("obj3 is true");
                else
                        Console.WriteLine("obj3 is false);

                if (obj4)
                        Console.WriteLine("obj4 is true");
                else
                        Console.WriteLine("obj4 is false);

                Console.WriteLine();
```

```
        Console.Writeline(" Controlling a while loop using a complex object:)
        while (! obj3)
        {
                obj3.display();
                obj3++;
        }
        // display and increment obj3 until it becomes non-zero

        Console.WriteLine();

        Console.Writeline(" Controlling a do-while loop using a complex object:)
        do
        {
                obj4.display();
                - -obj4;
        } while (obj4);
        // display and decrement obj4 until it becomes zero
    }
}
```

Output:

```
obj1= 3 + i0
obj2 =  0 + i3
obj3 = 0 + i0
obj4 = 3 + i3

obj1 is true
obj2 is true
obj3 is false
obj4 is true

Controlling a while loop using a complex object:
0 + i0

Controlling a do-while loop using a complex object:
3 + i3
2 + i2
1 + i
```

/* *Carefully, note how complex objects are used to control the if statements, and while & do-while loops.* The if statement succeeds if the evaluation of the complex object happens to be *true* (at least one of its real and imaginary parts is non-zero). In the case of the while loop, the condition succeeds if the evaluation of the complex object *obj3* happens to be false and the loop continues as long as *obj3* returns false. Similarly, the do-while loop continues to run as long as *obj4* evaluates as true; each iteration of the loop decrements *obj4* and when *obj4* evaluates as false (both its real and imaginary parts become zero), the loop stops. */

3.6 OVERLOADING LOGICAL OPERATORS

C# defines the logical operators: |, &, !, &&, and | |. Out of these five logical operators, the two short-circuit operators, && and | |, cannot be overloaded, and, only !, &, and ! can be overloaded, as already mentioned in section 3.2. By following certain rules, though, we can still obtain the benefits of these two short-circuit operators. In the following two subsections, we discuss each of these two situations.

3.6.1 Overloading Logical Operators - A Simple Approach

In the first approach, we shall not be enabling the two short-circuit logical operators and only overloading the remaining three logical operators, viz., |, &, and !, with each of them returning a boolean result. Here is a version of *complex* in *Example 58* that overloads |, &, and !, for the class of complex numbers. As before, we shall be assuming that a complex number is *true* if at least one of its coordinates (real and imaginary parts) is non-zero. If both the real and imaginary parts are zero, then, the complex number is *false*.

<u>Example 58</u>

```
/* Logical Operator Overloading - A Simple Approach */
/* Author: Arunesh; Date: 23/03/2011 */
using System;
class complex
{
        int a, b;                              // a + ib form

        public complex()
        { a = b = 0;}

        public complex(int i, int j)
        { a = i; b = j; }

        public void display()
        {
                Console.WriteLine(a + " i" + b);
        }

        /* Overloading | */

        public static bool operator | (complex op1, complex op2)
        {
                if ((op1.a != 0) | | (op1.b != 0)) | ((op2.a != 0) | | (op2.b != 0)
                        return true;
                else
                        return false;
        }
```

```
        /* Overloading & */

        public static bool operator & (complex op1, complex op2)
        {
                if((op1.a != 0) && (op1.b != 0)) & ((op2.a != 0) && (op2.b != 0))
                        return true;
                else
                        return false;
        }

        /* Overloading ! */

        public static bool operator ! (complex op)
        {
                if((op.a != 0) || (op.b != 0))
                        return false;
                else
                        return true;
        }
}
class Logical_Operator_Overloading1
{
        static void Main()
        {
                complex obj1 = new complex(3, 0);
                complex obj2 =  new complex(0, 3);
                complex obj3 = new complex(0, 0);

                Console.Write("obj1 = ");
                obj1.display();
                Console.Write("obj2 = ");
                obj2.display();
                Console.Write("obj3 = ");
                obj3.display();

                Console.WriteLine();

                if(!obj1)
                        Console.WriteLine("obj1 is false");
                else
                        Console.WriteLine("obj1 is true);
```

```
        if (!obj2)
                Console.WriteLine("obj2 is false");
        else
                Console.WriteLine("obj2 is true");
        if (!obj3)
                Console.WriteLine("obj3 is false");
        else
                Console.WriteLine("obj3 is true);
        Console.Writeline();

        if (obj1 | obj2)
                Console.WriteLine("obj1 | obj2 is true");
        else
                Console.WriteLine("obj1 | obj2 is false);
        if (obj1 | obj3)
                Console.WriteLine("obj1 | obj3 is true");
        else
                Console.WriteLine("obj1 | obj3 is false);
        Console.WriteLine();

        if (obj1 & obj2)
                Console.WriteLine("obj1 & obj2 is true");
        else
                Console.WriteLine("obj1 & obj2 is false);
        if (obj1 & obj3)
                Console.WriteLine("obj1 & obj3 is true");
        else
                Console.WriteLine("obj1 & obj3 is false);
    }
}
```

Output:

```
obj1= 3 + i0
obj2 = 0 + i3
obj3 = 0 + i0

obj1 is true
obj2 is true
obj3 is false

obj1 |  obj2 is true
obj1 | obj3 is true

obj1 & obj2 is true
obj1 & obj3 is false
```

/ Carefully, note how in Example 58, each of the |, &, and ! operator methods return a bool result.* This is essential for the normal usage of these operators. You may note that for all the built-in types, the outcome of a logical operation is a *bool* data type. So, the simple approach adopted in *Example 58* is a rational and logical approach. However, this approach doesn't work if we have to enable the short-circuit operators, && and ||. In the next subsection we demonstrate how to go about enabling these two short-circuit operators. */

3.6.2 Enabling the Short-Circuit Operators && and || (Overloading Logical Operators - A Better Approach)

To enable the two short-circuit operatos, we need to follow the following four rules:

(1) The class must overload | and &.
(2) The return type of the overloaded | and & must be the same as their class.
(3) Each parameter has to be a reference to the object of the class for which the operator is being overloaded.
(4) The *true* and *false* operators must be overloaded for the class.

After taking care of the above four conditions, the short-circuit operators, *&&* and | |, become available for use by themselves. The following example (*Example 59*) demonstrates how to properly carry out the implementation of overloading |, &, and ! so as to enable the short-circuit operators - *&&* and | |.

Example 59

```
/* Logical Operator Overloading - A Better Approach */
// This approach enables the short-circuit operators - && and | | - automatically
/* Author: Arunesh; Date: 23/03/2011 */
using System;
class complex
{
        int a, b;                          // a + ib form

        public complex()
        { a = b = 0;}

        public complex(int i, int j)
        { a = i; b = j; }

        public void display()
        {
                Console.WriteLine(a + "  i" + b);
        }
```

```
/* Overloading | for short-circuit evaluation */

public static bool operator | (complex op1, complex op2)
{
        if((op1.a != 0) || (op1.b != 0)) | ((op2.a != 0) || (op2.b != 0)
                return new complex(1, 1);
        else
                return new complex(0, 0);
                        /* note carefuly how true and false complex objects are being
                        returned, respectively */
}

/* Overloading & for short-circuit evaluation */

public static bool operator & (complex op1, complex op2)
{
        if ((op1.a != 0) && (op1.b != 0)) & ((op2.a != 0) && (op2.b != 0))
                return new complex(1, 1);
        else
                return new complex(0, 0);
                        /* note carefuly how true and false complex objects are being
                        returned, respectively */
}

/* Overloading ! */

public static bool operator ! (complex op)
{
        if (op)
                return false;
        else
                return true;
}

/* Overloading true */

public static bool operator true(complex op)
{
        if ((op.a != 0) || (op.b != 0))
                return true;
                        // at least one of the real and imaginary parts is non-zero
        else
                return false;
}
```

```
        /* Overloading false */

        public static bool operator false(complex op)
        {
                if ((op.a == 0) && (op.b == 0))
                        return true;
                                // both the real and imaginary parts are zero
                else
                        return false;
        }
}
class Logical_Operator_Overloading2
{
        static void Main()
        {
                complex obj1 = new complex(3, 0);
                complex obj2 =  new complex(0, 3);
                complex obj3 = new complex(0, 0);

                Console.Write("obj1 = ");
                obj1.display();
                Console.Write("obj2 = ");
                obj2.display();
                Console.Write("obj3 = ");
                obj3.display();

                Console.WriteLine();

                if (!obj1)
                        Console.WriteLine("obj1 is false");
                else
                        Console.WriteLine("obj1 is true);
                if (!obj2)
                        Console.WriteLine("obj2 is false");
                else
                        Console.WriteLine("obj2 is true");
                if (!obj3)
                        Console.WriteLine("obj3 is false");
                else
                        Console.WriteLine("obj3 is true);

                Console.Writeline();
```

```
        Console.WriteLine("First, use & and |");

        if (obj1 & obj2)
                Console.WriteLine("obj1 & obj2 is true");
        else
                Console.WriteLine("obj1 & obj2 is false);
        if (obj1 & obj3)
                Console.WriteLine("obj1 & obj3 is true");
        else
                Console.WriteLine("obj1 & obj3 is false);
        if (obj1 | obj2)
                Console.WriteLine("obj1 | obj2 is true");
        else
                Console.WriteLine("obj1 | obj2 is false);
        if (obj1 | obj3)
                Console.WriteLine("obj1 | obj3 is true");
        else
                Console.WriteLine("obj1 | obj3 is false);

        Console.WriteLine();

        Console.WriteLine("Now, use Short-Circuit operators && and | |");

        if (obj1 && obj2)
                Console.WriteLine("obj1 && obj2 is true");
        else
                Console.WriteLine("obj1 & obj2 is false);
        if (obj1 && obj3)
                Console.WriteLine("obj1 && obj3 is true");
        else
                Console.WriteLine("obj1 & obj3 is false);
        if (obj1 | | obj2)
                Console.WriteLine("obj1 | | obj2 is true");
        else
                Console.WriteLine("obj1 | | obj2 is false);
        if (obj1 || obj3)
                Console.WriteLine("obj1 | | obj3 is true");
        else
                Console.WriteLine("obj1 | | obj3 is false);

    }
}
```

Output:

obj1= 3 + i0
obj2 = 0 + i3
obj3 = 0 + i0

obj1 is true
obj2 is true
obj3 is false

First, use & and |
obj1 & obj2 is true
obj1 & obj3 is false
obj1 | obj2 is true
obj1 | obj3 is true

Now, use Short-Circuit operators && and ||
obj1 && obj2 is true
obj1 && obj3 is false
obj1 || obj2 is true
obj1 || obj3 is true

/ Carefully, note how in Example 59 each of the | and & operator methods returns an object of type complex.* If the result of the operation is true, then a true *complex* object (in which at least one of the real or imaginary parts is non-zero) is generated and returned. Otherwise, a false *complex* object (in which both the real and imaginary parts are zero) is generated and returned.

Also, note that the necessary four conditions have been met and whence, the short-circuit operators, && and ||, are now available for use on *complex* objects.They operate as follows: The first operand is tested by using operator *true* (for ||) or operator *false* (for &&). If it can find out the result of the operation, then the corresponding & or | is not invoked; otherwise, the corresponding & or | is used to find out the result. Thus, using a && or || leads to evaluating the corresponding & or | only if the first operand cannot determine the result of the expression. *For instance, take the following statement from the example program:*

```
if(obj1 || obj3)
        Console.WriteLine("obj1 || obj3 is true");
```

The true operator is first invoked on obj1. Since obj1 is true in this case, there is no need to use the | operator method.

But, if the statement had been written like this:

```
if(obj3 || obj1)
        Console.WriteLine("obj3 || obj1 is true");
```

*Then, the true operator would have been first invoked on obj3, which happens to be false in this case so that the | operator method would have been used to check if a was true (which it is, in this situation). */*

3.7 CONVERSION OPERATORS

Certain situations warrant the use of an object of a class in an expression involving other data types. In some cases, as we have seen earlier (*int* + *complex* etc.), operator overloading can help to do this. But, in other cases, you simply want a type conversion from the class type to the target type. To manoeuvre such cases, C# allows the creation of special *operator methods* referred to as *convesion operators*. These *conversion operators* help in fully integrating the class types into the C# programming zone/domain by allowing the class objects to be freely interspersed with other types of data so long as conversions to these other data types are defined.There are two kinds of *conversion operators*, namely, implicit and explicit. We shall examine both of these one by one in the coming two subsections.

3.7.1 Implicit Conversion Operators

An *implicit conversion* is invoked automatically such as when an object is used in an expression with the target type. The most general form of an *implicit conversion operator* is:

```
public static implicit operator target_type(source_type st)
{
        return val;
}
```

where, *source_type* is the data type you are converting from; *target_type* is the type you are converting to; and, *val* is the value of the calss after conversion. The *conversion operator* returns data of type *target_type,* and no other return type specifier is permitted.

We shall illustrate the concept of an *implicit conversion operator* by creating one for the class *complex*. Let us say, you wish to convert a complex number into an integer sothat it can be used in an integral expression. Moreover, the conversion shall occur by taking the product of the real and imaginary parts. Here is a program *(Example 60)* that accomplishes this convesion.

Example 60

```
/* Illustration of Implicit Conversion*/
/* Author: Arunesh; Date: 23/03/2011 */
using System;
class complex
{
        int a, b;                       // a + ib form

        public complex()
        { a = b = 0;}

        public complex(int i, int j)
        { a = i; b = j; }
```

```
        public void display()
        {
                Console.WriteLine(a + "  i" + b);
                Console.WriteLine();
        }

        /* Overloading binary + for complex*/

        public static complex operator +(complex op1, complex op2)
        {
                complex result = new complex();
                result.a = op1.a +  op2a;
                result.b = op1.b +  op2.b;
                return result;
        }


        /* Implicit Conversion from complex to int*/

        public static implicit operator int(complex op)
        {
                return op.a * op.b;
        }
}
class Implicit_Conversion
{
        static void Main()
        {
                complex obj1 = new complex(5, 15);
                complex obj2 =  new complex(3, 30);
                complex obj3 = new complex();

                int N;

                Console.Write("obj1 = ");
                obj1.display();
                Console.Write("obj2 = ");
                obj2.display();

                obj3 = obj1 + obj2;       // add obj1 and obj2
                Console.Write("obj3 = obj1 + obj2 = ");
                obj3.display();
```

```
            N = obj1;          // implicitly convert to int
            Console.WriteLine("N = obj1 = " + N);
            Console.WriteLine();

            N = obj1 * 4 - obj2;      // implicitly convert to int
            Console.WriteLine("N = obj1 * 4 - obj2 = " + N);
        }
}
```

<u>Output</u>:

```
    obj1 = 5 + i15

    obj2 = 3 + i30

    obj3 = obj1 + obj2 = 8 + i45

    N = obj1 = 75

    N = obj1 * 4 - obj2 = 210
```

/* As the above output indicates, when a complex object is used in an integer expression, such as *N = obj1,* the conversion is applied to the complex object. In ths particular case, the implicit conversion returns the value *75*, which is the product of the real and imaginary parts of *obj1*. However, in cases, when an expression does not need a conversion to *int*, the conversion operator is not invoked. It is for this reason that *obj3 = obj1 + obj2* does not call upon the operator *int()*.

You might wonder as to how the expression *N = obj1 * 4 - obj2* evaluates to *210*. Well, *obj1* and *obj2* are implicitly converted to the integers *75* and *90* respectively, which are the products of their real and imaginary parts. After this, the expression simply becomes:

*N = 75 * 4 - 90*
= 300 - 90
= 210

*/

There is one more interesting point regarding *conversion operators*, in general (implicit as well as explicit). *And, that is you may define as many conversion operators as you like to meet all your divergent needs.* Thus, you may create a second *conversion operator* that translates *complex* to *double*, let us say.

Each conversion is applied independently. Further, each conversion is invoked automatically in the case of *implicit conversion* and by means of an explicit cast in the case of *explicit conversion*, as we shall see in the next subsection.

3.7.2 Explicit Conversion Operators

An *explicit conversion* is not invoked automatically and is called into play only in case an explicit cast is used such as when an object is used in an expression with the target type. The most general form of an *implicit conversion operator* is:

```
public static explicit operator target_type(source_type st)
{
        return val;
}
```

where, *source_type* is the data type you are converting from; *target_type* is the type you are converting to; and, *val* is the value of the calss after conversion. The *conversion operator* returns data of type *target_type,* and no other return type specifier is permitted.

We shall illustrate the concept of an *explicit conversion operator* by creating one for the class *complex.* In fact, we shall rework the previous example program (*Example 60*) for accomplishing this as follows in *Example 61.*

<u>Example 61</u>

```
/* Illustration of Explicit Conversion*/
/* Author: Arunesh; Date: 23/03/2011 */
using System;
class complex
{
        int a, b;                       // a + ib form

        public complex()
        { a = b = 0;}

        public complex(int i, int j)
        { a = i; b = j; }

        public void display()
        {
                Console.WriteLine(a + " i" + b);
                Console.WriteLine();
        }

        /* Overloading binary + for complex*/

        public static complex operator +(complex op1, complex op2)
        {
                complex result = new complex();
                result.a = op1.a +  op2a;
                result.b = op1.b +  op2.b;
                return result;
        }
```

```
/*Explicit Conversion from complex to int*/

    public static explicit operator int(complex op)
    {
        return op.a * op.b;
    }
}
class Explicit_Conversion
{
    static void Main()
    {
        complex obj1 = new complex(5, 15);
        complex obj2 = new complex(3, 30);
        complex obj3 = new complex();

        int N;

        Console.Write("obj1 = ");
        obj1.display();
        Console.Write("obj2 = ");
        obj2.display();

        obj3 = obj1 + obj2;      // add obj1 and obj2
        Console.Write("obj3 = obj1 + obj2 = ");
        obj3.display();

        N = (int) obj1;  // explicitly convert to int (cast required)
        Console.WriteLine("N = obj1 = " + N);
        Console.WriteLine();

        N = (int) obj1 * 4 - (int) obj2;   // explicitly convert to int (casts required)
        Console.WriteLine("N = obj1 * 4 - obj2 = " + N);
    }
}
```

Output:

```
obj1 = 5 + i15

obj2 = 3 + i30

obj3 = obj1 + obj2 = 8 + i45

N = obj1 = 75

N = obj1 * 4 - obj2 = 210
```

/* You can easily infer that the output has not changed from the previous example program *(Example 60)*.

So, you might ask - "What's the difference between the two example programs?".Well, the conversion operator is now specified as explicit so that conversion to int has to be explicitly cast, e.g., in the two lines:

N = (int) obj1; // explicitly convert to int (cast required)
*N = (int) obj1 * 4 - (int) obj2; // explicitly convert to int (casts required)*
if the casts are peeled off, the program shall refuse to compile!
*/

3.7.3 Conversion Operators: Tips And Restrictions

The use of *conversion operators* widens the scope of the C# programming environment to a great extent by allowing for full class integration, as already stated. However, there are a few restrictions on their use. First, either the target type or the source type of the conversion has to be the class for which the *conversion operator* is declared so that the conversion from *double* to *int* cannot be redefined, for example. Second, a conversion from or to *object* (for a detailed discussion of the universal data type - *object* - consult chapter 5) cannot be specified. Third (and very significantly), both an implicit as well as an explicit conversion cannot be declared for the same source and target types. Fourth, a conversion from a base class to a derived class cannot be specified (base and derived classes are discussed at length in chapter 5). Finally, a conversion from or to an interface cannot be defined (interfaces are described in chapter 6).

Apart from these restrictions, there are some tips for byou to follow while choosing between implicit and explicit *conversion operators*:

(1) Implicit conversions are convenient to use but should only be used in cases where the conversion is, by its very nature, error-free and bug-free.

(2) For using implicit conversions, two rules of the thumb must be taken into account:

   (i) No *loss* of important data takes place such as overflow, loss of sign, truncation or it should be the case that such *loss* of information is acceptable under the given circumstances.

   (ii) The conversion should not result in raising an *exception* (exception handling is discussed in detail in chapter 7).

(3) If any of the two conditions above are not met, you must resort to explicit conversion.

Operator Overloading - A CASE STUDY

Throughout this chapter you have seen the use of the class *complex* to illustrate and demonstrate operator overloading and we are confident that it has served you well. However, before concluding this chapter, it might prove to be useful and pretty much handy to work out another example as a case study. The general principles and guidelines remaining the same, the study shows the immense power of operator overloading especially in the areas of *type extensibility*. The example develops a class called *Spherical* and defines different varied operations for it. The class maintains the coordinates of an object in three-dimensional spherical space. The case study uses the *Spherical* class to implement a spherical data type. It uses an *int* for its underlying storage. It defines the following eight *operators/operations*:

(1) Addition of a *Spherical* to a *Spherical*
(2) Addition of an *int* to a *Spherical*
(3) Addition of a *Spherical* to an *int*
(4) Greater than (>) and Less than (<)
(5) The *increment operator (++)*
(6) The *decrement operator (--)*
(7) *Conversion* to *int* from *Spherical*
(8) *Conversion* to *Spherical* from *int*

These *operators/operations* are sufficient to illustrate how a class type can be fully integrated into the C# type system althuogh for a complete *Spherical* implementation, you will need to specify all of the other operators as well; you can take it as an exercise to try adding these on your own. Meanwhile, our aforesaid *Spherical* class is as shown in *Example 62* along with a *SphericalDemo*, which demonstrates and illustrates its use.

Example 62

```
/* Operator Overloading - A case Study */
/* Author: Arunesh; Date: 23/03/2011 */
using System;
class Spherical
{
    int a, b, c;                          // spherical coordinates

    public complex()
    { a = b = c= 0;}

    public complex(int i, int j, int k)
    { a = i; b = j; c = k}
```

```
public void display()
{
        Console.WriteLine(a + ", " + b + ", " + c);
        Console.WriteLine();
}

/* Overloading binary + for Spherical*/

public static Spherical operator +(Spherical op1, Spherical op2)
{
        Spherical result = new Spherical();
        result.a = op1.a +  op2a;
        result.b = op1.b +  op2.b;
        result.c = op1.c  + op2.c;

        return result;
}

/* Overloading binary + for Spherical + int*/

public static Spherical operator +(Spherical op1, int op2)
{
                Spherical result = new Spherical();
                result.a = op1.a +  op2;
                result.b = op1.b +  op2;
                result.c = op1.c + op2;

                // note the adition of op2 to all the coordinates of op1
                // this operation can be used to translate the three axes

                return result;
}

/* Overloading binary + for int + Spherical */

public static Spherical operator +(int op1, complex op2)
{
                Spherical result = new Spherical();
                result.a = op2.a +  op1;
```

```
                result.b = op2.b +  op1;
                result.c = op2.c + op1;

                // note the adition of op1 to all the coordinates of op2
                // this operation can be used to translate the three axes

                return result;
}

/* Overloading  unary ++ for Spherical */

public static Spherical operator ++(Spherical op)
{
        complex Spherical = new Spherical();
        result.a =  op.a + 1;
        result.b =  op.b + 1;
        result.c = op.c + 1;

        return result; // return the incremented result
}

/* Overloading unary -- for complex */

public static Spherical operator --(Spherical op)
{
        Spherical result  = new Spherical();
        result.a =  op.a - 1;
        result.b =  op.b - 1;
        result.c = op.c - 1;

        return result; // return the decremented result
}

/* Overloading relational operator < for Spherical */

public static bool operator <(Spherical op1, Spherical op2)
{
        if (Math.sqrt(op1.a * op1.a +  op1.b * op1.b  + op1.c * op1.c) <
                Math.sqrt (op2.a * op2.a + op2.b * op2.b + op2.c + op2.c))
```

```
                return true;

        /* op1 < op2 if  the distance of op1 from the origin is less
        than the distance of op2 from the origin.
        In such a case, op2 lies on the larger sphere. */

        else
                return false;
}

/* Overloading relational operator > for Spherical */

public static bool operator <(Spherical op1, Spherical op2)
{
    if (Math.sqrt(op1.a * op1.a +  op1.b * op1.b + op1.c * op1.c) >
        Math.sqrt (op2.a * op2.a + op2.b * op2.b + op2.c + op2.c))

                return true;

    /* op1 > op2 if  the distance of op1 from the origin is greater
        than the distance of op2 from the origin.
    In such a case, op1 lies on the larger sphere. */

        else
                return false;
}

/* If neither of the above two relational operators, viz., < and >, returns
true, then, op1 and op2 are at the same distance from the origin, and
whence, lie on the same sphere. */
// Of course, you may devise other ordering schemes

/* Implicit Conversion from Spherical to int*/

public static implicit operator int(Spherical op)
{
    return op.a * op.b * op.c;

    /* Carefully, note how the Spherical operand op has been used to
        convert to int as a product of its three coordinates */
}
```

```
        /* Implicit Conversion from int to Spherical */

        public static implicit operator Spherical(int op)
        {
                return new Spherical(op, op, op);

                /* Carefully, note how the int operand op has been used to convert
                        to Spherical */
        }
}
class SphericalDemo
{
        static void Main()
        {
                Spherical obj1 = new Spherical(5, 10, 15);
                Spherical obj2 =  new Spherical(10, 20, 30);
                Spherical obj3 = new Spherical();

                Console.Write("obj1 = ");
                obj1.display();
                Console.Write("obj2 = ");
                obj2.display();

                obj3 = obj1 + obj2;   // add obj1 and obj2
                Console.Write("obj3 = obj1 + obj2 = ");
                obj3.display();

                int N = 5;
                Console.WriteLine("N = " + N);
                Console.WriteLine();

                obj2 = obj3 +  N;
                Console.Write("obj2 = obj3 + N = ");
                obj2.display();

                obj2 = N + obj1;
                Console.Write("obj2 = N + obj1 = ");
                obj2.display();
```

```
obj3 = obj2++;                    // post-increment obj1
Console.Write("obj3 = obj2++ = ");
obj3.display();

Console.Write("obj2 = ");
obj2.display();

obj3 = --obj1;           // pre-decrement obj1
Console.Write("obj3 = --obj1 = ");
obj3.display();

Console.Write("obj1 = ");
obj1.display();
        if (obj1 <  obj2)
        Console.WriteLine("obj1 < obj2 is true");
else if (obj1 >  obj2)
        Console.WriteLine("obj1 > obj2 is true");
else
        Console.WriteLine("obj1 and obj2 are at the same distance
                from the origin");
Console.WriteLine();

if (obj1 <  obj3)
        Console.WriteLine("obj1 > obj3 is true");
else if (obj1 >  obj3)
        Console.WriteLine("obj1 < obj3 is true");
else
        Console.WriteLine("obj1 and obj3 are at the same distance
                from the origin");
Console.WriteLine();

Spherical obj4 = new Spherical(15, 20, 25);
obj4.display();

if (obj4 <  obj2)
        Console.WriteLine("obj4 < obj2 is true");
else if (obj4 >  obj2)
        Console.WriteLine("obj4 > obj2 is true");
```

```
        else
                Console.WriteLine("obj4 and obj2 are at the same distance
                        from the origin");
        Console.WriteLine();

        N = obj4;       // implicitly convert to int
        Console.WriteLine("N = obj4 = " + N);
        Console.WriteLine();

        N = obj4 / 30 - obj1 + 250;   // implicitly convert to int
        Console.WriteLine("N = obj4 / 30 - obj1 + 250 = " + N);
        Console.WriteLine();

        obj2 = N;       // implicitly convert to Spherical
        Console.WriteLine("obj2 = N = ");
        obj2.display();
    }
}
```

Output:

obj1 = 5 , 10, 15

obj2 = 10, 20, 30

obj3 = obj1 + obj2 = 15, 30, 45

N = 5

obj2 = obj3 + N = 20, 35, 50

obj2 = N + obj1 = 10, 15, 20

obj3 = obj2++ = 10, 15, 20

obj2 = 11, 16, 21

obj3 = --obj1 = 4, 9, 14

obj1 = 4, 9, 14

obj1 < obj2 is true

obj1 and obj3 are at the same distance from the origin

obj4 = 15, 20, 25

obj4 > obj2 is true

N = obj4 = 7500

N = obj4 / 30 - obj1 + 250 = -4

obj2 = N = -4, -4, -4

/* Most of the operations of *Spherical* should be easy to comprehend. However, you must note one interesting and important feature. The conversion operatos have made it easy to integrate *Spherical* into the C# type system or the C# programming environment, so to say. Since conversions have been specified for both *Spherical* to *int* and from *int* to *Spherical*, a *Spherical* object can be freely intermingled in arithmetic expressions. For example, take the following expression from the example program as a case in point:

N = obj4 / 30 - obj1 + 250;

Here, *N* is an *int*, as are *30* and *250*, but *obj4* and *obj2* are *Spherical*. These two types are compatible in the above expression only because of the fact that *implicit conversion* from *Spherical* to *int* has been defined. In this specific case,because the rest of the expression is of type *int*, *obj4* and *obj2* are converted to *int* by the corresponding conversion method.

Similarly, the conversion method from *int* to *Spherical* allows for a *Spherical* object to be assigned an int value. For example, take the folowing statement from the example program as a case in point:

obj2 = N;

It works in the following manner: The conversion operator from *int* to *Spherical* is invoked, which causes a new *Spherical* object to be generated that contains as its three coordinates, the value of int *N*, which is *-4* in this case. This newly created *Spherical* object is then assigned to *obj2*. It is needless to add that without such conversion operatos, these expressions are not permissiible and are not allowed.

***/**

PRACTICAL SESSION

#1 Pick out the correct alternative(s) from the following multiple choce problems:

(i) Which of the following unary operators can be overloaded?
- (a) *false*
- (b) *is*
- (c) *true*
- (d) *new*
- (e) All of the above
- (f) None of the above

(ii) Which of the following operators cannot be overloaded?
- (a) |
- (b) &&
- (c) &
- (d) ||
- (e) All of the above
- (f) None of the above

(iii) Which of the following is the correct way to overload the binary - operator?
- (a) *public s_type operator - (s_type x, s_type y)*
- (b) *public abstract operator - (s_type x, s_type y)*
- (c) *public abstract s_type operator - (s_type x, s_type y)*
- (d) *public static s_type operator - (s_type x, s_type y)*
- (e) All of the above
- (f) None of the above

#2 State True (T) or False (F):
- (i) We can change the meaning of an operator using the operator overloading principle.
- (ii) The concept of operator overloading works only when applied to class objects.
- (iii) The compound assignment operator *= can be overloaded.
- (iv) Relational operators must be overloaded in pairs.
- (v) By overloading an opertator, we can change its precedence.
- (vi) An operator method must be declared as public.
- (vii) An operator method must be declared as static.
- (viii) While overloading a relational operator, the return type must be bool type.

#3 (a) Is operator overloading necessary? Why or why not? Elaborate.

(b) Elucidate the most general *syntax* of overloading a binary operator.

#4 (a) Point out the error(s), if any, in the following program:

```
using system;
class vacuum
{
        int ctr;
        public vacuum()
        {
                ctr = 0;
        }
        public static vacuum operator++()
        {
                ctr++;
                return vacuum(ctr);
        }
}
class vaccum_obj
{
        static void Main()
        {
                vacuum obj;
                obj++;
        }
}
```

(b) Design a class **polar** that defines a point in the plane using *polar coordinates*, viz., *radius and angle.*

Use the overloaded increment operator ++ to increment a **polar** object.

{ Tip: We cannot directly increment *polar values*. First, we shall have to convert *polar coordinates* into *rectangular* ones, then increment them, and finally, convert these *rectangular coordinates* into *polar* ones. If *X* (*x-coordinate*) & *Y* (*y-coordinate*) are the *rectangular coordinates* while *R* (*radius*) & *A* (*angle*) are the corresponding *polar coordinates*, then, you shall find the following *formulae* useful:

(I) $X = R * cosA$
(II) $Y = R * sinA$
(III) $A = tan^{-1}(Y/X)$
(IV) $R = sqrt(X * X + Y * Y)$

}

#5 (a) Implement a class called *Quatret* that develops a four-bit integer type and defines the following eight *operators/operations* for it:

(i) Addition of a *Quatret* to a *Quatret*
(ii) Addition of an *int* to a *Quatret*
(iii) Addition of a *Quatret* to an *int*
(iv) Greater than (>) and Less than (<)
(v) The *increment operator (++)*
(vi) The *decrement operator (--)*
(vii) *Conversion* to *int* from *Quatret*
(viii) *Conversion* to *Quatret* from *int*

Use the *Quatret* class to implement a quatret data type. It should use an *unsigned int* for its underlying storage but should restrict the values that can be held from 0 through 15.

Develop the complete *Quatret* class along with *QuatretDemo*, which should illustrate and demonstrate its use.

(b) In section 3.8, we had developed the class *Spherical*. Make use of this class to overload both the binary and unary minus opertors '-'.

{Tip: *If x(a1, b1, c2) and y(a2, b2, c2) are two spherical coordinates, then,*
x -y = (a1 - a2, b1 - b2, c1 - c2).
Similarly, if x(a, b, c) is a spherical coordinate, then,
-x = (-a, -b, -c).
}

CHAPTER 4

INDEXERS AND PROPERTIES

4.0 INTRODUCTION

Indexers and properties are two special types of class members that are related to each other by means of another very important feature of C#, namely, "accessors". These three, namely, indexers, properties, and accessors, form the topic of discussion for us in this chapter.

You can think of an indexer as a smart array in much the same way as you can think of a property as a smart field. Whereas a property encapsulates a single value in a class, an indexer encapsulates a set of values. While properties provide a streamlined and effective approach to control and manage access to a class' instance information/data, indexers offer the means by which an object can be indexed just like an array. Both enhance the power of a class by expanding its integration into C# type system or programming environment as well as by multi-fold increase in its resilience. They are related to each other as both of them are based and rely upon another feature of C# , viz., "accessors", as already mentioned.

Accessors are similar to methods with the sole exception that neither do they have any return type nor do they take any parameters. We shall learn more about indexers, properties, and accessors in the coming sections.

4.1 INDEXERS

We know that array indexing is done using the [ ] operator. We cannot overload this operator for the classes we create but C# allows us to achieve and accomplish the same results by using indexers instead. Indexers provide for an object to be indexed like an array. Another interesting point of note about indexers is that they can be overloaded just like methods.

The primary use of indexers lies in the creation of specialized versions of arrays, which are constrained by one or more conditions. However, an interesting point to note about indexers is that they can be used and employed in any situation or purpose for which an array-like syntax can prove beneficial.

Indexers can be one-dimensional or multi-dimensional, that is to say, they can have one or more dimensions. Thus, we can have as many dimensions as we wish for an indexer according to our needs, suitability, and purposes.

4.1.1 One-Dimensional Indexers

The most general form of one-dimensional indexers is as given below:

```
access_specifier element_type this[int index]
{
        get
                // the get accessor
        {
                // return value specified by index
        }
        set
                // the set accessor
        {
                // set value specified by index
        }
}
```

where, *element_type* is the base type for the indexer. Inside the body of the indexer are two accessors, viz., *get* and *set* that are automatically called when the indexer is used with both the accessors receiving *index* as a parameter. Also, the *access_specifier* can be private or public. It is private, by default.

If the indexer is on the right side of an assignment statement, the *get* accessor is called with the value associated with index being returned. Otherwise, if the indexer is on the left side of an assignment statement, the *set* accessor is called with the value associated with index being set. However, it is not essential for an indexer to support both the accessors, that is, *get* and *set*. A read-only indexer can be created by providing only the *get* accessor while a write-only accessor can be created by providing and implementing only the *set* accessor.

Although the concept of indexers would seem to suggest that there should always be an array underlying an indexer,but, it is indeed not necessary, as seen in *Example 63*. Here, the indexer does not operate on an actual array but only acts like a read-only array that contains the powers of 5 from 0 to 19. In reality, no actual array exists. In fact, the indexer only computes the proper value for a given specific index. Thus, it is important to understand that an indexer simply must provide functionality that appears to be array-like to the user of the indexer.

Also, note that the indexer in this example is read-only as it has a *get* accessior but no *set* accessor. This, in turn, implies that the indexer can only be used only on the right side of an assignment statement, and not on its left. It is, for this reason, that the following statement in the example program has been commented out:

```
//      power[0] = 13;
```

If we had not commented out the above statement, it shall result in a compile-time error due to the fact that no *set* accessor has been defined for the indexer.

<u>*Example 63*</u>

/ Illustration of one-dimensional Indexer */*

/ Author: Arunesh; Date: 23/03/2011 */*

```
using System;
class Powers_of_5
{
        /* access a logical array that contains powers of 5 from 0 to 19 */
        // this is the one-dimensional Indexer for Powers_of_5
        public int this[int index]
        {
                // COMPUTE AND RETURN POWER OF 5: get accessor
                get
                {
                        if ((index >= 0) && (index < 20))
                                return power(index);
                        else
                                return -1;
                }
                // NO set accessor
        }

        int power(int pw)
        {
                int r = 1;
                for (int a = 0; a < pw; a++)
                        r *= 5;
                return r;
        }
}
class Powers_of_5_Demo
{
        static void Main()
        {
                Powers_of_5 pow = new Powers_of_5( );

                Console.WriteLine("The first four powers of 5 are as given below:");
                for (int a = 0; a< 4; a ++)
                        Console.WriteLine(power[a]);

                Console.WrieLine("Two errors due to wrong index are:");
                Console.WriteLine(power[-1] + "/t" + power[20]);

                //      power[0] = 13;          // compilation error! NO set accessor
        }
}
```

Output:

The first four powers of 5 are as given below:
1
5
25
125
Two errors due to wrong index are:
-1 -1

4.1.2 Multi-Dimensional Indexers

We can have indexers for multi-dimensional arrays too. The most general form of a two-dimensional indexer is as given below:

```
access_specifier element_type this[int index1, int index2]
{
        get
                // the get accessor
        {
                // return value specified by index1 and index 2
        }
        set
                // the set accessor
        {
                // set value specified by index1 and index 2
        }
}
```

where, *element_type* is the base type for the indexer. Inside the body of the indexer are two accessors, viz., *get* and *set* that are automatically called when the indexer is used with both the accessors receiving *index* 1 and *index2* as parameters. Also, the *access_specifier* can be private or public. It is private, by default.

One of the gains or benefits of an indexer is that access to an array can be controlled precisely and accurately and improper access can be prevented without causing the program to terminate abnormally. This is demonstrated in *Example 64*. In this example program, the *Array2D* class implements an array that traps boundary errors and whence, prevents run-time exceptions (exception handling is discussed separately in chapter 7) if the array is indexed out-of-bounds. This is achieved by encapsulating the two-dimensional array as a private member of the class and allowing for access to the array only via the indexer. By using such an approach, attempts to gain access to the array beyond its boundaries can be prevented. Moreover, such attempts are made to fail softly and gracefully without resulting in a program/system crash. Further, since *Array2D* employs and uses an indexer, the array can be accessed normally using the conventional, usual and normal array notation.

Example 64

```
/* Illustration of Two-Dimensional Indexer */
/* Author: Arunesh; Date: 23/03/2011*/
using System;
class Array2D
{
        /* reference to underlying array */
        int [ ,] i;
        /* dimensions of underlying array */
        int r, c;
        public int l;     // Length : declared as public
        public bool err;          // boolean result of last operation: also public

        public Array2D(int rows, int cols)
                // construct array given its dimensions
        {
                r = rows;
                c = cols;
                i = new int[r, c];
                l = r * c;
        }

        /* indexer for Array2D follows */
        public int this[int index1, int index2]
        {
                // get accessor
                get
                {
                        if (okay(index1, index2))
                        {
                                err = false;
                                return i[index1, index2];
                        }
                        else
                        {
                                err = true;
                                return 0;
                        }
                }
                // set accessor
                set
                {
```

```
                    if (okay(index1, index2))
                    {
                              i[index1, index2] = value;
                              err = false;
                    }
                    else
                              err = true;
          }
     }

     // CHECKING BOUNDS
     private bool okay(int index1, int index2)
     {
          if (index1 >= 0 & index1 < r  & index2 >= 0 & index2 < c)
                    return true;
          else
                    return false;
     }
}
//        Demonstrate a Two-Dimensional (2D) Indexer
class Indexer2D
{
     static void Main( )
     {
          Array2D  a2d = new Array2D( 2, 3);
          int i;

          /* quiet failures */
          Console.WriteLine("Quiet Failures:");
          for (int x = 0; x < 4; x++)
                    a2d[x, x] = x * 100;
          for (int x = 0; x < 4; x++)
          {
                    i = a2d[x, x];
                    if (i != -1)
                              Console.WriteLine(i);
          }

          Console.WriteLine();

          /* fail with error reports */
          Console.WriteLine("Fail with Error Reports:");
```

```
        for (int x = 0; x < 4; x++)
        {
            a2d[x, x] = x * 100;
            i = a2d[x, x];
            if(!a2d.err)
                Console.WriteLine(i);
            else
                Console.WriteLine("a2d[" + x + ", " + x +
                                        "] out-of-bounds");
        }
    }
}
```

Output:

```
    Quiet Failures:
    0
    100
    0
    0

    Fail with Error Reports:
    0
    100
    a2d[2, 2] out-of-bounds
    a2d[3, 3] out-of-bounds
```

/* The 2Dindexer prevents the array boundaries from being overrun. Let us look carefully at each part of the indexer. It begins with the line:

public int this[int index1, int index2]

which declares a two-dimensional indexer that operates on *int* elements. The two indexes are passed in *index1* and *index2* respectively. Also, the indexer is public allowing for its use by code outside of its class. The indexer has two accessors, namely, *get* and *set*. Thus, it is a read-write (both read and write) indexer. The *get* accessor is shown next:

```
get
{
        if (okay(index1, index2))
        {
                err = false;
                return i[index1, index2];
        }
        else
        {
                err = true;
```

```
            return 0;
        }
    }
```

which prevents array boundary errors by first checking and confirming that the indexes are not out-of-bounds. This range checking is performed by the *okay()* method, that returns *true* if the indexes are valid and *false* otherwise. If the given indexes are within bounds, the element corresponding to the indexes is returned while in case of their being out of bounds, no operation occurs and no overrun takes place. Another interesting point to note here is that a boolean variable *err* contains the result/outcome of each operation. This variable/field can be checked/examined after each operation to assess the success/failure of the operation (in chapter 7, we shall look at a better approach to error handling by use of the C# exception subsystem, but for the time being, using an error flag variable like *err* is an acceptable way).

The *set* accessor is shown next:

```
set
{
        if (okay(index1, index2))
        {
                i[index1, index2] = value;
                err = false;
        }
        else
                err = true;
}
```

which also prevents a boundary error. In this case, if *index1* and *index2* are within bounds, then, the value passed in *value* is assigned to the corresponding element. Otherwise, *err* is set to *true*. You may note that in an accessor method, *value* is an implicit parameter containing the value being assigned. Further, you need not to (in fact, nor can you) declare it.

*/

4.1.3 Indexer Constraints & Restrictions

There are primarily two restrictions to using indexer enumerated as follows:

(1) Since an indexer does not define a storage location, therfore, a value produced by the indexer cannot be passed as a *ref* or *out* parameter to a method.

(2) An indexer cannot be declared to be *static*; indeed, it has to be an instance member of its class.

4.2 PROPERTIES

Property is another type of class member that combines a field with the methods that access it. Suppose, we wish to limit the range of values for a field; we can do so by using a private variable along with methods to access its value. But, properties offer a more sophisticated and better technique.

Properties are similar to indexers. A property consists of a name along with the *get* and *set* accessors, which are used for getting and setting the values of a variable. The main benefit of a property is that its name can be used in expressions and assignments just like a normal variable, but in reality, the *get* and *set* accessors are called instinctively. This is ver much similar to the case when the get and set accessors of an indexer are automatically called into play.

The most general form of a property is as shown below:

```
access_specifier type name
{
        get
                // the get accessor
        {
                // code for get accessor
        }
        set
                // the set accessor
        {
                // code for set accessor
        }
}
```

where, *type* specifies the type of property, e.g., *int* while *name* is the name of the property. Once the property is defined, any use of its name results in a call to its appropriate accessor. Also, the *access_specifier* can be private or public. It is private, by default.

It should be clear to you that a property does not define a storage location *per se*. A property only manages access to a field and, does not provide that field, itself. The field has to be declared independent of the property (the only exception to this is the *auto-implemented* property, which is described in the next subsection).

We now illustrate the concept of properties with a simple example (*Example 65*) that defines a property called *Example_Property*, which is used to access the field *myprop*. In this case, *Example_Property* allows only integer values greater than 99 to be assigned. The type of property defined by *Example_Property* is a read-write property as it allows for its underlying field *myprop* to be both read and written. But, we can have read-only and write-only properties as well. To define a read-only property, provide only the *get* accessor while in order to define a write-only property, implement only the *set* accessor.

Example 65

```
/* Illustration of a Simple Property*/
/* Author: Arunesh; Date: 23/03/2011*/
using System;
class Prop_Simple
{
        int myprop;        // field managed by Example_Property, which is given ahead

        public Prop_Simple()     { myprop = 0; }
                           // constructor for the class Prop_Simple

                /* the following property supports access to the private instance variable
myprop;
        it allows only integer values greater than 99 */
        public int Example_Property
        {
                get
                        // the get accessor
                {
                        return myprop;
                }
                set
                        // the set accessor
                {
                        if (value > 99)
                                myprop = value;
                }
        }
}

//      Demonstrate a simple property
class Prop_Simple_Demo
{
        static void Main()
        {
                Prop_Simple psobj = new Prop_Simple( );

                Console.WriteLine("The initial or original value of psobj.myprop = "
                                                                        + psobj.myprop);

                psobj.myprop = 101;     // assign a value
                Console.WriteLine("The NEW value of psobj.myprop = " + psobj.myprop);
```

```
            // VALUES LESS THAN 100 annot be assigned to myprop
            Console.WriteLine("trying to assign 99 to psobj.myprop");
            psobj.myprop = 99;
            Console.WriteLine("The value of psobj.myprop = " + psobj.myprop);
      }
}
```

Output:

```
      The initial or original value of psobj.myprop = 0
      The NEW value of psobj.myprop = 101
      trying to assign 99 to psobj.myprop
      The value of psobj.myprop = 101
```

/* Let us now examine this example program (*Example 65*) closely. The program specifies one private field, named *myprop*, and a property named *Example_Property*, which manages and controls access to *myprop*. Moreover, since *myprop* is declared as private, it can be accessed only through *Example_Property*, which is, in turn, declared to be public so as to enable it to be accessed by code outside of its class. This makes logical sense as it controls and manages access to *myprop*, which is a private field. The *get* accessor simply returns the value of *myprop* while the *set* accessor sets the value of *myprop* if and only if the value is greater than *99*. In this manner, *Example_Property* controls the values that *myprop* can have. This, in fact, is the core, sum and substance of the importance of properties.

*/

We can use the concept of properties to further refine and improve upon the *Array2D* class (*Example 64*). Now, we know that all arrays have a *Length* property associated with them In *Example 64*, we had use a public integer field called *l* for this purpose but it is not good practicece to do so as it allows *l* to be set to any value other than the length of the actual array in question (a person with malafide intentions can corrupt its value, for example). To remedy this situation, we transform *l* into a read-only *Length* property. Further, the *err* member is also a key candidate to be converted into a property as access to it should be limited to read-only. So, we create a property called *Error* that uses the original *err* variable as its storage, and *err* is made private to *Array2D*. Here is the final improved version (*Example 66*) with the aforesaid two changes incrporated into the previous version of *Array2D* class in *Example 64*.

Example 66

```
/* Using the concept of properties to Refine & improve upon Example 64 */
/* Converting err (see Example 64) into read-only Error property;
Also, adding read-only Length property */
/* Author: Arunesh; Date: 23/03/2011*/
using System;
class Array2D
{
      /* reference to underlying array */
      int [ ,] i;
      /* dimensions of underlying array */
      int r, c;
```

```
int l;          // now private: underlies Length property
bool err;       // now private

public Array2D(int rows, int cols)
// construct array given its dimensions
{
        r = rows;
        c = cols;
        i = new int[r, c];
        l = r * c;
}

/* Read-only Length and Error Properties follow */
public int Length
{
        get
        {
                return l;
        }
        //      NO set accessor
}

public bool Error
{
        get
        {
                return err;
        }
        //      No set accessor again
}

/* indexer for Array2D follows */
public int this[int index1, int index2]
{
        // get accessor
        get
        {
                if (okay(index1, index2))
                {
                        err = false;
                        return i[index1, index2];
                }
```

```
                    else
                    {
                              err = true;
                              return 0;
                    }
          }
          // set accessor
          set
          {
                    if (okay(index1, index2))
                    {
                              i[index1, index2] = value;
                              err = false;
                    }
                    else
                              err = true;
          }
     }
     // CHECKING BOUNDS
     private bool okay(int index1, int index2)
     {
          if (index1 >= 0 & index1 < r  & index2 >= 0 & index2 < c)
                    return true;
          else
                    return false;
     }
}
class Indexer_Property_Demo
{
     static void Main( )
     {
          Array2D  a2d = new Array2D( 2, 3);
          int i;
          //        a2d.Length − 5;          // WRONG! Length is read-only
          /* quiet failures */
          Console.WriteLine(“Quiet Failures:”);
          for (int x = 0; x < a2d.Length - 2; x++)
                    // a2d.Length = l = 2 * 3 = 6; Whence, a2d.Length - 2 = 6 - 2 = 4
                    a2d[x, x] = x * 100;
          for (int x = 0; x < a2d.Length - 2; x++)
          {
                    i = a2d[x, x];
                    if (!a2d.Error)
                    Console.WriteLine(i);
          }
```

```
            Console.WriteLine();

            /* fail with error reports */
            Console.WriteLine("Fail with Error Reports:");

        for (int x = 0; x < a2d.Length - 2; x++)
            {
                    a2d[x, x] = x * 100;
                    i = a2d[x, x];
                    if(!a2d.Error)
                            Console.WriteLine(i)
                    else
                            Console.WriteLine("Error with indexes " + x + ", " + x );
            }
        }
}
```

Output:

```
        Quiet Failures:
        0
        100
        0
        0

        Fail with Error Reports:
        0
        100
        Error with indexes 2, 2
        Error with indexes 3, 3
```

/* As you can see for yourself, by using the concept of properties, we have been able to improve upon the previous example program (*Example 64*) significantly. The creation of the *Error* property has caused two changes to be made to *Array2D*. First, *err* has now been made private as it is now used as the underying storage for the *Error* property. And, second, the read-only *Error* property has been introduced. Programs needing to detect errors shall now interrogate *Error* as seen in *Main ( )*, where a boundary error is generated intentionally, and the *Error* property is used to detect the boundary error.

Also, notice the sophisticated use of the read-only *Length* property in *Main ( )*, where the statement:

```
// a2d.Length = 5;
```

has been commented out since *Length* is a read-only property, and as such, it shall result in a compile-time error.

*/

4.2.1 Auto-Implemented Properties

Version 3.0 of C# made it possible to implement very simple properties without having to explicitly specify the variable managed by the property. Such a property is referred to as *auto-implemented* property in which the compiler supplies the underlying variable on its own.

The most general form of an *auto-implemented* property is as shown below:

access_specifier type name { get; set; }

where, *type* specifies the type of property, e.g., *int* while *name* is the name of the property. Also, the *access_specifier* can be private or public. It is private, by default. You may note that the two accessors, *get* and *set*, are immediately followed by semicolons and have no bodies. Such a syntax informs the compiler to automatically create and supply a storage location (called a *backing field*, sometimes), which holds the value. This *backing field* or variable neither has a name nor is it directly available to the user of the *auto-implemented* property. Rather, it can be accessed only throgh the property.

For example, a property called *Counter* is declared using an *auto-implemented* property as follows:

public int Counter { get; set; }

You may note that no variable is explicitly specified. Instead, the compiler, as already explained, creates and generatyes an anonymous unnamed field that holds the value. Otherwise, *Counter* is used and acts like any other property. However, unlike normal properties, an *auto-implemented* property such as *Counter* cannot be read-only or write-only as both the accessors, *get* and *set*, have to be specified in all cases of *auto-implemented* properties. But, at the same time, it must be pointed out that the same effect can be approximated by declaring *get* or *set* as *private*, as explained in section 4.3.

Auto-implemented properties, even though they offer convenience, their use is limited to situations where no control over the getting or setting of the *backing field* is required. In other words, these situations are those cases where you need not constrain the value an *auto-implemented* property can have. This is due to the fact that you cannot access the *backing field* directly. *Auto-implemented* properties offer the use of their name as a proxy for the field itself. But, there are situations where what is required is exactly this. Further, *auto-implemented* properties can prove pretty handy to expose functionality to a third party (e.g., via a design tool).

4.2.2 Using Object Initializers with Properties

As already discussed in chapter 2, *Object initializers* provide an alternative way to explicitly calling a class' constructor. They provide an alternative way to create an object and initialize its fields and/or properties. The object initialization syntax remains the same for both properties and fields. For instance, here is the object intializer illustration program (*Example 45*) from chapter 2, reworked to demonstrate the use of *object initializers* with properties (*Example 67*).The only difference between the two example programs is that x, s, and d have been converted from fields into properties with the object initializer sytntax remaining the same.

Example 67

```
/* Using Object Initializers with Properties*/
/* Author: Arunesh; Date: 27/03/2011 */
using System;
class cl
{
        public int x { get; set; }          // x is now a property
        public string s {get; set; }        // s is now a property
        public double d {get; set; }        // d is now a property
}
class cl_obj_init
{
        static void Main()
        {
                cl c = new cl {x = 99, s = "game", d = 999.999};
                                // construct a cl object c by use of object initializers
                Console.WriteLine(c.x);
                Console.WriteLine(c.s)
                Console.WrriteLine(c.d);
        }
}
```

Output:

```
99
game
999.999
```

As you can see for yourself, the properties *x, s,* and *d* are set through object initializer expressions. Also, the output remains unchanged from the one in *Example 45*.

As already outlined in chapter 2, *object initializers* are mostly to be used with anonymous types generated by a LINQ expression. And, in most of the other cases, you shall be using the normal constructor syntax instead of *object initializers.*

4.2.3 Property Constraints & Restrictions

Just like indexers, there are a few restrictions to using properties as well, in fact; three primary restrictions enumerated as follows:

(1) Since a property does not define a storage location, therfore, it cannot be passed as a *ref* or *out* parameter to a method.

(2) A property cannot be overloaded (there may be two different properties accessing the same variable but this is rather unusual).

(3) A property cannot alter the state of the underlying variable when the *get* accessor is called. Even though this rule is not set by the compiler, its violation is wrong as per the semantics of C#. A *get* operation must not be intrusive.

4.3 USING ACCESS MODIFIERS WITH ACCESSORS

The *get* and *set* accessors, by default, have the same accessibility as the indexer/property of which they are a part. For instance, if indexer/property is specified as *public*, then, the *get* and *set* accessors are also *public*, by default. However, it is possible to assign *get* or *set* its own access modifier, such as *private*. The access modifier for an accessor must be more restrictive than the access level of its property/indexer in all cases.

There are numerous reasons for restricting the accessibility of an accessor, e.g., you may wish to allow anyone to obtain the value of a property, but let only members of its class to set the property. In order to carry this out, declare the *set* accessor as *private*, e.g., *Example 68* uses a property called *Prop_Access* that has its *set* accessor declared to be *private*.

Example 68

```
/* Illustration of the use of an Access Modifier with an Accessor*/
/* Author: Arunesh; Date: 23/03/2011*/
using System;
class Prop
{
        int myprop;        // field managed by Prop_Access, which is given ahead

        public Prop()   { myprop = 0; }
                        // constructor for the class Prop

        /* the following property supports access to the private instance variable myprop;
        it allows any code to obtain/get the value of myprop, but lets only other class members
        to modify/set the value of myprop */
        public int Prop_Access
        {
                get
                        // the get accessor
                {
                        return myprop;
                }
                private set
                        // the set accessor: note the access specifier private
                {
                        myprop = value;
                }
        }
        // the following class member decrements the value of myprop
        public void DecrementProp
        {
                --myprop;       // okay, member of same class
        }
}
```

```
//      Demonstrate Accessor with Access Modifier
class Prop_Demo
{
        static void Main()
        {
                Prop  pobj = new Prop( );

                Console.WriteLine("The initial or original value of pobj.myprop = "
                                                        + pobj.myprop);
                //      pobj.myprop = 1;        // Wrong! cannot access set as it is private

                pobj.DecrementProp();
                Console.WriteLine("The NEW value of pobj.myprop after Decrement = "
                                                        + psobj.myprop);

        }
}
```

Output:

```
        The initial or original value of pobj.myprop = 0
        The NEW value of pobj.myprop after Decrement = -1
```

/* In the *Prop* class, the *set* accessor is declared *private*. This implies that it can be accessed by other class members, such as *DecrementProp()*, but it cannot be accessed by code outside of *Prop*. It is for this reason that trying to assign a value of *1* to *pobj.myprop* inside *Prop_Demo* has been commented out as it shall result in a compile-time error..
*/

We would like to mention here that one of the most important uses of restricting an accessor's access is found while working with *auto-implemented* properties. As already pointed out, unlike normal properties, an *auto-implemented* property cannot be read-only or write-only as both the accessors, *get* and *set*, have to be specified in all cases of *auto-implemented* properties. But, the same effect can be approximated by declaring *get* or *set* as *private*, e.g., the following is a declaration of a read-only (in effect), *auto-implemented Length* property for the *Array2D* class shown in *Example 66*:

```
public int Length { get; private set; }
```

Since *set* is private, *Length* can only be set by code within its class. Outside this class, any attempt to change/modify *Length* is invalid/illegal. In this way, outside its class, *Length* is effectively a read-only *auto-implemented* property. The same mechanism/technique can be applied to *Error* property as well in the following manner:

```
public bool Error {get; private set; }
```

This allows for *Error* to be read, but not set, by code outside the *Array2D* class. You may want to try the *auto-implemented* versions of *Length* and *Error* with *Array2D* . For this, first remove the *l* and *err* variables as they are no longer required. After this, replace each use of *l* with *Length* and each use of *err* with *Error* within/inside *Array2D* in *Example 66*.

4.3.1 Using Access Modifiers with Accessors - Constraints & Restrictions

Just like indexers and properties, there are a few restrictions to using access modifiers with accessors as well, in fact, three primary restrictions enumerated as follows:

(1) Only one of the *get* and *set* accessors can have an access modifier; not, both of them together.

(2) As already stated, the access modifier used must be more restrictive than the access specification of the indexer/property.

(3) An access modifier cannot be used while specifying an accessor within an interface or while implementing an accessor declared by an interface (Interfaces are discussed at length in chapter 6).

Indexers & Properties - A CASE STUDY

The preceding examples have given a fair idea of the basic mechanism of indexers and properties. However, they have not given a complete picture of their full potential. Before bringing this chaspter to a close, it might prove to be useful to take up a case study in which a class named *ArbitraryIndexedArray* is developed that uses the concept of indexers and properties to create an array type which allows indexes to begin at any arbitrary point. You may recall that in C#, array indexing starts at *zero*. However, in certain situations, it might be more suitable for an array to begin indexing at *1*. Similarly, in another case, it might be more handy to allow negative indexes, such as an array that runs from *-10* to *10*. The *ArbitraryIndexedArray* class developed in this case study allows this and other types of indexing.

Using *ArbitraryIndexedArray*, a sample code can be written as:

```
ArbitraryIndexedArray aia = new ArbitraryIndexedArray(-2, 3);
                    // array with indexes from -2 to 3 inclusive
for (int k = -2; k <=3; k++)
        aia[k] = k;
```

As you can possibly decipher, the first line constructs an *ArbitraryIndexedArray*, which runs from *-2* to *3*, inclusive. The first argument/ parameter indicates the beginning index while the second argument/parameter indicates the ending index. Once *aia* has been generated, it can be indexed from *-2* to *3* as demonstrated by the *for* loop.

The complete *ArbitraryIndexedArray* class is shown in *Example 69* along with *ArbitraryIndexedArray_Demo*, which demonstrates and illustrates the array. As per our implementation, *ArbitraryIndexedArray* supports and creates arrays of type *int*, but you might like to change the underlying data type.

Example 69

```
/* Indexers & Properties - A case Study */
/* Create an arbitrarily specifioed indexes array; indexing can begin at values
other than 0; In fact, the array is created starting from the specified beginning
index and ending at the specified ending index; allows specified indexes to be
negative as well; thus, you can create arrays that index/run from -2 to 2, 1 to 5, or,
25 to 30, both indexes inclusive, for example */
/* Author: Arunesh; Date: 23/03/2011*/
using System;
class ArbitraryIndexedArray
{
    // Private data
    int [,] i;        /*  reference to underlying array */
    int lb, ub;; // lower and upper bounds indicating smallest and largest
indexes respectively

    /* Auto-implemented Read-only Length and Error Properties follow */
    public int Length { get; private set; }
    public bool Error { get; private set; }
        // notice the use of the private access modifier with the set accessor

    /* construct array given its size */
    public ArbitraryIndexedArray(int lo, int hi)
    {
        hi++;
        if (hi <= lo)
        {
            Console.WriteLine("invalid indexes");
            hi = 1; // create a minimal array to be on the safe side
            lo = 0;
        }
        i = new int [hi - lo];
        Length = hi - lo;
        lb = lo;
        ub = --hi;
    }
```

```
        /* indexer for ArbitraryIndexedArray follows */
        public int this[int index]
        {
                // get accessor
                get
                {
                        if (okay(index))
                        {
                                Error = false;
                                return i[index - lb];
                        }
                        else
                        {
                                Error = true;

                                        return 0;
                        }
                }
                // set accessor
                set
                {
                        if (okay(index))
                        {
                                i[index - lb] = value;
                                Error = false;
                        }
                        else
                                Error = true;
                }
        }

        // CHECKING BOUNDS
        private bool okay(int index)
        {
                if (index >= lb  & index <= ub)
                        return true;
                else
                        return false;
        }
}
```

```
//      Demonstrate the arbitrary-indexed array
class ArbitraryIndexedArray_Demo
{
        static void Main( )
        {
                ArbitraryIndexedArray aia1 = new ArbitraryIndexedArray(-2, 3);
                ArbitraryIndexedArray aia2 = new ArbitraryIndexedArray( 1, 4);
                ArbitraryIndexedArray aia1 = new ArbitraryIndexedArray(-5,-1);


                // Demonstrate aia1
                Console.WriteLine("Length of aia1 = " + aia1.Length);
                for (int x = -2; x <=3; x++)
                        aia1[x] = x;
                Console.Write("Contents of aia1: ");
                for (int x = -2; x <=3; x++)
                        Console.Write(aia1[x] + "\t");
                Console.WriteLine('\n");
                // Demonstrate aia2
                Console.WriteLine("Length of aia2 = " + aia2.Length);
                for (int x = 1; x <=4; x++)
                        aia1[x] = x;
                Console.Write("Contents of aia2: ");
                for (int x = 1; x <=4; x++)
                        Console.Write(aia2[x] + "\t");
                Console.WriteLine('\n");

                // Demonstrate aia3
                Console.WriteLine("Length of aia3 = " + aia3.Length);
                for (int x = -5; x <=-1; x++)
                        aia3[x] = x;
                Console.Write("Contents of aia3: ");
                for (int x = -5; x <=-1; x++)
                        Console.Write(aia3[x] + "\t");
                Console.WriteLine('\n");
        }
}
```

Output:

Length of aia1 = 6
Contents of aia1: -2 -1 0 1 2 3

Length of aia2 = 4
Contents of aia2: 1 2 3 4

Length of aia3 = 5
Contents of aia3: -5 -4 -3 -2 -1

/* As you can see for yourself, objects of type *ArbitraryIndexedArray* can be indexed in ways other than starting at *0*. Let us take a good look at how *ArbitraryIndexedArray* is implemented.

***ArbitraryIndexedArray* begins by defining the following private instance variables:**

```
// Private data
int [,] i;        /*  reference to underlying array */
int lb, ub;
// lower and upper bounds indicating smallest and largest indexes
// respectively
```

The underlying array is referred to by *i*. This array is allocated by the *ArbitraryIndexedArray* constructor. The index of the lower bound of the array is stored in *lb* while the index of the upper bound of the array is stored in *ub*.

The two auto-implemented, read-only properties, *Length* and *Error* are declared next:

```
/* Auto-implemented Read-only Length and Error Properties follow */
public int Length { get; private set; }
public bool Error { get; private set; }
// notice the use of the private access modifier with the set accessor
```

As mentioned above, the *set* accesor is private for both the properties. As already explained in this chapter, this creates what are effectively read-only auto-implemented properties.

Next comes the *ArbitraryIndexedArray* constructor as shown here:

```
/* construct array given its size */
public ArbitraryIndexedArray(int lo, int hi)
{
        hi++;
        if (hi <= lo)
        {
                Console.WriteLine("invalid indexes");
```

```
            hi = 1; // create a minimal array to be on the safe side
            lo = 0;
        }
        i = new int [hi - lo];
        Length = hi - lo;
        lb = lo;
        ub = --hi;
}
```

An *ArbitraryIndexedArray* is constructed by passing the lower bound index in *lo* and the upper bound index in *hi*. The value of *hi* is then incremented since the given indexes are inclusive. After this, a check is made to confirm that the upper index is greater than the lower index. If this is not the case, an error is reported and a one-element array is generated. Next, the array is allocated its storage and assigned to *i*. After this, the *Length* property is set equal to the number of elements in the array. And, finally, the *lb* and *ub* are set.

After this, the *ArbitraryIndexedArray* implements its indexer as shown by the following code:

```
/* indexer for ArbitraryIndexedArray follows */
public int this[int index]
{
    // get accessor
    get
    {
        if (okay(index))
        {
            Error = false;
            return i[index - lb];
        }
        else
        {
            Error = true;
            return 0;
        }
    }
    // set accessor
    set
    {
        if (okay(index))
        {
            i[index - lb] = value;
```

```
                Error = false;
            }
            else
                Error = true;
        }
    }
```

This indexer is similar to the one used by *Array2D* except for two things. First, this indexer is one-dimensional as compared to the two-dimensional indexer used by *Array2D*. And, second, and much more importantly, note the expression that indexes *i*. It goes like this:

index - lb

This expression translates/transforms the index passed in *index* into a zero-based index suitable/convenient for use on *i*. Whether *lb* is positive, negative, or zero, in all of these three cases, this expression works alike.

Finally, the *okay()* method for checking the bounds is as shown here:

```
// CHECKING BOUNDS
private bool okay(int index)
{
        if (index >= lb  & index <= ub)
                return true;
        else
                return false;
}
```

Again, this method is similar to the one used by *Array2D* except for two things. First, this method has only one parameter as compared to the two-parameter method used by *Array2D*. And, seccond, and much more importantly, the range is checked by testing it against the values in *lb* and *ub*, both inclusive.

***/**

Remark: The above case study illustrates just one kind of custom arrays that can be created using *indexers* and *properties*. There are several others such as *dynamic arrays*, which expand and contract as per the requirements, You might like to try your hands at creating these on your own.

PRACTICAL SESSION

#1 Pick out the correct alternative(s) from the following multiple choce problem:
Suppose a library class has an indexed property that is used to store/retrieve values to/from an array of 10 integers, then which of the following are the correct ways to use this indexed property?

(a) library[10] = 5;
(b) Console.WriteLine(library[5]);
(c) library Lib = new library( );
Lib[5] = 10;
(d) library.this Lib = new library.this( );
Lib[5] = 10;
(e) All of the above
(f) None of the above

#2 Point out the error(s), if any, in the following C# codes:

(a)
```
using System;
class vacuum
{
        int len;
        public int Length
        {
                get
                {
                        return Length;
                }
        }
}
```

(b)
```
using System;
class vacuum
{
        int len;
        public int Length
        {
                set
                {
                        Length = value;
                }
        }
}
```

#3 State True (T) or False (F):

(a)
- (i) Every property mut have a set accessor and a get accessor.
- (ii) Properties cannot be overloaded.
- (iii) Properties of a class are actually methods that work like data members.
- (iv) A property has to be either read only or write only.
- (v) Properties are used to store and retrieve the values to and from the data members of a class.
- (vi) A property can simultaneously be read only and write only.
- (vii) A write only property will only have a set accessor.
- (viii) A write only property will always return a value.
- (ix) A read only property will only have the get accessor.

(b)
- (i) The signature of an indexer consists of the number and types of its formal parameters.
- (ii) Indexers are similar to properties except that their accessors take parameters.
- (iii) The type of an indexer and the type of its parameters must be at least as accessible as the indexer itself.
- (iv) We cannot have multi-dimensional indexers.

#4 A library class has a property called books. Lib is a reference to a library object and

(i) suppose we declare the books property with only the get accessor. What shall be the result of the following statement:

Lib.books = 1000;

(ii) suppose we declare the books property with only the set accessor. What shall be the result of the following statement:

Console.WriteLine(Lib.books);

(iii) suppose we declare the books property with both the get and set accessors. What shall be the result of the following statements:

Lib.books = 1000;
Console.WriteLine(Lib.books);

#5 (a) Suppose á class vaccuum has an indexer. Write down this indexer to make the following C# code snippet work successfully:

vaccuum v = new vaccuum( );
v[1, 2] = 10;

(b) Suppose a class vaccuum has an indexed property that is used to set/ retrieve values to / from an array of 10 integers called numbers[ ]. The property should give an appropriate message if the bounds of the array are exceeded. Write down the proper way to implement this property.

CHAPTER 5

INHERITANCE / POLYMORPHISM

5.0 INTRODUCTION

As already explained in chapter 1, inheritance and polymorphism are the two pillars of object-oriented programming (OOP). The concept of inheritance allows us to create generalized classes that define attributes common to a set of related items. Such classes can then be inherited by other less general classes adding features unique to the inheriting classes. The class that is inherited is referred to as the *base/super* class while the inheriting class is known as the *derived/sub* class. In this way, it can be seen that a *derived class* is a more specialized version of the *base class*. On one hand, it inherits all the public and protected members of the base class such as variables, methods, indexers and properties. On the other, it adds its own unique elements and features. The main advantage of inheritance is *reusability* of code.

As you are already aware, 'poly' means "many". In this chapter, we shall also discuss virtual methods and method overriding as also abstract methods and classes that allow C# to implement the "one interface, multiple methods" aspect of *polymorphism* at run-time.

5.1 FUNDAMENTALS OF INHERITANCE

The most general form of a class declaration that inherits a base class is as given below:

```
class derived_class_name : base_class_name
{
        // body of derived class
}
```

Unlike C++, C# does not support multiple inheritance and so, we can specify only one base class for any derived class we create. But, we can have an hierarchy of classes where a derived class acts as a base class for another derived class. Also, no class can be a base class of itself directly or indirectly. In all cases, a derived class inherits all the public and protected members of its base class including instance variables, methods, indexers, and properties.

To begin with, let us take an example. Consider the following class named/called *ThreeDshapes* that stores and displays the length, width, and height of a three-dimensional object, such as a cube, cuboid , and so on..

```
// A class for three-dimensional objects
class ThreeDshapes
{
        public double length;
        public double width;
        public double height;

        public void dispdim()
        {
                System.Console.WriteLine("Length, width & height are: "
                                + "\t" + length + '\t" + width + "\t" + height);
        }
}
```

ThreeDshapes can be used as a base class (i.e., a starting/beginning point) for classes that portray specific types of three dimensional objects, e.g., the following example program (*Example 70*) makes use of *ThreeDshapes* to derive a class called *Cuboid.*

Example 70

```
/* Illustrates a simple class hierarchy */
/* Author: Arunesh;  Date: 23/03/2011 */
using System;

// A class for three-dimensional objects
class ThreeDshapes
{
        public double length;
        public double width;
        public double height;

        public void dispdim()
        {
                Console.WriteLine("Length, width & height are: "
                                + "\t" + length + '\t" + width + "\t" + height);
        }
}

// Cuboid is derived from ThreeDshapes
class Cuboid : ThreeDshapes
{
        public string colour;     // colour of cuboid
```

```
        // display colour of cuboid
        public void dispclr( )
        {
                Console.WriteLine("Colour of cuboid is " + colour);
        }

        // display volume of cuboid
        public void dispvol( )
        {
                Console.WriteLine("Volume of cuboid is " + (length * width * height));
        }
}
class Forms1
{
        static void Main( )
        {
                Cuboid c1 = new Cuboid( );
                Cuboid c2 = new Cuboid( );

                c1.length = 3;
                c1.width = 2;
                c1.height = 5;
                c1. colour = "red";

                c2.length = 4;
                c2.width = 3;
                c2.height = 6;
                c2.colour = "green";

                Console.Writeline("Particulars about c1:");
                c1.dispclr( );
                c1.dispdim( );
                c1.dispvol( );

                Console.WriteLine();

                Console.Writeline("Particulars about c2 :");
                c2.dispclr( );
                c2.dispdim( );
                c2.dispvol( );
        }
}
```

Output:

Particulars about c1:
Colour of cuboid is red
Length, width & height are 3.0 2.0 5.0
Volume of cuboid is 30.0

Particulars about c2:
Colour of cuboid is green
Length, width & height are 4.0 3.0 6.0
Volume of cuboid is 72.0

/* The *Cuboid* class creates a particular type of *ThreeDshapes*, in this case, a cuboid. The *Cuboid* class inherits all of *ThreeDshapes* and adds its unique elements, viz,, the field, *colour*, and the two methods, *dispclr()* & *dispvol()*. While *dispclr()* displays the colour of the cuboid, *dispvol()* computes and displays its volume. Since *Cuboid* inherits and includes all of the members of its base class, *ThreeDshapes*, it can access *length*, *width*, and *height* inside *dispvol()*. Further, inside *Main()*, the two objects, *c1* & *c2*, can refer to *length*, *width*, and *height* directly, as if they were part of *Cuboid*.

There is one more interesting point to note about *Example 70*. Although, *ThreeDshapes* acts as the base class for *Cuboid*, it is a completeltely stand-alone independent class as well. In other words, there is nothing to prevent a base class to be used by itself even though other classes are derived from it, e,g., the following code is absolutely fine and okay:

```
ThreeDshapes shape = new ThreeDshapes();
shape.length = 10;
shape.width = 20;
shape.height = 30;
Console.WriteLine("Particulars about shape:");
shape.dispdim();
```

As stated above, this code is absoluteltely legitmate and results in the following:

Output:

Particulars about shape:
Length, width & height are 10.0 20.0 30.0

At the same time, there is a caveat. An object of *ThreeDshapes,* such as *shape,* has no know-how or access to any classes derived from *ThreeDshapes*, such as *Cuboid*.

We would like to make one final point before rouding off this section. And, that is, once you have a base class, which caters to the common attributes for a set of objects, it can be tailored to create any number of specific derived classes according to the requirements of each such derived class. Further, there can be a multilevel hierarchy in which a derived class can act as a base class for more refined derived classes. For, example, as we shall see later on in this chapter, the class *Cube* can be derived from *Cuboid*.

*/

5.1.1 Inheritance and Member Access

We have already discussed and explained in chapter 2 that we can declare members of a class to be private to limit access to them only up to other members of the class. When a class having certain private members is inherited, this access restriction still applies. This, in turn, implies that a derived class inherits and includes all members of the base class but still, it does not have access to those members of the base class which are specified as private. In short, a private class member shal remain private to its class. It is inaccessible to any code outside its class, inclusive of derived classes, e.g., consider the following version of the base class *ThreeDshapes* and derived class *Cuboid.*

<u>*Example 71*</u>

```
/* Illustrates inaccessible Private members in a simple hierarchy */
/* Author: Arunesh;  Date: 23/03/2011 */
using System;
// A class for three-dimensional objects
class ThreeDshapes
{
        // the three dimensions of ThreeDshapes are now private
        private double length;
        private double width;
        private double height;

        public void dispdim()
        {
                Console.WriteLine("Length, width & height are: "
                                + "\t" + length + "\t" + width + "\t" + height);
        }
}
// Cuboid is derived from ThreeDshapes
class Cuboid : ThreeDshapes
{
        public string colour;     // colour of cuboid
        // display colour of cuboid
        public void dispclr( )
        {
                Console.WriteLine("Colour of cuboid is " + colour);
        }
        // display volume of cuboid
        public void dispvol( )
        {
                Console.WriteLine("Volume of cuboid is " + (length * width * height));
                // Compile-time error! Cannot access private members of base class
        }
}
```

Thus, as indicated by the comment inside *Cuboid*, this program shall not compile and access to private members is not inherited. It might, at first, seem to be a severe restriction but C# provides various solutions, in fact, two, to be precise. One solution is the use of *protected* members, which we shall take up in the next section. For now, we shall consider the second solution, which is the use of public properties to access private members.

We have already discussed, in the previous chapter, the role of properties in managing access to instance variables, e.g., you can put constraints on their values, or make them read-only. A derived class cannot directly access the underlying private variable but can have access to it indirectly by using the overlying property declared to be public, e,g., here is *ThreeDshapes* reworked (*Example 72*) to convert *length, width,* and *height* into properties. Along with other things, it also ensures that the values of *length, width*, and *height*, will be positive, which would, in the process, help you to specify them using the coordinates of the shape in any octant of the 3-dimensional space without having to first compute their absolute values.

<u>*Example 72*</u>

```
/* Illustrates the use of Properties to access (set & get) Private data/members */
/* Author: Arunesh;  Date: 23/03/2011 */
using System;
// A class for three-dimensional objects
class ThreeDshapes
{
        // the three dimensions of ThreeDshapes are now private
        private double pvt_length;
        private double pvt_width;
        private double pvt_height;

        public void dispdim()
        {
                Console.WriteLine("Length, width & height are: "
                                + "\t" + length + '\t" + width + "\t" + height);
        }
        // Public properties for length, width, and height follow
        public double length
        {
                get
                {
                        return pvt_length;
                }
                set
                {
                        pvt_length = value >= 0 ? value : - value;
                }
        }
```

```
        public double width
        {
                get
                {
                        return pvt_width;
                }
                set
                {
                        pvt_width = value >= 0 ? value : - value;
                }
        }
        public double height
        {
                get
                {
                        return pvt_height;
                }
                set
                {
                        pvt_height = value >= 0 ? value : - value;
                }
        }
}

// Cuboid is derived  from ThreeDshapes
class Cuboid : ThreeDshapes
{
        public string colour;     // colour of cuboid

        // display colour of cuboid
        public void dispclr( )
        {
                Console.WriteLine("Colour of cuboid is " + colour);
        }

        // display volume of cuboid
        public void dispvol( )
        {
                Console.WriteLine("Volume of cuboid is " + (length * width * height));
        }
}
```

```
class Forms2
{
    static void Main( )
    {
        Cuboid c1 = new Cuboid( );
        Cuboid c2 = new Cuboid( );

        c1.length = 3;
        c1.width = 2;
        c1.height = 5;
        c1. colour = "red";

        c2.length = 4;
        c2.width = 3;
        c2.height = 6;
        c2.colour = "green";

        Console.Writeline("Particulars about c1:");
        c1.dispclr( );
        c1.dispdim( );
        c1.dispvol( );

        Console.WriteLine();

        Console.Writeline("Particulars about c2:");
        c2.dispclr( );
        c2.dispdim( );
        c2.dispvol( );
    }
}
```

Output:

```
Particulars about c1:
Colour of cuboid is red
Length, width  & height are      3.0      2.0      5.0
Volume of cuboid is 30.0

Particulars about c2:
Colour of cuboid is green
Length, width  & height are      4.0      3.0      6.0
Volume of cuboid is 72.0
```

/* In this example program (*Example 72*), the properties, viz., *length, width,* and *height*, provide access to the corresponding *private* members, viz., *pvt_length, pvt_width,* and *pvt_height*, respectively, which actually store the values. Thus, even though *pvt_length, pvt_width*, and *pvt_height* are *private* to *ThreeDshapes*, their values can still be *set* and obtained (*got*) *via* their corresponding properties (declared *public*), viz., *length, width*, and *height*, by the derived class *Cuboid.*
*/

5.1.1.1 The Access Mode: Protected

We have already explained the fact that a private member of a base class is inaccessible to the derived class. Does it imply that we would have to declare the member as public for it to become accessible to the derived class? Of course, declaring a member as public has its own implications and ramifications. It means that the public member does not become avaialable not only to the derived class but to all code, even outside the class hierarchy. Such an eventuality may not be entirely desirable, except in a few cases. So, what is the solution out for us? Fortunately, C# comes to our aid by providing for *protected* access. A *protected* member is public within a class hierarchy and private outside the class hierarchy. A *protected* member is created by use of the *protected* access modifier. When a member of a class is specified as *protected*, that member is by all means private except for one case.This one exception occurs when a *protected* member is inherited. In such a case, a *protected* member of the base class becomes a *protected* member of the derived class and whence, accessible to the derived class. This, in turn, implies that by using *protected*, we can create class members that remain private to their own class but can still be inherited and accessed by the derived class. An example follows (*Example 73*).

Example 73

```
/* Illustrate Protected Access */
/*Author: Arunesh; Date: 23/03/2011 */
using system;
class b                       // base class
{
        protected int m, n;        // private to base class but accessible by derived class

        public void init (int i, int j)
        {
                m = i;
                n = j;
        }
        void disp( )
        {
                Console.WriteLine(m + "\t" + n);
        }
}
```

```
class d : b                    // derived class
{
    int z;   // private
    public void init_z()
    {
        z = m + n;             // d may access b's m & n
    }
    public void disp_z()
    {
        Console.WriteLine(z);
    }
}
class ProtectedAccess
{
    static void Main( )
    {
        d obj = new d( );
        obj.init(3, 4);        // known to d
        obj.disp();            // known to d
        obj.init_z();          // part of d
        obj.disp_z();          // part of d
    }
}
```

Output:

```
    3       4
    7
```

/* In this example program (*Example 73*), since *b* is inherited by *d*, and since *m* and *n* are declared as *protected* in *b*, the *init_z()* method can access them. If *m* and *n* had been declared as private by *b*, then, *d* would not have been able to access them and as a result, the program would have given a compile-time error!

Just like *public* and *private*, the *protected* status stays and remains with a member irrespective of the number of layers of inheritance involved. Whence, when a derived class is used as a base class for another derived class, any *protected* members of the first base class that is inherited by the first derived class are also inherited as *protected* by the second derived class.

*/

A Useful Tip: Sometimes, you might have to choose between *protected* and *private access* as also between using *protected access* and a *property*. In such cases, you must use *protected* when you require to create a member which is accessible throughout a class hierarchy, but otherwise you should use *private*. Again, to manage access to a value, you must use a *property*.

5.1.2 Inheritance & Constructors

It is possible, in a hierarchy, for both the base classes and derived classes to have their own constructors. So, which constructor is responsible for building an object of the derived class? The answer is simple: "The constructor for the derived class builds the derived class part and the constructor for the base class builds the base class part!". This is logical as the base class has no information about or access to any element in the derived class. So far, all the examples have used the default constructors provided by C#. But, in actual practice, most of the classes shall define their own constructors. When only the derived class defines a constructor, the process is quite straightforward. Just construct the derived class object. The base class part of the object is created automatically using its default constructor. This situation is illustrated in *Example 74*. In this example program, we have a reworked version of *Cuboid* that provides a constructor explicitly. Here, *colour* is also declared private as it is now set by the constructor.

Example 74

```
/* Explicitly define a Constructor for Cuboid */
/* Author: Arunesh;  Date: 23/03/2011 */
using System;
// A class for three-dimensional objects
class ThreeDshapes
{
        // the three private dimensions of ThreeDshapes
        private double pvt_length;
        private double pvt_width;
        private double pvt_height;

        public void dispdim()
        {
                Console.WriteLine("Length, width & height are: "
                                + "\t" + length + '\t" + width + "\t" + height);
        }
        // Public properties for length, width, and height follow
        public double length
        {
                get
                {
                        return pvt_length;
                }
                set
                {
                        pvt_length = value >= 0 ? value : - value;
                }
        }
```

```
        public double width
        {
                get
                {
                        return pvt_width;
                }
                set
                {
                        pvt_width = value >= 0 ? value : - value;
                }
        }
        public double height
        {
                get
                {
                        return pvt_height;
                }
                set
                {
                        pvt_height = value >= 0 ? value : - value;
                }
        }
}
// Cuboid is derived  from ThreeDshapes
class Cuboid : ThreeDshapes
{
        string colour;   // colour of cuboid: now private
        // Explict constructor
        public Cuboid{string c, double l, double w, double h)
        {
                length = l; width = w; height = h; // initialize the base class ThreeDshapes
                colour = c;      // initialize the derived class Cuboid
        }
        // display colour of cuboid
        public void dispclr( )
        {
                Console.WriteLine("Colour of cuboid is " + colour);
        }
        // display volume of cuboid
        public void dispvol( )
        {
                Console.WriteLine("Volume of cuboid is " + (length * width * height));
        }
}
```

```
class Forms3
{
        static void Main( )
        {
                Cuboid c1 = new Cuboid( "red", 3.0, 2.0, 5.0);
                Cuboid c2 = new Cuboid( "green", 4.0, 3.0, 6.0);

                Console.Writeline("Particulars about c1:");
                c1.dispclr( );
                c1.dispdim( );
                c1.dispvol( );

                Console.WriteLine();

                Console.Writeline("Particulars about c2:");
                c2.dispclr( );
                c2.dispdim( );
                c2.dispvol( );
        }
}
```

Output:

```
Particulars about c1:
Colour of cuboid is red
Length, width & height are     3.0     2.0     5.0
Volume of cuboid is 30.0

Particulars about c2:
Colour of cuboid is green
Length, width & height are     4.0     3.0     6.0
Volume of cuboid is 72.0
```

/* In this example program (*Example 74*), the *Cuboid*'s constructor initializes the members of *ThreeDshapes* that it inherits along with its own *colour* field.
*/

If both the base class and the derived class define constructors, things get a bit complicated since in such a case, both the base class as well as the derived class constructors must be invoked/executed. For this, we have to use the C# keyword, *base*, which can be used in two distinct ways. Its first use is to call/invoke a base class constructor (we shall examine this use in the following subsection). Its second use lies in accessing a member of the base class that has been hidden by a member of the derived class (we shall examine this use a little while later in this chapter, section 5.1.3.1, to be precise).

5.1.2.1 Invoking Base Class Constructors

A derived class can call a constructor defined in its base class by using an expanded form of the derived class' constructor declaration and the base keyword as given below:

```
derived_class_constructor(parameter_list) : base(argument_list)
{
        // body of constructor
}
```

where, *argument_list* specifies any arguments needed by the constructor in the base class. As an example, consider the following (*Example 75*).

Example 75

```
/* Illustration of invoking a base class Constructor */
/* Author: Arunesh;  Date: 23/03/2011 */
using System;
// A class for three-dimensional objects
class ThreeDshapes
{
        // the three private dimensions of ThreeDshapes
        private double pvt_length;
        private double pvt_width;
        private double pvt_height;
        // Explicit constructor for ThreeDshapes
        public ThreeDshapes(double l, double w, double h)
        {
                length = l; width = w; height = h;
                        // properties length, width, and height are defined ahead
        }
        public void dispdim()
        {
                Console.WriteLine("Length, width & height are: "
                                + "\t" + length + "\t" + width + "\t" + height);
        }
        // Public properties for length, width, and height follow
        public double length
        {
                get
                {
                        return pvt_length;
                }
                set
                {
                        pvt_length = value >= 0 ? value : - value;
                }
        }
```

```
public double width
        {
                get
                {
                        return pvt_width;
                }
                set
                {
                        pvt_width = value >= 0 ? value : - value;
                }
        }
        public double height
        {
                get
                {
                        return pvt_height;
                }
                set
                {
                        pvt_height = value >= 0 ? value : - value;
                }
        }
}
// Cuboid is derived from ThreeDshapes
class Cuboid : ThreeDshapes
{
        string colour;   // colour of cuboid: private, by default
        // invoke the base class constructor
        public Cuboid(string c, double l, double w, double h) : base (l, w, h)
        {
                colour = c;
        }
        // display colour of cuboid
        public void dispclr( )
        {
                Console.WriteLine("Colour of cuboid is " + colour);
        }
        // display volume of cuboid
        public void dispvol( )
        {
                Console.WriteLine("Volume of cuboid is " + (length * width * height));
        }
}
```

```
class Forms4
{
        static void Main( )
        {
                Cuboid c1 = new Cuboid( "red", 3.0, 2.0, 5.0);
                Cuboid c2 = new Cuboid( "green", 4.0, 3.0, 6.0);

                Console.Writeline("Particulars about c1:");
                c1.dispclr( );
                c1.dispdim( );
                c1.dispvol( );

                Console.WriteLine();

                Console.Writeline("Particulars about c2:");
                c2.dispclr( );
                c2.dispdim( );
                c2.dispvol( );
        }
}
```

<u>Output</u>:

```
Particulars about c1:
Colour of cuboid is red
Length, width  & height are     3.0     2.0     5.0
Volume of cuboid is 30.0

Particulars about c2:
Colour of cuboid is green
Length, width  & height are     4.0     3.0     6.0
Volume of cuboid is 72.0
```

/* In this example program (*Example 75*), the *Cuboid*'s constructor is declared as follows:

```
public Cuboid(string c, double l, double w, double h) : base (l, w, h)
{
        colour = c;
}
```

Here, *Cuboid()* invokes *base* with the parameters *l, w,* and *h,* which, in turn, causes the *ThreeDshapes()* constructor to be invoked, initializing *length, width*, and *height*, with these values. Thus, *Cuboid* no longer needs to initialize these values itself; rather, it only initializes the value unique to it, viz., *colour*. This leaves *ThreeDshapes* ample scope to construct its subobject in any way it chooses. Moreover, *ThreeDshapes* can add functionality about which existing derived classes have no know-how; this, in turn, prevents existing code from breaking.
*/

There is another interesting point about *base*. And, that is, any form of base class constructor can be invoked by it. The constructor that shall be executed is the one that matches the arguments, e.g., consider the following example program (*Example 76*) that contains expanded versions of *ThreeDshapes* as well as *Cuboid*, including default constructors as also constructors taking just one argument.

<u>Example 76</u>

```
/* Illustration of multiple Constructors */
/* Author: Arunesh;  Date: 23/03/2011 */
using System;
// A class for three-dimensional objects
class ThreeDshapes
{
        // the three private dimensions of ThreeDshapes
        private double pvt_length;
        private double pvt_width;
        private double pvt_height;

        // Default constructor for ThreeDshapes
        {
                length = width = height = 0.0;
                        // properties length, width, and height are defined ahead
        }

        // Explicit constructor for ThreeDshapes
        public ThreeDshapes(double l, double w, double h)
        {
                length = l; width = w; height = h;
        }

        // Construct object with equal length, width, and height
        public ThreeDshapes(double e)
        {
                length = width = height = e;
        }

        public void dispdim()
        {
                Console.WriteLine("Length, width & height are: "
                                + "\t" + length + "\t" + width + "\t" + height);
        }
```

```
        // Public properties for length, width, and height follow
        public double length
        {
                get
                {
                        return pvt_length;
                }
                set
                {
                        pvt_length = value >= 0 ? value : - value;
                }
        }
        public double width
        {
                get
                {
                        return pvt_width;
                }
                set
                {
                        pvt_width = value >= 0 ? value : - value;
                }
        }
        public double height
        {
                get
                {
                        return pvt_height;
                }
                set
                {
                        pvt_height = value >= 0 ? value : - value;
                }
        }
}
// Cuboid is derived  from ThreeDshapes
class Cuboid : ThreeDshapes
{
        string colour;   // colour of cuboid: private, by default

        /*Default constructor for Cuboid; this shall invoke the default constructor of
        ThreeDshapes automatically. */
```

```
        public Cuboid()
        {
                colour = "null";
        }

        // Constructor for Cuboid that takes four arguments
        public Cuboid{string c, double l, double w, double h) : base (l, w, h)
        {
                colour = c;
        }

        // Construct a Cube
        public Cuboid(string c, double e) : base(e)
        {
                colour = c;
        }

        // display colour of cuboid
        public void dispclr( )
        {
                Console.WriteLine("Colour is " + colour);
        }

        // display volume of cuboid
        public void dispvol( )
        {
                Console.WriteLine("Volume is " + (length * width * height));
        }
}
class Forms5
{
        static void Main( )
        {
                Cuboid c = new Cuboid();
                Cuboid c1 = new Cuboid("red", 3.0, 2.0, 5.0);
                Cuboid c2 = new Cuboid( "green", 4.0, 3.0, 6.0);
                Cuboid c3 = new Cuboid("blue", 10.0);

                c = c3;
                Console.Writeline("Particulars about c:");
                c.dispclr( );
                c.dispdim( );
                c.dispvol( );
```

```
        Console.WriteLine();

        Console.Writeline("Particulars about c1:");
        c1.dispclr( );
        c1.dispdim( );
        c1.dispvol( );

        Console.WriteLine();

        Console.Writeline("Particulars about c2:");
        c2.dispclr( );
        c2.dispdim( );
        c2.dispvol( );
    }
}
```

Output:

```
Particulars about c:
Colour is blue
Length, width & height are    10.0    10.0    10.0
Volume is 1000.0

Particulars about c1:
Colour is red
Length, width & height are    3.0    2.0    5.0
Volume of is 30.0

Particulars about c2:
Colour is green
Length, width & height are    4.0    3.0    6.0
Volume is 72.0
```

/* The above output is more or less self-explanatory. Herein, we sum up the key ideas about/behind *base*.

A derived class specifying a *base* clause is invoking the constructor of its immediate base class. In fact, *base* always refers to the base class that is immediately above the invoking/calling class. This holds good in a multilevel hierarchy as well.

Arguments are passed to the base constructor by specifying them as arguments to *base*.

Finally, if no *base* clause is present, in that case, the default constructor of the base class is invoked/called by itself or, so to say, automatically.

*/

5.1.3 Inheritance & Name Hiding

It may happen that a member in a derived class has the same name as a member in the base class. If and when this happens, the member in the base class is hidden inside the derived class. Even though, not a technical error, a warning message shall be issued by the compiler in such a case. The purpose of the warning is clear and sound, viz., alerting the user to the fact that a name is being hidden. If you really want to hide a base class member, the derived class member must be preceded by the keyword *new* in order to prevent this warning. You must understand and be absolutely clear in your mind that this use of *new* is not the same, but is completely separate and distinct from its use while creating an instance of an object. An example of name hiding follows (*Example 77*).

Example 77

```
/* Illustrates Name Hiding as Related to Inheritance */
/*Author: Arunesh; Date: 23/03/2011 */
using system;
class b                     // base class
{
        public int m = 0;
}
class d : b                 // derived class
{
        new int m;          // this m in d hides the m in b; notice the use of new

        public d(int z)     // constructor
        {
                m = z;              // m in d
        }
        public void disp()
        {
                Console.WriteLine("m in derived class = " + m);
        }
}
class Inherit_Name_Hiding
{
        static void Main( )
        {
                d obj = new d( 16);

                obj.disp();
        }
}
```

Output:

```
        m in derived class = 16
```

/* Since the derived class *d* defines its own instance variable *m*, it hides the *m* in base class *b*. Whence, when *disp()* is invoked on an object of type *d*, it is not the value of *m* as defined in *b* that is displayed, but the one as defined by *d*.

Also, carefully note the use of *new* in the statement:

new int m;   // this m in d hides the m in b; notice the use of new

The sum and substance of this use is that it informs the compiler that a new variable *m* is being created which hides the *m* in the base class *b*. Leaving *new* out would generate a warning message from the compiler, as already explained.

*/

5.1.3.1 Accessing a Hidden Name Using 'base' Keyword

We have already told you about one use of *base* in the previous section, viz., invoking base class constructors. Now, we introduce you to a second use of *base* that acts in a manner similar to *this* except for the fact that it always refers to the base class of the derived class in which it is used. The most general form of this usage is:

base.member

where, *member* can either be an instance variable or a method. This form of *base* applies mostly to cases in which member names of a derived class hide members by the same name in the base class, e.g., we shall see in *Example 78* how to overcome name hiding (as seen in *Example 77*) by use of the keyword *base*.

Example 78

```
/* Illustrates use of base to overcome Name Hiding as Related to Inheritance */
/*Author: Arunesh; Date: 23/03/2011 */
using system;
class b                 // base class
{
    public int m = 0;
}
class d : b             // derived class
{
    new int m;          // this m in d hides the m in b; notice the use of new

    public d(int y, int z)      // constructor
    {
        base.m = y;             // use of base uncovers the m in b
        m = z;                  // m in d
    }
    public void disp()
    {
        Console.WriteLine("m in base class = " + base.m); // displays m in b
        Console.WriteLine("m in derived class = " + m);       // displays m in d

    }
}
```

```
class Name_Uncovering
{
        static void Main( )
        {
                d obj = new d( 15, 16);

                obj.disp();
        }
}
```

Output:

```
        m in base class = 15
        m in derived class = 16
```

/* As the above output suggests and indicates, even though the insatance variable *m* in the derived class *d* hides the *m* in the base class *b*, the use of the *base* keyword has allowed for access to the instance variable *m* as defined in *b*.
*/

We had said while outlining the general form of the usage of base that even hidden methods could be uncovered by its use. Consider *Example 79* as a case in point. Herein, class *d* inherits *b*, and both *b* and *d* declare a method called *disp()*. Inside *d's disp()*, the version of *disp()* defined by *b* is called via the use of *base*. There is one more point of note in this example program. And, that is, the use of the *new* keyword preceding *disp()*'s declaration in *d*.. It is used to inform the compiler that a new method named *disp()* is being created/declared in the derived class *d* which hides the *disp()* in the base class *b* lest a warning message be generated, as already explained.

Example 79

```
/* Illustrates use of base to overcome Name Hiding in methods as Related to Inheritance */
/*Author: Arunesh; Date: 23/03/2011 */
using system;
class b                 // base class
{
        public int m = 0;

        public void disp()        // disp() in b
        {
                Console.WriteLine("m in base class = " + m); // displays m in b
        }
}
class d : b             // derived class
{
        new int m;        // this m in d hides the m in b; notice the use of new
```

```
        public d(int y, int z)      // constructor
        {
                base.m = y;          // use of base uncovers the m in b
                m = z;               // m in d
        }
        new public void disp()  // this disp() in d hides the disp() in b; notice the use of new
        {
                base.disp();    // calling disp() in b; use of base uncovers the disp() in b
                Console.WriteLine("m in derived class = " + m);          // displays m in d
        }
}
class Method_Name_Uncovering
{
        static void Main( )
        {
                d obj = new d( 15, 16);

                obj.disp();
        }
}
```

<u>Output</u>:

```
        m in base class = 15
        m in derived class = 16
```

/* As the above <u>output</u> suggests and indicates, even though the method *disp()* in the base class *b* is hidden by the method *disp()* in the derived class *d*, the use of the *base* keyword has allowed for its use inside *d* without ambiguity. In fact, the following line:

```
base.disp(); // calling disp() in b; use of base uncovers the disp() in b
```

calls and invokes the base class version of *disp()*.

Again, carefully note the use of the *new* keyword preceding the method declaration in the following lines of code:

```
new public void disp()
        // this disp() in d hides the disp() in b; notice the use of new
{
        base.disp();
        // calling disp() in b; use of base uncovers the disp() in b
        Console.WriteLine("m in derived class = " + m);
        // displays m in d
}
```

As already excplained, this use of *new* is totally different from its use when creating an object instance. Its role is to tell the compiler that a new method *disp()* is being defined in the derived class *d* which hides the previously defined *disp()* in the base class *b*. Leaving it out shall result in a compiler warning to this effect, as already pointed out.

*/

5.1.4 Multilevel Inheritance / Hierarchy

So far, we have been using a simple class hierarchy consisting of only one derived class and one base class. But we can have as many layers of inheritance as we like. Thus, if **X, Y,** and **Z** are three classes, then it is, in general, possible to derive **Y** from **X** and **Z** from **Y**. In such a case, **Z** shall inherit all traits and aspects of **Y** and **X**.

The class *Cuboid* can be used as a base class to encapsulate still more special types of three dimensional objects such as cubes as seen in *Example 80*.

Example 80

```
/* Illustration of multilevel hierarchy */
/* Author: Arunesh;  Date: 23/03/2011 */
using System;
// A class for three-dimensional objects
class ThreeDshapes
{
        // the three private dimensions of ThreeDshapes
        private double pvt_length;
        private double pvt_width;
        private double pvt_height;

        // Default constructor for ThreeDshapes
        {
                length = width = height = 0.0;
                        // properties length, width, and height are defined ahead
        }

        // Explicit constructor for ThreeDshapes
        public ThreeDshapes(double l, double w, double h)
        {
                length = l; width = w; height = h;
        }

        // Construct object with equal length, width, and height
        public ThreeDshapes(double e)
        {
                length = width = height = e;
        }

        public void dispdim()
        {
                Console.WriteLine("Length, width & height are: "
                        + "\t" + length + "\t" + width + "\t" + height);
        }
```

```
        // Public properties for length, width, and height follow
        public double length
        {
                get
                {
                        return pvt_length;
                }
                set
                {
                        pvt_length = value >= 0 ? value : - value;
                }
        }
        public double width
        {
                get
                {
                        return pvt_width;
                }
                set
                {
                        pvt_width = value >= 0 ? value : - value;
                }
        }
        public double height
        {
                get
                {
                        return pvt_height;
                }
                set
                {
                        pvt_height = value >= 0 ? value : - value;
                }
        }
}
// Cuboid is derived  from ThreeDshapes
class Cuboid : ThreeDshapes
{
        string colour;    // colour of cuboid: private, by default

        /*Default constructor for Cuboid; this shall invoke the default constructor of
        ThreeDshapes automatically. */
```

```
        public Cuboid()
        {
                colour = "null";
        }
        // Constructor for Cuboid that takes four arguments
        public Cuboid{string c, double l, double w, double h) : base (l, w, h)
        {
                colour = c;
        }
        // Construct a Cube
        public Cuboid(string c, double e) : base(e)
        {
                colour = c;
        }
        // display colour of cuboid
        public void dispclr( )
        {
                Console.WriteLine("Colour is " + colour);
        }
        // display volume of cuboid
        public void dispvol( )
        {
                Console.WriteLine("Volume is " + (length * width * height));
        }
}
// class Cube is further derived from Cuboid
class Cube : Cuboid
{
        public Cube (string c, double e) : base (c, e)
        {
                // no CONSTRUCTOR BODY
        }
}
// Demonstrate multilevel hierarchy
class MultilevelHierarchy
{
        static void Main( )
        {
                Cube c1 = new Cube("red", 10.0 );
                Cube c2 = new Cube("green", 4.0 );

                Console.Writeline("Particulars about c1:");
                c1.dispclr( );
                c1.dispdim( );
```

```
c1.dispvol( );

        Console.WriteLine();

        Console.Writeline("Particulars about c2:");
        c2.dispclr( );
        c2.dispdim( );
        c2.dispvol( );
    }
}
```

Output:

```
Particulars about c1:
Colour is red
Length, width  & height are      10.0      10.0      10.0
Volume is 1000.0

Particulars about c2:
Colour  is green
Length, width  & height are      4.0       4.0       4.0
Volume is 64.0
```

/* Because of inheritance, the class *Cube* can reuse the code of the previously defined classes, *ThreeDshapes* and *Cuboid,* adding only the specific extra information it requires for its own, particular application.

There is one more important point to note: the *base* clause always refers to the constructor in the nearest and closest base class. In this particular case/example, the *base* clause in *Cube* calls the relevant constructor in *Cuboid*. The *base* clause in *Cuboid* calls the relevant constructor in *ThreeDshapes.* Further, in such a multilevel class hierarchy, if a base class constructor needs some parameters, then all derived classes must pass all those parameters from the bottom-up, that is to say - up the line. This holds good whether or not a derived class requires parameters of its own.

*/

5.1.4.1 Order of Constructor Execution

In a multilevel hierarchy, another important question is: when a derived class object is created, whose constructor is executed first? The base class one or the derived class one? For instance, if **X** is the base class and **Y** is the derived class, then, is **X**'s constructor called before **Y**'s, or **Y**'s constructor called before **X'**s? The answer is quite logical and simple, i.e. constructors are called in the order of derivation from the base class to the derived class. Again, this order remains unchanged irrespective of the fact whether the *base* clause is used or not. In the event of its not being used, the default (parameterless) constructor of each base class shall be executed. *Example 81* illustrates the order of constructor execution which is in the order of derivation from the uppermost base class down to to the derived class at the lowest rung of the class hierarchy.

Example 81

```
/* Illustrates the order of Constructor execution */
/* Author: Arunesh; Date: 23/03/2011 */
using System;
class b                    // base class
{
        public b( )
        {
                Console.WriteLine("Constructor b( ) called");
        }
}
class d1 : b                       // derived class 1
{
        public d1( )
        {
                Console.WriteLine("Constructor d1( ) called");
        }
}
class d2 : d1                      // derived class 2 derived from d1
{
        public d2( )
        {
                Console.WriteLine("Constructor d2( ) called");
        }
}
class Order_of_Constructors
{
        static void Main( )
        {
                d2 obj = new d2( );
        }
}
```

Output:

```
        Constructor b( ) called
        Constructor d1( ) called
        Constructor d2( ) called
```

/* Thus, it can be seen that the constructors are called in the order of derivation from *b( )* down to *d2( )*. And, it makes logical sense as well that the constructors are executed in the order of derivation. Since a base class has no know-how of any derived class, any initialization it needs to do is distinct, separate and possibly a prelude to any initialization by the derived class; whence, it must be executed first.

*/

5.1.5 Derived Objects & Base Class References

C# being a strongly typed language, a reference variable for one class type cannot, in general, refer to an object of another class type. But, a reference variable of a base class can be assigned a reference to an object of any class derived from that particular base class. Thus, even though **A** and **B** be two classes that are physically exactly the same, we cannot assign a **B** reference to an **A** object unless **B** is derived from **A**. Consider the following two example programs (*Example 82* & *Example 83*) in this context.

Example 82

```
/* Illustrates two classes identical in their composition; yet, reference variable for one class
type cannot refer to an object of the other class type; in general, an object reference variable
can refer only  to objects of its own type*/
/* Author: Arunesh; Date: 23/03/2011 */
using System;
class A                          // first class
{
        int i;

        public A(int m )
        {
                i = m;
        }
}
class B                          // second class
{
        int i;

        public B( int m)
        {
                i = m;
        }
}
class Incompatible_Reference
{
        static void Main( )
        {
                A a  = new A(30);
                A a1;
                B b = new B(10);
                a1 = a; // okay; a1 and a are of same class type
                a1 = y; // compile-time mismatch & error; a1 and y not of same class type
        }
}
```

Example 83

```
/* Illustrates the exception to the strict type enforcement in C#; a reference variable of a base
class can be assigned a reference to an object of any class derived from that base class*/
/* Author: Arunesh; Date: 23/03/2011 */
using System;
class A                 // base class
{
        public int i;

        public A(int m )
        {
                i = m;
        }
}
class B : A             // derived class
{
        public int j;

        public B( int m, int n) : base(n)
        {
                j = m;
        }
}
class Base_Reference
{
        static void Main( )
        {
                A a  = new A(30);
                A a1;
                B b = new B(10, 20);
                a1 = a; // okay; a1 and a are of same class type
                Console.WriteLine("a1.i = " + a1.i);
                a1 = b; // okay; class B is derived from class A
                Console.WriteLine("a1.i = + a1.i);
                // A references know about A members only
                a1.i = 5;          // okay; class A has a member i
                //      a1.j = 6;          // Error; class A does not have member j
        }
}
```

Output:

```
        a1.i = 30
        a1.i = 20
```

/* There are two important points to note in *Example 83*. First, note how the last line has been commented out. Second, and more importantly, note that the following assignment: *a1 = b; // okay; class B is derived from class A*

is permissible, legal, and valid since a base class reference, *a1* in this particular case, can refer to a derived class object, which is the object referred to by *b*.

*/

What is important here is to understand the fact that it is the type of the reference variable and not the type of the object it is referring to which determines the members that are accessible. When a reference to a derived class object is made to a base class reference variable, only those parts of object shall be accessible which are defined by the base class. This makes logical sense as well since the base class is not in the know-how of what a derived class has added to it.

You might be wondering as to what is the practical use of all that we have described so far in this section. It all seems so abstract and abstruse. Well, it has several important applications. One of them is discussed next (the other is covered in the section on virtual methods later in this chapter).

A significant and noteworthy place whee derived class references are assigned to base class variables is the one where constructors are invoked in a class hierarchy. In fact, it is commonplace for a class to specify a constructor tat takes an object of its class as a parameter. This helps the class to make/construct a copy/clone of an object. Classes that are derived from such a class can take advantage or gain from this feature, viz., derived objects and base class references as illustrated in *Example 83*, e.g., take the following versions of *ThreeDshapes* and *Cuboid*, both of which use constructors that take an object as a parameter (*Example 84*).

<u>*Example 84*</u>

```
/* Illustration of Passing A Derived class Reference to a Base class Reference*/
/* Author: Arunesh; Date: 23/03/2011 */
using System;
// A class for three-dimensional objects
class ThreeDshapes
{
        // the three private dimensions of ThreeDshapes

        private double pvt_length;
        private double pvt_width;
        private double pvt_height;

        // Default constructor for ThreeDshapes
        {
                length = width = height = 0.0;
                        // properties length, width, and height are defined ahead
        }
```

```
// Explicit constructor for ThreeDshapes
public ThreeDshapes(double l, double w, double h)
{
        length = l; width = w; height = h;
}

// Construct object with equal length, width, and height
public ThreeDshapes(double e)
{
        length = width = height = e;
}

// Construct a copy/clone of  a ThreeDshapes object
public ThreeDshapes(ThreeDshapes obj)
{
        length = obj.length; width = obj.width; height = obj.height;
}

public void dispdim()
{
        Console.WriteLine("Length, width & height are: "
                    + "\t" + length + "\t" + width + "\t" + height);
}

// Public properties for length, width, and height follow
public double length
{
        get
        {
                return pvt_length;
        }
        set
        {
                pvt_length = value >= 0 ? value : - value;
        }
}
public double width
{
        get
        {
                return pvt_width;
        }
```

```
            set
            {
                pvt_width = value >= 0 ? value : - value;
            }
        }
        public double height
        {
            get
            {
                return pvt_height;
            }
            set
            {
                pvt_height = value >= 0 ? value : - value;
            }
        }
}
// Cuboid is derived from ThreeDshapes
class Cuboid : ThreeDshapes
{
        string colour;    // colour of cuboid: private, by default

        /*Default constructor for Cuboid; this shall invoke the default constructor of
        ThreeDshapes automatically. */
        public Cuboid()
        {
            colour = "null";
        }

        // Constructor for Cuboid that takes four arguments
        public Cuboid{string c, double l, double w, double h) : base (l, w, h)
        {
            colour = c;
        }

        // Construct a Cube
        public Cuboid(string c, double e) : base(e)
        {
            colour = c;
        }
```

```
        // Construct a copy/clone of  a Cuboid object
        public Cuboid(Cuboid obj) : base (obj)
        {
                colour = obj.colour;
        }
        // display colour of cuboid
        public void dispclr( )
        {
                Console.WriteLine("Colour is " + colour);
        }

        // display volume of cuboid
        public void dispvol( )
        {
                Console.WriteLine("Volume is " +  (length *  width *  height));
        }
}
class Forms6
{
        static void Main( )
        {
                Cuboid c1 = new Cuboid( "red", 3.0, 2.0, 5.0);
                Cuboid c2 = new Cuboid( c1);   // make a copy/clone of c1

                Console.Writeline("Particulars about c1:");
                c1.dispclr( );
                c1.dispdim( );
                c1.dispvol( );

                Console.WriteLine();

                Console.Writeline("Particulars about c2:");
                c2.dispclr( );
                c2.dispdim( );
                c2.dispvol( );
        }
}
```

Output:

```
        Particulars about c1:
        Colour is red
        Length, width  & height are      3.0      2.0      5.0
        Volume is 30.0
```

Particulars about c2:
Colour is red
Length, width & height are 3.0 2.0 5.0
Volume is 30.0

/* As this output indicates and confirms, *c1* and *c2* are identical. This is because *c2* is constructed from *c1*. Take special note of this *Cuboid* constructor:

```
// Construct a copy/clone of a Cuboid object
public Cuboid(Cuboid obj) : base (obj)
{
        colour = obj.colour;
}
```

It receives an object of type *Cuboid*, and passes that object to the following *ThreeDshapes* constructor (of course, via/through *base*):

```
// Construct a copy/clone of a ThreeDshapes object
public ThreeDshapes(ThreeDshapes obj)
{
        length = obj.length; width = obj.width; height = obj.height;
}
```

The noteworthy point is that even though the *ThreeDshapes()* constructor outlined above is expecting to recive a *ThreeDshapes* object, the *Cuboid()* constructor outlined above passes it a *Cuboid* object. As we have already discussed and explained, this works alright because a base class reference can refer to a derived class object so that it is absolutely fine to pass *ThreeDshapes()* a reference to an object of a class derived from *ThreeDshapes*, in this case *Cuboid*. The *ThreeDshapes()* constructor only initializes those parts and components of the *Cuboid* object that are members of *ThreeDshapes*; whence, it is of no concern whatsoever that this object also has other members added by the derived class *Cuboid*.

*/

5.2 VIRTUAL & OVERRIDDEN METHODS AND POLYMORPHISM

A virtual method is one that is declared as virtual in a base class and redefined in one or more derived classes. It is possible for each derived class to have its own version of a virtual method. Virtual methods are important considering the fact what happens when one is called through a base class reference. C# decides at run-time in such a situation as to which version of the virtual method to call depending upon the type of the object referred to by the reference. We can declare a method as virtual inside a base class by preceding its declaration by the keyword virtual. And, when a virtual method is redefined by a derived class, we use the override keyword/ modifier. This concept is known as *method overriding*. The concept of method overriding, thus allows C# to support *run-time polymorphism*. And, polymorphism is essential to OOP as it allows a general class to specify methods that shall be common to all of its derivatives, while allowing the derived classes to have their own implementation of some or all of those methods. In this way, C# supports the "one interface, multiple methods" aspect of polymorphism through overridden methods.

While overriding a method, the name, return type, and signature of the overriding method has to be the same as that of the virtual method being overridden. Further, a virtual method cannot be declared *static* or *abstract* (in chapter 2, we have already discussed static methods; abstract ones, we shall take up later in this chapter itself). Method overriding is at the core of one of C#'s most potent concepts, viz., *dynamic method dispatch*. This (*dynamic method dispatch*) forms the technique by means of which a call to an overridden method is resolved at run-time, rather than compile-time. Its importance is overwhelming since it is the mechanism by which C# is able to implement run-time polymorphism.

In order to enforce polymorphism successfully, it is of paramount importance to understand that the base classes and derived classes form a class hierarchy moving from lesser to greater specialization. In fact, the base class provides all the components and elements which a derived class can make use of directly. By means of virtual methods, it also specifies and defines those methods that the derived class can implement by itself, that is to say, on its own. In this manner, the derived class is allowed maximum flexibility without compromising on the consistency of the interface. Whence, a base class, by a suitable combination of inheritance and overridden methods, can define the broad and general outline of the methods that shall be put to use by all of its derived classes.

Before moving on to the three example programs (*Example 85 - Example 87*) illustrative of the basic concepts of virtual methods and overriding, we would like to inform you that even properties and indexers can be modified by the virtual keyword and overridden using the override modifier/keyword.

Example 85

```
/* Illustrates Virtual Methods & Overriding*/
/* Author: Arunesh; Date: 23/03/2011 */
using System;
class b                     // base class
{
        public virtual void disp()          // Virtual method in base class: note the use of virtual
        {
                Console.WriteLine("disp() in base class");
                Console.WriteLine();
        }
}

class d1 : b                // derived class 1
{
        public override void disp() // Override disp() in derived class 1: note the use of override
        {
                Console.WriteLine("disp() in derived class 1");
                Console.WriteLine();
        }
}
```

```
class d2 : b                    // derived class 2
{
        public override void disp() // Override disp() in derived class 2: note the use of override
        {
                Console.WriteLine("disp() in derived class 2");
                Console.WriteLine();
        }
}
class Virtual_Override_Demo1
{
        static void Main( )
        {
                b bobj = new b();         // object of type b
                d1 d1obj = new d1();      // object of type d1
                d2 d2obj = new d2();      // object of type d2
                b bReference;             // reference of type base class b

                bReference = bobj;        // bReference refers to b object
                bReference.disp();        // call b's version of disp()

                bReference = d1obj;       // bReference refers to d1 object
                bReference.disp();        // call d1's version of disp()

                bReference = d2obj;       // bReference refers to d2 object
                bReference.disp();        // call d2's version of disp()
        }
}
```

Output:

```
        disp() in base class

        disp() in derived class 1

        disp() in derived class 2
```

Example 86

```
/* Illustrates the situation when a virtual method is not overridden*/
/* Author: Arunesh; Date: 23/03/2011 */
using System;
class b                         // base class
{
        public virtual void disp()        // Virtual method in base class: note the use of virtual
        {
```

```
            Console.WriteLine("disp() in base class");
            Console.WriteLine();
        }
}

class d1 : b                // derived class 1
{
        public override void disp() // Override disp() in derived class 1: note the use of override
        {
            Console.WriteLine("disp() in derived class 1");
            Console.WriteLine();
        }
}
class d2 : b                // derived class 2
{
        // NO overriding of disp() here
}
class Virtual_Override_Demo2
{
        static void Main( )
        {
            b bobj = new b();
            d1 d1obj = new d1(0;
            d2 d2obj = new d2();
            b bReference;           // reference of type base class b

            bReference = bobj;
            bReference.disp();

            bReference = d1obj;
            bReference.disp();

            bReference = d2obj;
            bReference.disp();      // invokes disp() in b since d2 doesn't override disp()
        }
}
```

Output:

```
        disp() in base class

        disp() in derived class 1

        disp() in base class
```

Example 87

```
/* Illustrates the situation when a virtual method is not overridden in a multilevel hierarchy*/
/* Author: Arunesh; Date: 23/03/2011 */
using System;
class b                         // base class
{
    public virtual void disp()          // Virtual method in base class: note the use of virtual
    {
        Console.WriteLine("disp() in base class");
        Console.WriteLine();
    }
}

class d1 : b                    // derived class 1
{
    public override void disp() // Override disp() in derived class 1: note the use of override
    {
        Console.WriteLine("disp() in derived class 1");
        Console.WriteLine();
    }
}
class d2 : d1                   // derived class 2 derived from d1
{
    // NO overriding of disp() here
}
class d3 : d2                   // derived class 3 further derived from d2
{
    // NO overriding of disp() here again
}

class Virtual_Override_Demo3
{
    static void Main( )
    {
        b bobj = new b();
        d1 d1obj = new d1(0;
        d2 d2obj = new d2();
        d3 d3obj = new d3();
        b bReference;                   // reference of type base class b

        bReference = bobj;
        bReference.disp();
```

```
            bReference = d1obj;
            bReference.disp();

            bReference = d2obj;
            bReference.disp();      // invokes disp() in d1 since d2 doesn't override disp()

            bReference = d3obj;
            bReference.disp(); // invokes disp() in d1 since d3 & d2 don't override disp()
      }
}
```

Output:

disp() in base class

disp() in derived class 1

disp() in derived class 1

disp() in derived class 1

/* *Example 85* illustrates the concept of virtual methods and overriding in a very simple manner.

It creates a base class *b*, and two derived classes, *d1* and *d2*; *b* specifies a method *disp()*, and, *d1* and *d2* override it, that is to say, provide their own overridden version of *disp()*; inside *Main()*, objects of type *b, d1,* and *d2* are declared; a reference of type *b,* viz., *bReference*, is declared as well; a reference to each type of the three objects, *b, d1,* and *d2*, is then assigned to *bReference* and further, that reference, in turn, is used to invoke *disp()*; and, as the output shows and verifies, the form of *disp()* that is activated is related to the type of the object being referred to at the time of invocation, not by *bReference*'s class type.

Example 86 illustrates the fact that it is not mandatory for a virtual method to be overridden. If a derived class does not provide its own implementation of a virtual method, then its version in the base class is the one that is executed.

Herein, *d2* doesn't override *disp()*; so, when *disp()* is invoked on a *d2* object, the version of *disp()* in *b* is used.

Example 87 is illustrative of the situation in a multilevel hierarchy where a derived class does not override a virtual method. In this case, the first overide of the virtual method that is found while moving up the hierarchy is the one put to use.

Herein, class *d3* inherits *d2* which, in turn, inherits *d1*, which, in its turn, inherits *b*, thus forming a multilevel hierarchy. As the output confirms, since *disp()* is neither overidden by *d3* nor by *d2*, it is the override of *disp()* in *d1* that gets executed, as it is the first form of *disp()* that is encounterted while moving up the hierarchy.

*/

Virtual Methods - A CASE STUDY

We now take up a case study for a better understanding of the full potential of virtual methods. In fact, we shall apply them to the *ThreeDshapes* class. For the sake of convenience and better demonstration, the case study (*Example 88*) also adds a property called *term* to *ThreeDshapes*.

Example 88

```
/* Virtual Methods - A case Study*/
/* Author: Arunesh;  Date: 23/03/2011 */
using System;
// A class for three-dimensional objects
class ThreeDshapes
{
        // the three private dimensions of ThreeDshapes
        private double pvt_length;
        private double pvt_width;
        private double pvt_height;

        // Default constructor for ThreeDshapes
        {
                length = width = height = 0.0;
                term = "null";
                // properties term, length, width, and height are defined ahead
        }

        // Explicit constructor for ThreeDshapes
        public ThreeDshapes(double l, double w, double h, string t)
        {
                length = l; width = w; height = h;
                term = t;
        }

        // Construct object with equal length, width, and height
        public ThreeDshapes(double e, string t)
        {
                length = width = height = e;
                term = t;
        }
```

```
// Construct a copy/clone of  a ThreeDshapes object
public ThreeDshapes(ThreeDshapes obj)
{
        length = obj.length; width = obj.width; height = obj.height;
        term = obj.term;
}

public void dispdim()
{
        Console.WriteLine("Length, width & height are: "
                        + "\t" + length + '\t' + width + "\t" + height);
}

public void dispterm()
{
        Console.WriteLine("Object is of type:\t" + term);
}

// dispvol( ) must be overridden
public virtual void dispvol( )
{
        Console.WriteLine("MUST OVERRIDE dispvol( ));
        Console.WriteLine("Volume is: \t 0.0");
}

// Auto-implemented public property term
public string term { get; set; }

// Public properties for length, width, and height follow
public double length
{
        get
        {
                return pvt_length;
        }
        set
        {
                pvt_length = value >= 0 ? value : - value;
        }
}
```

```
    public double width
    {
        get
        {
            return pvt_width;
        }
        set
        {
            pvt_width = value >= 0 ? value : - value;
        }
    }
    public double height
    {
        get
        {
            return pvt_height;
        }
        set
        {
            pvt_height = value >= 0 ? value : - value;
        }
    }
}
// Cuboid is derived  from ThreeDshapes
class Cuboid : ThreeDshapes
{
    string colour; // colour of cuboid: private, by default
    /*Default constructor for Cuboid; this shall invoke the default
    constructor of ThreeDshapes automatically. */
    public Cuboid()
    {
        colour = "null";
    }
    // Constructor for Cuboid that takes four arguments:
    // Parameterized constructor
    public Cuboid{string c, double l, double w, double h) : base (l, w, h,
                                                            "cuboid")
    {
        colour = c;
    }
```

```
        // Construct a Cube
        public Cuboid(string c, double e) : base(e, "cube")
        {
                colour = c;
        }
        // Construct a copy/clone of  a Cuboid object
        public Cuboid(Cuboid obj) : base (obj)
        {
                colour = obj.colour;
        }
        // display colour
        public void dispclr( )
        {
                Console.WriteLine("Colour is: \t " + colour);
        }
        //  override dispvol( ) for Cuboid
        public override void dispvol( )
        {
                Console.WriteLine("Volume is: \t" +  (length *  width *  height));
        }
}
class Virtual_PolyForms_Demo
{
        static void Main( )
        {
                ThreeDshapes [ ] forms = new ThreeDshapes[3];

                forms[0] = ThreeDshapes(10.0, 20.0, 30.0, "Generic");
                forms[1] = new Cuboid("red", 1.0, 2.0,3.0);
                forms[2] = new Cuboid("green", 5.0);

                for (int k =0; k < forms.Length; k++)
                // notice the use of the property Length
                {
                        forms[k].dispterm();
                        forms[k].dispdim( );
                        forms[k].dispvol( );
                        Console.WriteLine( );
                }
        }
}
```

<u>Output</u>:

Object is of type: Generic
Length, width & height are: 10.0 20.0 30.0
MUST OVERRIDE dispvol( )
Volume is: 0.0

Object is of type: cuboid
Length, width & height are: 1.0 2.0 3.0
Volume is: 6.0

Object is of type: cube
Length, width & height are: 5.0 5.0 5.0
Volume is: 125.0

/* This <u>case study</u> reveals some interesting facets, two in particular. First, *dispvol()* is declared as <u>virtual</u> in *ThreeDshapes* class and is overridden by the derived class *Cuboid*. Within *ThreeDshapes*, *dispvol()* is simply a placeholder informing the user that it must be overridden by a derived class. Further, each override of *dispvol()* requires an implementation specifically suitable for the type of object encapsulated by the derived class, e.g., if you were to implement a *Sphere* class, then *dispvol()* would need to compute the volume of a sphere.

Second, in *Main()*, forms is said to be an array of *ThreeDshapes* objects; but, the elements of this array are assigned *Cuboid* as well as *ThreeDshapes* references. This works here because a base class reference can refer to a derived class object. The program then makes its way throgh the array, displaying particulars about each object. This looks and is actually simple; yet, it demonstrates the potential of inheritance as also method overriding.

The key point here is that the type of object stored in a base class reference variable is found out at run-time and acted upon accordingly. In case of any object derived from *ThreeDshapes*, its volume can be computed and obtained by invoking *dispvol()*. This is the basis of *polymorphism* as well since the *interface* to this operation is consistent, in fact, is the same, irrespective of the type of *shape/ form* being used.

Another point to note is that we have not used the method *dispclr( )* to display the colour of the objects created in *Main( )* as it not applicable to objects of type *ThreeDshapes*.

***/**

5.3 ABSTRACT METHODS / ABSTRACT CLASSES

We, at times, need to create a base class that defines only a generalized form that shall be shared by all its derived classes, leaving it to each derived class to fill in its own details for the type of implementation it wants. *Example 88* was a case in point. The definition of *dispvol( )* is just a placeholder as it does not calculate the actual volume and only displays a warning message along with a default value of zero in case none of the derived classes override it. Sometimes, we need to ensure that each derived class does indeed override all the necessary methods. An abstract method is C#'s solution to this problem. To declare an abstract method, we use the following general form:

abstract type name(parameter_list); // note that no method body is there

where, *name* refers to the name of the method, *type* specifies its return type, and *parameter_list* includes all its parameters/arguments.Here, we must sound a caveat, i.e., only instance methods (and not static methods) can be abstract. Also, it is an error to specify virtual along with abstract (in fact, an abstract method is, by itself, virtual and whence, there is no need too to specify them together as such). Indexers and properties can also be declared as abstract. Further, a class that contains one or more abstract methods must also be preceded by the abstract keyword before its name and declared to be abstract. Since an abstract class does not provide a complete implementation, no objects of an abstract class can be created and trying to do so by using *new* shall generate a compiler error instead.Furthermore, when a derived class inherits an abstract class, it must implement all the abstract methods in the base class. In case it does not, then it must also be declared as abstract. This chain continues and the abstract attribute keeps on getting inherited until and unless a full implementation is accomplished.

Take *Example 89* as an illustration of the concept of abstract classes and methods. It improves upon the previous version of ThreeDshapes as in *Example 88* by declaring the method *dispvol()* inside *ThreeDshapes* as well as the class *ThreeDshapes* as abstract.This would, of course, make it mandatory for all classes derived from *ThreeDshapes* to override *dispvol()*. "Why is it an improvement?", you might ask. The simple reason is that the concept of volume for an undefined three-dimensional figure has virtually no useful meaning.

Example 89

```
/* Demonstrates & Illustrates Abstract Methods & Classes*/
/* Author: Arunesh;  Date: 23/03/2011 */
using System;
// A class for three-dimensional objects
abstract class ThreeDshapes      // notice the use of abstract keyword
{
        // the three private dimensions of ThreeDshapes
        private double pvt_length;
        private double pvt_width;
        private double pvt_height;
```

```
// Default constructor for ThreeDshapes
{
        length = width = height = 0.0;
        term = "null";
                // properties term, length, width, and height are defined ahead
}
// Explicit constructor for ThreeDshapes
public ThreeDshapes(double l, double w, double h, string t)
{
        length = l; width = w; height = h;
        term = t;
}
// Construct object with equal length, width, and height
public ThreeDshapes(double e, string t)
{
        length = width = height = e;
        term = t;
}
// Construct a copy/clone of  a ThreeDshapes object
public ThreeDshapes(ThreeDshapes obj)
{
        length = obj.length; width = obj.width; height = obj.height;
        term = obj.term;
}

public void dispdim()
{
        Console.WriteLine("Length, width & height are: "
                        + "\t" + length + "\t" + width + "\t" + height);
}

public void dispterm()
{
        Console.WriteLine("Object is of type:\t" + term);
}

// dispvol( ) is now abstract and must necessarily be overrdden by all derived classes
public abstract void dispvol( );

// Auto-implemented public property term
public string term { get; set; }
```

```
        // Public properties for length, width, and height follow
        public double length
        {
                get
                {
                        return pvt_length;
                }
                set
                {
                        pvt_length = value >= 0 ? value : - value;
                }
        }
        public double width
        {
                get
                {
                        return pvt_width;
                }
                set
                {
                        pvt_width = value >= 0 ? value : - value;
                }
        }
        public double height
        {
                get
                {
                        return pvt_height;
                }
                set
                {
                        pvt_height = value >= 0 ? value : - value;
                }
        }
}
// Cuboid is derived  from ThreeDshapes
class Cuboid : ThreeDshapes
{
        string colour;   // colour of cuboid: private, by default

        /*Default constructor for Cuboid; this shall invoke the default constructor of
        ThreeDshapes automatically. */
```

```
public Cuboid()
{
        colour = "null";
}

// Constructor for Cuboid that takes four arguments; Parameterized constructor
public Cuboid{string c, double l, double w, double h) : base (l, w, h, "cuboid")
{
        colour = c;
}

// Construct a Cube
public Cuboid(string c, double e) : base(e, "cube")
{
        colour = c;
}

// Construct a copy/clone of  a Cuboid object
public Cuboid(Cuboid obj) : base (obj)
{
        colour = obj.colour;
}

// display colour
public void dispclr( )
{
        Console.WriteLine("Colour is:\t" + colour);
}

//  override dispvol( ) for Cuboid
public override void dispvol( )
{
        Console.WriteLine("Volume is: \t" + (length * width * height));
}
}

class AbstractForms_Demo
{
    static void Main( )
    {
        ThreeDshapes [ ] forms = new ThreeDshapes[2];
```

```
        forms[1] = new Cuboid("red", 1.0, 2.0,3.0);
        forms[2] = new Cuboid("green", 5.0);

        for (int k =0; k < forms.Length; k++)    //notice the use of the property Length
        {
                forms[k].dispterm();
                forms[k].dispclr( )
                forms[k].dispdim( );
                forms[k].dispvol( );
                Console.WriteLine( );
        }
    }
}
```

<u>Output</u>:

```
    Object is of type:        cuboid
    Colour is:        red
    Length, width & height are:    1.0    2.0    3.0
    Volume is:        6.0

    Object is of type:        cube
    Colour is:        green
    Length, width & height are:    5.0    5.0    5.0
    Volume is:        125.0
```

/* This example program (*Example 89*) amply illustrates the concept of abstract classes and methods. First, the base class *ThreeDshapes* is specified to be <u>abstract</u> since it contains an abstract method, viz., *dispvol()*. Second, the derived class, *Cuboid*, has overridden *dispvol()*, as it must (or be declared itself as <u>abstract</u> too). Again, it is still possible to create an object reference of type *ThreeDshapes*, and the program does create this reference. But, it is no longer possible to create objects of type *ThreeDshapes* since *ThreeDshapes* is an abstract class. It is, for this very reason, that the *forms* array in *Main()* has been cut down to 2; the "Generic" *ThreeDshapes* object is not created as was done in the previous example.

We would like to mention just one more point before rounding off this section. And, that is, an abstract class is free to contain concrete methods (other than abstract ones) which a derived class can make use of without any need for overriding. It is just that only the methods specified to be <u>abstract</u> have to be necessarily overridden by derived classes. This is once again amply illustrated by the concrete methods *dispdim()* and *dispterm()* besides the <u>abstract</u> method *dispvol()* in the base class *ThreeDshapes*.

*/

5.4 CAN WE PREVENT INHERITANCE / OVERRIDING?

The answer is: "YES", by using the keyword sealed. An example of a sealed class is:

```
sealed class X
{
        // relevant code goes here
}
```

Now, X cannot be inherited and the following is illegal:

```
class Y : X        // Error as Y cannot inherit X (it is sealed)
{
        // ......
}
```

It is, of course, illegetimate to declare a class as both abstract and sealed. This is becauise an abstract class is incomplete in itself and depends upon its derived classes for providing full implementations.

We can also prevent further overriding by using the keyword sealed on virtual methods. This is illustrated by the following code:

```
class b // base class
{
        public virtual void disp() { /* ............ */ }
}
class d1 : b     // derived class d1 derived from base class b
{
        .sealed public override void disp() { /* ............ */ }
                   // this seals disp() and prevents it from being further overridden
}
```

Now, *disp()* cannot be overridden and the following is illegal:

```
class d2 : d1    // derived class d2 further derived from d1
{
        public override void disp() { /* ............ */ }
                   // Error as disp() is already sealed
}
```

5.5 THE object CLASS

As pointed out succinctly in chapter 1, C# specifies a specialized class named *object* that acts as the underlying base class for all other classes and all other types inclusive of the value types as well. In short, all other types are derived from this special base class called *object*. This implies that a reference variable of type *object* can refer to an object of any other type. Moreover, since arrays are implemented as objects in C#, a variable of type *object* can refer to any array as well. In technical terms, the C# name *object* is just another name for *System.Object*, which is part of the .NET Framework class library.

Table 5.1 Methods of the *object* class

Method	Purpose
public virtual bool Equals(object obj)	*Determines whether the invoking object is the same as the one referred to by obj.*
public static bool Equals(object objA, object objB)	*Determines whether objA is the same as objB.*
protected virtual Finalize()	*Performs shutdown actions prior to garbage collection. In C#, Finalize() is accessed through a destructor.*
public virtual int GetHashCode()	*Returns the hash code associated with the invoking object*
public Type GetType()	*Returns the type of an object at run-time.*
protected object MemberwiseClone()	*Makes a "shallow copy" of the object. This is one in which the members are copied, but objects referred to by objects are not.*
public static bool ReferenceEquals(object objA, object objB)	*Determines whether objA and obB refer to the same object.*
public virtual string ToString()	*Returns a string that describes the object.*

The special C# class *object* defines the methods as enumerated in Table 5.1. Thus, these methods are available in every object.

A few of these methods need some extra and additional explanation. By default, the *Equals(object)* method finds out if the invoking object refers to the same object as the one referred to by its argument, i.e., it finds out whether the two references are the same. In case the objects are the same, it returns true. If not, it returns false. This method can be overridden in the classes created by you. Doing this permits you to specify as to what equality means relatrive to a class, e.g., *Equals(object)* can be so defined that it compares the contents of two objects for equality. Again, the *GetHashCode()* method returns a hash code associated with the invoking object. A hash code is required by any algorithm that uses hashing as a way of accessing stored objects. What is important is to understand the fact that the default implementation of *GetHashCode()* is not sufficient for all uses. As already mentioned in chapter 3, overloading the = = operator requires the overriding of *Equals(object)* and *GetHashCode()* methods since the = = operator and *Equals(object)* must function the same and when *Equals()* is overridden, *GetHashCode()* also needs to be overridden for compatibility between the two methods.

Before rounding off this section, a word about the *ToString()* method. *ToString()* returns a string containing the description of the object on which it is called. Further, *ToString()* is invoked automatically when an object is output using *WriteLine()*. Many classes override *ToString()* enabling them to customize a description in accordance with the type of objects which they create.

5.6 BOXING & UNBOXING

All C# types (inclusive of the value types) are derived from the *object* class (in fact, *object* is an *universal* data type in C#, as we shall see in the next section). Thus, a reference of type *object* can be used to refer to any type including value types. When an *object* reference refers to a value type, it is known as *boxing*. It causes the value of a value type to be stored in an instance of an object, that is to say, a value type is *boxed* inside an object. In all cases, boxing occurs automatically. We just assign a value to an *object* reference and the rest is done by C#. *Unboxing* is the reverse process of retrieving a value from a boxed object. This is done by using an explicit cast from an *object* reference to its corresponding value type (note that attempting to unbox an object into a different type shall result in a run-time error!). As an illustration of the concept of *boxing* and *unboxing*, consider *Example 90.*

Example 90

```
/* Illustrates Boxing & Unboxing */
/* Author: Arunesh; Date: 23/03/2011 */
using System;
class Boxing_Unboxing_Demo
{
        public static void Main( )
        {
                int i, j;

                object ob;

                        i = 80;
                ob = x;             // Boxing i into an object ob

                j = (int) ob;       // Unboxing ob into an int j

                Console.WriteLine(j);
        }
}
```

Output:

80

/* In this example program (*Example 90*), it is quite noticeable that the value in *i* is boxed simply by assigning it to *ob*, which is an *object* reference. The integer value in *ob* is unboxed/retrieved by casting *ob* to *int*.

*/

5.7 UNIVERSAL DATA TYPE - object

One of the strong features of C# is that it has a unified type system. Every type, including the simple built-in types such as *int*, are derived from *System.Object*. Thus, in C#, "Everything is an object"! A language such as Smalltalk also has such a feature , but pays the price of inefficiency for simple types. Languages, such as C++ and Java, treat simple built-in types as different from objects, thus obtaining efficiency but at the loss of a unified type system. C# enjoys the best of both worlds through boxing.

In fact, given that *object* is a base class for all other types and that boxing of value types takes place automatically, it is indeed possible to use *object* as a "universal generic" data type. Since an *object* reference can hold a reference to any other type of data, it is possible to use an *object* reference to refer to any type of data.

Although the "universal data type" feature or characteristic of *object* is potentially very powerful and can be put to use very effectively in certain situations, it is a grave mistake trying to use *object* as a way to penetrate the otherwise strong type checking system of C#. Thus, in general terms, if you need to store an *int*, employ an *int* variable; when you need to store a *string*, use a *string* reference; and so on.

Before rounding off this section and chapter, we would like to state a very moot point. Ever since version 2.0, true generic types have become avaiable to the C# programmer (As a point of interest, generics are not described in this book). The introduction of generics has enabled C# programmers to easily define classes and algorithms that automatically work with various different types of data in a type-safe manner. Generics have virtually eliminated the need to use *object* as a universal type when creating new code. As things stand today, it is in your best interests to reserve and keep *object*'s universal nature only for specialized rare occasions, situations and cases.

PRACTICAL SESSION

#1 Explain the concept of inheritance citing suitable examples wherever necessary.

#2 What do you mean by virtual methods and abstract classes? Elucidate.

#3 Write the C# syntax for the following base and derived class:
Base Class (Person): name, age, address, change_address()
Derived Class (Lecturer): basic_pay, provident_fund, house_rent_allowance, total_salary, compute_total_salary()
{Tip: You may assume appropriate rules wherever necessary. }

#4 What do you mean by polymorphism in C#? How is it achieved at run-time? Elaborate.

#5 Fill in the blanks:

(i) The common characteristics of a group of classes are separated in the form of a ______ class.
(ii) _________________ is an activity of defining a new class in terms of an ___________ class.
(iii) When we have a chain of classes, it is called __________ inheritance.

#6 State True (T) or False (F):

(i) The base class is, in fact, an existing class.
(ii) The derived class inherits all the members of the base class.
(iii) Protected members of the base class are not accessible to the derived class.

#7 Identify the erro(s), if any, in the following code fragments:

(i)

```
abstract class X
{
        public void show( );
}
```

(ii)

```
class X { }
class Y { }
class Z : X, Y
{
        ..........
        ..........
}
```

#8 (a) Some programmers do not like the *protected* access specifdier? What do you think might be their reasons?

(b) How would you prevent other programmers from extending (inheriting) one of your classes via inheritance?

#9 Pick out the correct alternative in each of the following multiple choice problems:

(i) In an inheritance chain, which of the following members of the base class are accessible to the derived class?
(a) private
(b) static
(c) shared
(d) protected
(e) None of the above

(ii) A derived class can stop virtual inheritance by declaring an override as:
(a) inherits
(b) extends
(c) sealed
(d) noninheritable
(e) None of the above

(iii) Which of the following statements are correct?
(a) Abstract methods can be virtual.
(b) It is necessary to override a virtual method.
(c) We can override virtual as well as non-virtual methods.
(d) When overriding a method, the names and type signatures of the override method must be the same as that of the virtual method being overridden.
(e) None of the above

(iv) To implement a 'like a'/'kind of' relationship betrween two entities, which of the following should be used?
(a) Containership.
(b) Polymorphism.
(c) Encapsulation.
(d) Inheritance.
(e) None of the above

#10 Attempt the following (*programming exercises*):

(i) Create a base class **shapes**. Use this class to store two float values that can be used to compute the area of figures. Derive two specific classes: **triangle** and **rectangle** from the base **shapes**. To the class **shapes**, add a member function *init( )* to initialize base class data members and another member function *display( )* to find out and print the area of the figures. Make *display( )* into a virtual method and redefine it suitably in the derived classes.
Using these classes, design a program to accept the dimensions of a triangle and a rectangle interactively and print out their areas.

{Tip: The two inputs in case of a triangle shall be the base *A* and height *B* and lengths *A and B of* the sides in case of a rectangle. Then, the required areas can be calculated using the following formulae:
*area(triangle) = (1/2) * A * B;* and,
*area(rectangle) = A * B.*
}

(ii) Expand the above program to print out the area of a given circle that requires the addition/inclusion of a new derived class **circle**.

{Tip: In case of a circle, you need only one dimension viz., the radius but the *init( )* function in the base class requires two values to be passed. So, you need to make the second parameter of the *init( )* function as a default one with value zero.
}

(iii) Execute the aforesaid program with the following modifications:

(a) Remove the definition of the *display( )* function from one of the derived classes, say **circle**; and

(b) Additionally, declare *display( )* as virtual in the base class **shapes**.

What do you note in the three outputs now?
Comment and *elucidate*.

CHAPTER 6

INTERFACES, STRUCTURES AND ENUMERATIONS

6.0 INTRODUCTION

We shall discuss in this chapter one of C#'s most important features, viz., the interface. An interface definers a set of methods that shall be implemented by a class, and does not, by itself, implement any method. In other words, we can say that an inteface is purely a logical construct describing functionality without specifying implementation.

We shall also discuss two more C# data types in this chapter, viz., structures and enumerations. Structures are very much similar to classes but for the fact that they are treated as value types rather than reference types. Enumerations are also value types that are nothing but lists of named integer constants. Structures and enumerations, especially enumerations, provide, as we shall see later on in this chapter, a covenient style of presentation.

6.1 INTERFACES

We have already learnt in the concept of abstract methods/classes what a class must do but not how it will do it. In other words, each derived class must provide its own version of the particular abstract method.

We can go a step futher in the concept of an interface and totally separate a class's interface from its implementation. Although an interface is syntactically similar to an abstract class, no method in an interface can have a body. In other words, every method in an interface is an abstract method. With the concept of an interface, C# allows us to fully use the "one interface, multiple methods" aspect of polymorphism. An interface is declared by the use of the keyword <u>interface</u> as follows:

```
interface name
{
        return_type method_name1(parameter_list);
        return_type method_name2(parameter_list);
        ..........................................................
        ..........................................................
        ..........................................................
        return_type method_nameN(parameter_list);
}
```

where, *name* specifies the interface name. All methods are abstract methods with only their return types and signatures. Also, each method is public implicitly and no explicit definition is permissible. In an interface, no method can have an implementation. Whence, each class which includes an interface has to necesssarily implement all of the methods. Apart from methods, an interface can define properties, indexers and events (events have been taken care of in chapter 9). An interface is neither alllowed to have data members nor can they have constructors, destructors, or operator methods. Further, no member in an interface can be static.

After an interface has been defined, one or more classes can implement it. When a class implements an interface, it must implement the entire interface; it cannot choose to implement certain paets of it, leaving the others, for instance. The general form of a class that implements an interface is as given below:

```
class class_name : interface_name
{
        // body of class
}
```

where interface_name stands for the name of the interface being implemented and class_name is the name of the implementing class. A class must fully implement the interface and no partial implementation is permissible. Also, a class can implement more than one interface separated by commas (in a comma-separated list of interfaces). Moreover, a class can inherit a base class as well as implement an interface (in such a case, the name of the base class must come first in the comma-separated list.).

The methods which implement an interface must be declared as public because within an interface, a method is implicitly public; whence its implementation must also be public. Further, the return type and signature of the implementing method must exactly match the return type and signature defined in the interface specification.

Next, we give an example of an interface called *Iser* that generates a series of numbers, a class called *ByFives*, which implements *Iser*, and a class called *ByFives_Demo* that demonstrates *ByFives* (*Example 91*).

Example 91

```
/* Illustrates an Interface and a Class that implements it*/
/* Author: Arunesh; Date: 27/03/2011 */
public interface Iser
{
        int getnext( );             // return next number
        void reset( );              // restart;
        void setstart(int i).       // set starting value
}
class ByFives : Iser                // ByFives implements the interface Iser
// Using Iser to implement a series of numbers, each five greater than the previous one
{
        int start;
        int value;
```

```
    public ByFives( )          // defaut constructor
    {
        start = 0;
        value = 0;
    }
    public int getnext( )
    {
        value += 5;
        return value;
    }
    public void reset( )
    {
        value = start;
    }
    public void setstart(int i)
    {
        start = i;
        value = start;
    }
}
// Demonstrate ByFives, which has implemented all the three methods defined by Iser
using System;
class ByFives_Demo
{
    static void Main( )
    {
        ByFives byfives = new ByFives( );

        for (int x = 0; x < 5; x++)         // first five numbers
            Console.WriteLine("Next value is: \t" + byfives.getnext( ));

        Console.WriteLine("\nResetting");
        byfives.reset( );
        for (int x = 0; x < 5; x++)         // first five numbers again
            Console.WriteLine("Next value is: \t" + byfives.getnext( ));

        Console.WriteLine("\n Starting at 51");
        byfives.setstart(51);
                    // first five numbers after51
        for (int x = 0; x < 5; x++)
            Console.WriteLine("Next value is: \t" + byfives.getnext( ));
    }
}
```

Output:

Next value is 5
Next value is 10
Next value is 15
Next value is 20
Next value is 25

Resetting
Next vaue is 5
Next value is 10
Next value is 15
Next value is 20
Next value is 25

Starting at 51
Next value is 56
Next value is 61
Next value is 66
Next value is 71
Next value is 76

/* To compile *ByFives_Demo*, you must have all the three files containing *Iser, ByFives,* and *ByFives_Demo* in the compilation. The compiler shall, by itself, compile all the three files to create the final executable file, e,g., if you have called these three files as *Iser.cs, ByFives.cs,* and *ByFives_Demo.cs*, then, you can compile them at the command prompt as: *>csc ByFives_Demo.cs Iser.cs ByFives.cs*

Of course, it is perfectly fine to put all of these three in the same file, say, *NewFile.cs* and then compile thois new file.

If you are using Visual Studio IDE, the three files can simply be addded to your C# project. */

It is both permissible and common for classes that implement interfaces to specify additional members of their own, e.g., the following version of *ByFives* (*Example 92*) adds the method *getprevious()*, which returns the previous value.

Example 92

```
/* Illustrates implementation of Iser and an additional method getprevious()*/
/* Author: Arunesh; Date: 27/03/2011 */
public interface Iser
{
        int getnext( );              // return next number
        void reset( );               // restart;
        void setstart(int i).        // set starting value
}
```

```
class ByFives : Iser
// ByFives implements the interface Iser and adds getprevious()
{
        int start;
        int value;
        int previous;

        public ByFives( )           // defaut constructor
        {
                start = 0;
                value = 0;
                previous = -2;
                }
        public int getnext( )
        {
                previous = value;
                value += 5;
                return value;
        }
        public void reset( )
        {
                value = start;
                previous = start - 2;
        }
        public void setstart(int i)
        {
                start = i;
                value = start;
                previous = value - 2;
        }

        public int getprevious() // a method not defined by Iser
        {
                return previous;
        }
}
```

/* You can note that the addition of *getprevious()* resulted in changed implementations of the methods specified by *Iser.* Still, the interface to those method has not changed and has not broken preexisting code. This is one of the major advantages of interfaces. */

As you know, any number of classes can implement the same interface. *Example 93* is a case in point. Here, we have a class called *Primes*, which generates a series of prime numbers. You may note that its implementation of the interface *Iser* is fundamentally different from that provided by *ByFives* in *Example 91*.

<u>*Example 93*</u>

```
/* Illustrates a different class implementing the same interface */
/* Author ; Arunesh; Date: 27/03/2011 */
public interface Iser
{
        int getnext( );              // return next number
        void reset( );               // restart;
        void setstart(int i).        // set starting value
}
class Primes : Iser        // class Primes implements the interface Iser
        // Using Iser to implement a series of Prime Numbers
{
        int start;
        int value;

        public Primes( )             // defaut constructor
        {
                start = 2;
                value = 2;
        }
        public int getnext( )
        {
                int a, b;
                bool isPri;

                value++;
                for (a = value; a < 10000; a ++)
                {
                        isPri = true;
                        for (b = 2; b < (a/b + 1); b++)
                        {
                                if (a % b ==0)
                                {
                                        isPri = false;
                                        break;
                                }
                        }
```

```
                    if (isPri)
                    {
                            value = a;
                            break;
                    }
            }
            return value;
    }
    public void reset( )
    {
            value = start;
    }
    public void setstart(int i)
    {
            start = i;
            value = start;
    }
}
// Demonstrate Primes, which has implemented all the three methods defined by Iser
using System;
class Primes_Demo
{
    static void Main( )
    {
            Primes primes = new Primes( );

            for (int x = 0; x < 5; x++)          // first five prime numbers
                    Console.WriteLine("Next value is: \t" + primes.getnext( ));

            Console.WriteLine("\nResetting");
            primes.reset( );
            for (int x = 0; x < 5; x++)          // first five prime numbers again
                    Console.WriteLine("Next value is: \t" + primes.getnext( ));

            Console.WriteLine("\n Starting at 51");
            primes.setstart(51);
                            // first five prime numbers after51
            for (int x = 0; x < 5; x++)
                    Console.WriteLine("Next value is: \t" + primes.getnext( ));
    }
}
```

<u>Output</u>:

Next value is 3
Next value is 5
Next value is 7
Next value is 11
Next value is 13

Resetting
Next vaue is 3
Next value is 5
Next value is 7
Next value is 11
Next value is 13

Starting at 51
Next value is 53
Next value is 57
Next value is 59
Next value is 61
Next value is 67

/* What is important here to understand is the fact that even though *ByFives* and *Primes* generate completely unrelated series of numbers, yet both implement the same interface, viz., *Iser.* This is because, an interface is totally silent about its implementation, leaving it to each class to implement the interface in any way it deems fit, suitable, and convenient. */

6.1.1 Using Interface References

We can declare a reference variable of an interface type, or, in other words, we can create an interface reference variable; such a reference can refer to any object that implements the interface. When a method is invoked on an object via an interface reference, the version of the method implemented by that object gets executed. This concept is just like the one for using a base class reference to access a derived class object, as already explained in the previous chapter.

Consider *Example 94* as a case in point. It uses the same interface reference variable to invoke methods on objects of both *ByFives* and *Primes.*

<u>Example 94</u>

```
/* Illustrates an Interface Reference */
/* Author ; Arunesh; Date: 27/03/2011 */
using System;
// specify the interface
public interface Iser
```

```
{
        int getnext( );              // return next number
        void reset( );               // restart;
        void setstart(int i).        // set starting value
}
class ByFives : Iser                 // ByFives implements the interface Iser
// Using Iser to implement a series of numbers, each five greater than the previous one
{
        int start;
        int value;
        public ByFives( )            // defaut constructor
        {
                start = 0;
                value = 0;
        }
        public int getnext( )
        {
                value += 5;
                return value;
        }
        public void reset( )
        {
                value = start;
        }
        public void setstart(int i)
        {
                start = i;
                value = start;
        }
}
class Primes : Iser        // class Primes implements the interface Iser
        // Using Iser to implement a series of Prime Numbers
{
        int start;
        int value;

        public Primes( )             // defaut constructor
        {
                start = 2;
                value = 2;
        }
```

```
public int getnext( )
{
        int a, b;
        bool isPri;

        value++;
        for (a = value; a < 10000; a ++)
        {
                isPri = true;
                for (b = 2; b < (a/b + 1); b++)
                {
                        if (a % b ==0)
                        {
                                isPri = false;
                                break;
                        }
                }
                if (isPri)
                {
                        value = a;
                        break;
                }
        }
        return value;
}
public void reset( )
{
        value = start;
}
public void setstart(int i)
{
        start = i;
        value = start;
}
}
class Series_Demo1
{
    static void Main( )
    {
        ByFives byfives = new ByFives( );
        Primes primes = new Primes( );
        Iser obj;
```

```
            for (int x = 0; x < 5; x++)
            {
                    obj = byfives;
                    Console.WriteLine("Next ByFives value is: \t" +  obj.getnext( ));

                    obj = primes;
                    Console.WriteLine("Next Primes value is: \t" +  obj.getnext( ));
            }
      }
}
```

Output:

```
    Next ByFives value is    5
    Next Prime number is     7
    Next ByFives value is    10
    Next Prime number is     11
    Next ByFives value is    15
    Next Prime number is     17
    Next ByFives value is    20
    Next Prime number is     23
    Next ByFives value is    25
    Next Prime number is     29
```

/* In this example program (*Example 94*), inside *Main(), obj* is specified as a reference to the interface *Iser* so that it can be employed to refer to any object that implements *Iser*. Herein, it is employed to refer to *byfives* and *primes*, which happen to be objects of type *ByFives* and *Primes*, respectively, and both of these implement *Iser*.
*/

Before rounding off this section, we would like to state just one more point. And, that is, an interface reference variable has the know-how of only the methods specified by its *interface* declaration, and whence, it cannot be employed to access any other variables/methods, which may be supported by the object in question.

6.1.2 Interface Properties

Just like methods, properties can also be declared in an interface without having any body. The most genral form of such a property declaration is:

```
// An INTERFACE Property
type name
{
        get; set;
}
```

where, *name* specifies the property name and *type* specifies its data type.Note that only one of the *get* or *set* accessors will be present for read-only or write-only properties, respectively.

You might be thinking that this declaration of an interface property is the same as an auto-implemented property is declared in a class. But, the two are completely different. In fact, the interface specification does not result in the property becoming auto-implemented; it only specifies the name and the type of the property while leaving out its implementation to the implementing class. Further, no access modifiers can be specified with the accessors in an interface property so that, for example, the *set* accessor cannot be specified to be *private* in an interface.

The following example program (*Example 95*) reworks *Example 91* (illustrating *Iser* interface and *ByFives* class) by using an interface property named *next* to obtain (get) and set the next element/value in the series. *Note that the property next is implicitly passed the parameter value; so, we have changed our variable name value in Example 91 to simply v in Example 95.*

Example 95

```
/* Illustrates an Interface Property*/
/* Author: Arunesh; Date: 27/03/2011 */
using System;
public interface Iser
{
        int next                        // an interface property
        {
                get;                    // return next number in series
                set.                    // set next number
        }
}
class ByFives : Iser        // ByFives implements the interface Iser
        // Using Iser to implement a series of numbers, each five greater than the previous one
{
        int v;
        public ByFives( )               // defaut constructor
        {
                v = 0;
        }
        public int next( )              // get or set value
        {
                get
                {
                        v + = 5;
                        return v;
                }
                set
                {
                        v = value;
                }
        }
}
```

```
// demonstrate the inteface property next
class series_Demo2
{
        static void Main( )
        {
                ByFives byfives = new ByFives( );

                for (int x = 0; x < 5; x++)        // access first five numbers through next
                        Console.WriteLine("Next value is: \t" + byfives.next);

                Console.WriteLine("\n Starting at 51");
                byfives.next =51;
                                // access  first five numbers after51 through next
                for (int x = 0; x < 5; x++)
                        Console.WriteLine("Next value is: \t" + byfives.next);
        }
}
```

Output:

```
        Next value is    5
        Next value is    10
        Next value is    15
        Next value is    20
        Next value is    25

        Starting at 51
        Next value is    56
        Next value is    61
        Next value is    66
        Next value is    71
        Next value is    76
```

6.1.3 Interface Indexers

An interface can also specify an indexer. A simple one-dimensional interface indexer has the most general form:

```
// An INTERFACE Indexer
element_type this[int index]
{
        get; set;
}
```

where, *element_type* specifies its underlying data type.Note that only one of the *get* or *set* accessors will be present for read-only or write-only indexers, respectively. Further, no access modifiers can be specified with the accessors in an interface indexer so that, for example, the *set* accessor cannot be specified to be *private*. This is just like interface properties.

The following example program (*Example 96*) reworks *Example 95* (illustrating interface property *next*) by using a read-only interface indexer, which returns the *i*-th element in the series.

Example 96

```
/* Illustrates an Interface Indexer*/
/* Author: Arunesh; Date: 27/03/2011 */
using System;
public interface Iser
{
        int next                        // an interface property
        {
                get;                    // return next number in series
                set.                    // set next number
        }

        int this[int index]                     // a read-only interface indexer
        {
                get;                    // return the specified number in series
        }
}
class ByFives : Iser        // ByFives implements the interface Iser
        // Using Iser to implement a series of numbers, each five greater than the previous one
{
        int v;

        public ByFives( )           // defaut constructor
        {
                v = 0;
        }

        public int next( )          // get or set value
        {
                get
                {
                        v + = 5;
                        return v;
                }
                set
                {
                        v = value;
                }
        }
```

```
        int this[int index]                    // get a value using an index
        {
                get
                {
                        v = 0;
                        for (int x = 0; x < index; x++)
                                v += 5;
                        return v;
                }
        }
}

// Demonstrate the inteface indexer
class series_Demo3
{
        static void Main( )
        {
                ByFives byfives = new ByFives( );

                for (int x = 0; x < 5; x++)  // access first five numbers through property next
                        Console.WriteLine("Next value is: \t" + byfives.next);

                Console.WriteLine("\n Starting at 51");
                byfives.next =51;
                        // access  first five numbers after 51 through property next
                for (int x = 0; x < 5; x++)
                        Console.WriteLine("Next value is: \t" + byfives.next);

                Console.WriteLine("\n Resetting to 0");
                byfives.next = 0;
                        // access  first five numbers through the interface indexer
                for (int x = 0; x < 5; x++)
                        Console.WriteLine("Next value is: \t" + byfives[x]);
        }
}
```

Output:

```
        Next value is    5
        Next value is    10
        Next value is    15
        Next value is    20
        Next value is    25
```

```
Starting at 51
Next value is    56
Next value is    61
Next value is    66
Next value is    71
Next value is    76

Resetting to 0
Next value is    0
Next value is    5
Next value is    10
Next value is    15
Next value is    20
```

6.1.4 Interfaces Can Be Inherited

Interfaces can be inherited just like classes. The syntax is exactly the same as for class inheritance. When a clsss implements an interface thast inherits another interface, it must provide complete implementation for all the members defined within the interface inheritance ladder. An example follows (*Example* 97).

Example 97

```
/* Illustrates Interface Inheritance*/
/* Author: Arunesh; Date: 27/03/2011 */
public interface I1                 // Inteface 1
{
        void M1( );                 // Method/Member 1
        void M2( );                 // Method/Member 2
}

public interface I2 : I1            // Inteface 2 inherits Interface 1
{
        void M3( );                 // Method/Member 3
}

class NewClass : I2                 // NewClass implements I2 which inherits I1
                                    // whence, it must implement all members of both I2 and I1
{
        public void M1()
        {
                Console.WriteLine("Implementation of M1() Done");
        }
```

```
        public void M2()
        {
                Console.WriteLine("Implementation of M2() Done");
        }

        public void M3()
        {
                Console.WriteLine("Implementation of M3() Done");
        }
}

class Interface_Inheritance
{
        static void Main()
        {
                NewClass obj = new NewClass();

                obj.M1();
                obj.M2();
                obj.M3();
        }
}
```

Output:

Implementation of M1() Done
Implementation of M2() Done
Implementation of M3() Done

/* An attempt to remove any of the implementations for *M1(), M2(),* or *M3()* in *NewClass* shall cause a compiler error. This is because a class implementing an interface must mecessarily implement all methods.members in that interface, inclusive of any inherited from other interfaces.*/

6.1.4.1 Name Hiding in Interface Inheritance

When one interface inherits another, there can be a case where a member in the inhrited interface has the same declartion as the one in the base interface. In such a case , the base interface name is hidden. As with inheritance in classes, this shall sound a compiler warning message unless and until the derived interface member is qualified with the keyword *new*, which informs the compiler that a new member is being created in the derived interface, which has the same name as a previously defined member in the base interface.

6.1.5 Explicit Interface Member Implementations

While implementing a member of an interface, you can fully *qualify* its name with that of the interface resulting in what is known as *explicit interface member implementation*, or just *explicit implementation*, to put it even more succinctly, e,g., given the following interface:

```
interface IsIF
{
        void M();
}
```

then, the following explicit implementation is perfectly fine and valid:

```
class C : IsIF
{
        void IsIF.M()
        {
                Console.WriteLine("Explicit Implementation!");
        }
}
```

What is important here is to note the fact that when the *M()* member of *IsIF* is implemented, its full name is qualified with that of its interface.

But, the question arises - "What is the pressing need for such an explicit implementation?". Well, there are two main reasons. For one, when an interface method is implemented using its fully qualified name, such an implementation cannot be accessed through an object of the class; rather, it must necessarily be accessed through an interface reference. In this way, an explicit implementation provides a technique to implement an interface method so that it is not a public member of the class providing the implementation. The second reason is removing ambiguity when a class implements two interfaces, both of which have methods with the same name and type signature. In such a situation, we can qualify their names with that of their intefaces and remove the ambiguity. *Examples 98* and *99* look at each of these two situations vividly.

<u>Example 98</u>

```
/* Illustrates Explicit Implementation of an Interface Member */
/* Author: Arunesh; Date: 27/03/2011 */
using System;
interface IsIF
{
        bool Even(int i);
        bool Odd(int i);
}
class C : IsIF
{
        /* Explicit Implementation; note that this member is private, by default */
        bool IsIF.Even(int i)
```

```
    {
        if ((i % 2) == 0)
                return true;
        else return false;
    }

    /* Normal Implementation */
    public bool Odd(int i)
    {
        Odd odd = this;          // interface reference to invoking object

        return !odd.Even(i);
    }
}
class IsIF_Demo
{
    static void Main()
    {
        class C c = new C();
        bool b;

        b = c.Odd(5);
        if (b)
                Console.WriteLine("5 is odd");

        // b = c.Even(6);  // ERROR! Even() not exposed as public member of C

        IsIF IsIFref = (IsIF) c; // this is fine; creates IsIf reference to a class C object
        b = IsIfref.Even(6);    // then, calls Even() via that reference
        if (b)
                Console.WriteLine("6 is even");
    }
}
```

<u>Output</u>:

```
    5 is odd
    6 is even
```

/* *Example 98* includes an inteface *IsIF* that specifies two methods, *Even()* and *Odd()*, which determine whether a given integer is even or odd, respectively. Class *C* implements *IsIF*, and in the process, implements *Even()* explicitly. And, since that is the case, *Even()* is not exposed as a public member of class *C*. Whence, *Even()* can be accessed only through an interface reference variable of type *IsIF* such as *odd* in the implementation for *Odd()*. */

Example 99

```
/* Illustrates Explicit Implementation to remove Ambiguity */
/* Author: Arunesh; Date: 27/03/2011 */
using System;

interface IsIF1
{
        int M(int i);
}

interface IsIF2
{
        int M(int i);
}

class C : IsIF1, IsIF2    // class C implements both interfaces
{
        /* Explicit Implementation of the two M()s */
        int IsIF1.M(int i)
        {
                return 2 * i;
        }
        int IsIF2.M(int i)
        {
                return 3 * i;
        }

        /* Invoke/call the two M()s through interface references */
        public int M1(int i)
        {
                IsIF1 obj1;
                obj1 = this;
                return obj1.M(i);          // invokes IsIF1.M()
        }
        public int M2(int i)
        {
                IsIF2 obj2;
                obj2 = this;
                return obj2.M(i);          // invokes IsIF2.M()
        }
}
```

```
class IsIF1_IsIF2_Demo
{
        static void Main()
        {
                class C c = new C();

                Console.Write("Invoking IsIF1.M(): /t");
                Console.WriteLine(c.M1(5));

                Console.WriteLine();

                Console.Write("Invoking IsIF2.M(): /t");
                Console.WriteLine(c.M2(5));
        }
}
```

Output:

```
        Invoking IsIF1.M():     10

        Invoking IsIF2.M():     15
```

/* *Example 99* includes two intefaces *IsIF1, IsIF2* with the method *M()* having the same signature in these two intefaces. Class *C* implements both *IsIF1, IsIF2*, and in the process, implements *M()* explicitly. And, since *an explicitly implemented* method can be invoked only through an interface reference, class C creates two such references, one for *IsIF1* and one for *IsIF2,* inside *M1()* and *M2(),* respectively.. Thereupon, it invokes these two methods, which, in turn, invoke the respective interface methods, thus removing and getting rid of the ambiguity. */

6.1.6 Interfaces vs. Abstract Classes

Choosing between interfaces and abstract classes can be an extremely tedious task especially in those cases where you want to have functionality without implementation. The common rule of the thumb is that you should use an interface if you are in full control of "what to do?" without having to worry about "how to do it?". However, if you cannot fully describe the vconcept without including some implementation part, then you must use an abstract class. As easy as that.

6.1.7 Standard Interfaces as Supported by the .NET Framework

The .Net Framework specifies a good number of interfaces, which C# programmers can easily make use of, e.g., *System.IComparable* specifies the *CompareTo()* method, which compares objects with respect to their ordering. Collection classes providing various kinds of storage such as stacks and queues etc. for groups of objects also contain some important interfaces, e.g., *System.Collections.ICollection* specifies the functionality of a collection while *System.Collections.IEnumerator* provides for sequencing through the elements of a collection.

6.1.8 Interface Restrictions

The key point to remember is that an inteface never contaiuns any implementation. The following six major restrictions are a natural corollary of this concept:

(1) No fields can be defined in an interface, not even static ones. This is because a field is an implementation detail of a class/structure.

(2) No constructors can be defined in an interface. This is because a constructor is also an implementation detail of a class/structure.

(3) No destructors can be defined in an interface. This is because a destructor contains code to destroy an object instance.

(4) No access modifier can be specified for any method in the inteface. This is because all methods in an interface are implicitly public.

(5) You are not allowed to nest any types (such as enumerations, structures, classes, or interfaces) inside an interface.

(6) An inteface cannot inherit from a structure/class although it is allowwed to inherit from another interface. This is because structures/classes contain implementation, which, in turn, implies that if an interface were allowed to inherit from structures/classes, it would, in fact, be inheriting some implementation.

6.2 STRUCTURES

We know that classes are reference types and that classobjects are accessed through a reference. But, in certain situations, it might be more beneficial to access object directly like values types are. One of the main reasons for this is efficiency as accessing class objects through a reference adds significant overhead. To take care of such situations, we have the structure. As already mentioned, a structure is similar to a class, but is a value type, rather than a reference type, which a class is. Structures are syntactically similar to classes and are declared using the keyword struct as follows:

```
struct struct_name : interfaces
{
        // member declarations
}
```

where, *struct_name* specifies the name of the particular structure.

Structures are neither not allowed to inherit other structures/classes nor can they be used as a base for other structures/classes (it is pertinent to note that all structures do inherit *System.ValueType*, which, in turn, inherits *object*). A structure can, however, implement one or morethan one interfaces, which are specified after the name of the structure using a comma-separated list

Structure members can be methods, fields, indexers, properties, operator methods, and events (events are discussed at length in chapter 9), just as in the case of classes. Structures may also have constructors, but no destructors. But, there is a caveat. And, that is, a structure cannot define a default, i.e., parameterless constructor, the reason being that a default constructor is automatically defined for all structures, which cannot be changed. This default constructor initializes all the fields of a structure to their default values. Note that structure members cannot be declared as *abstract*, *virtual*, or *protected*. The simple reason for this is that structures do not support inheritance, as already explained.

A structure object can be created using the operator *new* just like a class object, but it is not mandatory to do so. In fact, if *new* is not used, the object is still created but not initialized. Any initialization in such a case would have to be carried out manually.

Now, we take up an example program (*Example 100*) that uses a structure to hold information about a library.

Example 100

```
/* Illustrates a Structure */
/* Author: Arunesh; Date: 27/03/2011 */
using System;
struct Library
{
        public string Book;
        public string Author;
        public string Title;
```

```
        public Library(string b, string a, string t)
        {
                Book = b;
                Author = a;
                Title = t;
        }
}

// Demonstrate the structure Library
class StructLib
{
        static void Main()
        {
                Library lib1 = new Library("Computers", "Arunesh Goyal",
                                "The Essentials of C# 4.0");    // user-defined constructor

                Library lib2 = new Library();   // default constructor

                Library lib3;   // NO constructor

                Console.WriteLine("Subject: " + lib1.Book + " Author: " + lib1.Author
                                                                + " Title: " + lib1.Title);
                Console.WriteLine();

                if (lib2.Title == null)
                        Console..WriteLine("lib2.Title is empty");

                /* assign lib2 some data */
                lib2.Book = "Computers";
                lib2.Author = "Arunesh Goyal";
                lib2.Title = "The Essentials of JAVA";

                Console.WriteLine("lib2 now has the following data: ");
                Console.WriteLine("Subject: " + lib2.Book + " Author: " + lib2.Author
                                                                + " Title: " + lib2.Title);
                Console.WriteLine();

                // Console.WriteLine(lib3.Title); // Error! Must Initialize First
                lib3.Title = "Systems Analysis and Design";
                Console.WriteLine(lib3.Title);  // now, fine
        }
}
```

Output:

Subject: Computers Author: Arunesh Goyal Title: The Essentials of C# 4.0

lib2.Title is empty
lib2 now has the following data:
Subject: Computers Author: Arunesh Goyal Title: The Essentials of JAVA

Systems Analysis and Design

/* As this example program (*Example 100*) demonstrates, a structure can be created by using *new* to call a constructor or by just declaring an object. When *new* is used, the fields of the structure are either initialized to their defalut values by the default constructor, or initialized by a user-defined constructor. When *new* is not used, as is the case with *lib3*, the object is not initialized, and its fields must be set or assigned values prior to its use by the program. */

6.2.1 Distinction between Structures and Classes

The main distinction lies in the fact that structures are value types whereas classes are reference types. If you assign one structure to another, a copy of the object is created. This is a significant way in which structures differ from classes. As already elaborated in chapter 2, when a class reference is assigned to another, it simply makes the reference on the left side of the assignment refer to the same object as the one referred to by the reference on the right. However, when a structure variable is assigned to another, a copy of the object on the right is made. This would become clear in the light of the following two example programs (*Examples 101* and *102*).

Example 101

```
/* Illustrates the VALUE type concept of Structures */
/* Author: Arunesh; Date: 27/03/2011 */
using System;
struct s
{
        public char ch;
}

class StructureValue
{
        static void Main()
        {
                /* structure declarations */
                s s1;
                s s2;
```

```
            s1.ch = 'A';
            s2.ch = 'B';

            Console.WriteLine(s1.ch);
            Console.Writeline(s2.ch);

            s1 = s2;
            s2.ch = 'C';

            Console.WriteLine(s1.ch);
            Console.Writeline(s2.ch);
      }
}
```

<u>Output</u>:

```
      A
      B
      B
      C
```

/* From the output, it can be easily deciphered that even after the equality assignment, viz., *s1 = s2, s1* and *s2* are still separate and distinct. Thus, *s1* does not relate to or refer to *s2* in any way other than containing a copy of *s2*'s value.Whence, structures are value types. */

<u>*Example 102*</u>

```
/* Iillustrates the REFERENCE type concept of Classes */
/* Author: Arunesh; Date: 27/03/2011 */
using System;
class c
{
      public  char ch;
}

class ClassReference
{
      static void Main()
      {
            /* class declarations */
            c1 = new c();
            c2 = new c();;

            c1.ch = 'A';
            c2.ch = 'B';
```

```
            Console.WriteLine(c1.ch);
            Console.Writeline(c2.ch);

            c1 = c2;
            c2.ch = 'C';

            Console.WriteLine(c1.ch);
            Console.Writeline(c2.ch);
      }
}
```

Output:

```
      A
      B
      C
      C
```

/* From the output, it can be easily deciphered that after the equality assignment, viz., *c1* = *c2, c1* and *c2* refer to same object, that is, the one originally referred to by *c2*. Whence, classes are reference types.
*/

6.2.2 Need for Structures

Structures are especially handy to have when grouping data. You will say - "We can do that using classses also!" The major advantage of structures is efficiency and performance. Since structures are value types, they are accessed directly rather than through a reference. In this way, structures do not need the declaration of an additional reference variable as is the case with classes (recall that classes are reference types). This means that less memory is incurred in case of structures as compared to classes that require an additional overhead due to indirect reference. We can lay down a general guideline for you to follow while choosing between structures and classes. And, that is, structures can be a better and more efficient choice if you just want to store a group of related data, but neither require inheritance nor need to operate on this data via a reference.

Before rounding off this section, we have an interesting point to make as regards structures in C++. C++ also uses the *struct* keyword just like C# but structures in C# and C++ have different connotations. In C++, structures define a class type and therefore, in C++, structures and classes are almost equivalent, with the only difference being in the defaiult access of their members, which is *public* for structures and *private* for classes. However, as already explained again and again, in C#, structures define a value type while classes are reference types.

6.3 ENUMERATIONS

An enumeration is a way of assigning names to integer constants. To give you a practical example of the need for enumerations, imagine a scenario where you wanted to represent the seasons of the year in a program. You could very well use the integers 0, 1, 2, and 3 to represent spring, summer, autumn, and winter respectively. This solution would work but it is not very innovative, e.g., if you used the integer value 0 in the program code, it would not be very obvious that a particular 0 represented spring. Futhermore, it would also not be a very robust solution to the problem, e.g., if you declare an integer variable called *season* , there is nothing to prevent you from assigining the variable *season* any legal integer value other than 0, 1, 2, or 3. C# offers a much better solution. You can create an enumeration (sometimes called an *enum* type), whose values would be limited to a set of symbolic names, e,g., in this particular case, it could be: *enum season{spring, summer, autumn, winter};*

The most general form of an enumeration is:

enum enum_name {enum_list };

// notice the keyword '*enum*'!

where, *enum_name* is the name of the said enumeration and *enum_list* is a comma-separated list of identifiers. Take for instance the following enumeration, which enumerates various types of fruits.:

enum Fruit {Apple, Banana, Orange, Mango };

What is important to understand about an enumeration is that each of the symbols/identifiers stands for an integer value. But no implicit conversions are defined between an enum type and the built-in integer types; whence, an explicit cast must be employed. A cast is also required if you want to convert between two enumerations. Further, because an enumeration represents integer values, it can be used to control a for loop or a switch construct, for instance. Each enumeration symbol/identifier has a value one greater than the one immediately preceding it. Also, by default, the value of the first enumeration symbol/identifier is 0.

Whence, by default, in the *Fruit* enumeration:

Apple = 0, Banana = 1, ..., Mango = 3;

The members of an enumeration can be acccessed via their type name through the dot (.) operator, e.g.,

Console.,WriteLine("Fruit.Mango + " has the value " + (int) Fruit.Mango);

displays the following output:

Mango has the value 3

The above output confirms the fact that when an enumerated value is displayed, its name is used and in order to obtain its integer value, a cast to *int* has to be necessarily used.

The following example (*Example 103*) is illustrative of the above enumeration, namely, *Fruit.*

Example 103

```
/* Illustrates the ENUMERATION: Fruit */
/* Author: Arunesh; Date:27 /03/2011 */
using System;
class EnumIllustrative
{
        enum Fruit {Apple, Banana, Orange, Mango };

        static void Main()
        {
                string [ ] val = { "zero", "one", "two", "three" };

                Fruit F;
                        // enum variable

                for (F = Fruit.Apple; F <= Fruit.Mango; F++)
                        Console.WriteLine(F + " = " + (int)F);
                        // cycling through enumeration Fruit through variable F

                Console.WriteLine();

                for (F = Fruit.Apple; F <= Fruit.Mango; F++)
                        Console.Writeline("val[" + F + "] = " + val[(int)F]);
                        // indexing array  val using enumeration Fruit
        }
}
```

Output:

```
        Apple = 0
        Banana = 1
        Orange = 2
        Mango = 3

        val[0] = zero
        val[1] = one
        val[2] = two
        val[3] = three
```

/* In this example program (*Example 103*), the noteworthy thing is the controlling of the two *for* loops by the variable *F* of type *Fruit*. Since the enumerated values in *Fruit* begin with 0, these values can be employed to index the string array *val* to obtain the values stored in this array.

Another interesting point of note is that an explicit cast is required to index the *val* array since there are no implicit conversions defined between integers and enum types, as already explained. */

Before rounding off this section, we would like to state just one more point, by the way. And, that is, all enumerations implicitly inherit *System.Enum*, which, in turn, inherits *System.ValueType*, which ultimately inheris our universal data type *object*, as explained in the previous chapter..

6.3.1 Initializing an Enumeration

We can specify an initial value for one or more of the identifier symbols in an enumeration.we can do so by following the identifier symbol with an equal sign and an integer constant expression. Symbols/identifiers appearing after these initializers are assigned values greater than the previous initialization value. Consider the following modification of *Example 103* as a case in point (*Example 104*).

<u>*Example 104*</u>

```
/* Illustrates the INITIALIZATION of an Enumeration */
/* Author: Arunesh; Date: 27/03/2011 */
using System;
class EnumInitializer
{
    enum Fruit {Apple = 1, Banana, Orange = 10, Mango };

    static void Main()
    {
            Fruit F;
                    // enum variable

            for (F = Fruit.Apple; F <= Fruit.Mango; F++)
                    Console.WriteLine(F + " = " + (int)F);
                    // cycling through enumeration Fruit through variable F

    }
}
```

<u>Output</u>:

```
Apple = 1
Banana = 2
Orange = 10
Mango = 11
```

/* Use your own imagination and logic for the changed <u>output</u>, especially the values of *Banana* and *Mango*!
*/

6.3.2 Enumerations - Specifying Underlying Type

All enumerations, by default, are based upon type int, but you can specify an enumeration of any underlying integral type, except for char. In oder to specify a type other than the default int, just use the desired type after the name of the enumeration with a colon in between, e,g., the following statement:

enum Fruit : short {Apple, Banana, Orange, Mango };

converts *Fruit* into an enumeration based on *short* integer type, e.g., *Fruit.Banana* now, is a *short* entity.

6.3.3 A Real Life Example of Using an Enumeration

You might be thinking, in light of the precerding discussion, that enumerations are an interesting but relatively not so important in C#. Forget it. It is just not the case. Enumerations have a very useful role to play when a C# program is in need of one or more than one specialized symbols/ identifiers. In fact, if you have been careful enough, you should not have missed such a case, which we have already elaborated in the main section on enumerations (recall the variable, *season*).

We shall now use the *switch-case* construct to come up with another example simulating real life action by means of an enumeration (*Example 105*).

<u>Example 105</u>

```
/* Uses switch-case construct to Simulate real life action by nmeans of an Enumeration */
* Author: Arunesh; Date: 27/03/2011 */
using System;
class Rank
{
    public enum Position {First, Second, Third };
    // enumerate the three ranks
    public void RankControl(Position pos)
    {
            switch(pos)
            {
                    case pos.First:
                            Console.WriteLine("Person with Rank ONE");
                            break;
                    case pos.Second:
                            Console.WriteLine("Person with Rank TWO");
                            break;
                    case pos.Third:
                            Console.WriteLine("Person with Rank THREE");
                            break;
            }
    }
}
```

```
class EnumRealLifeSimulation
{
        static void Main()
        {
                Rank  r = new Rank();

                r.RankControl(Rank.Position.First);
                r.RankControl(Rank.Position.Second);
                r.RankControl(Rank.Position.Third);
        }
}
```

Output:

```
        Person with Rank ONE
        Person with Rank TWO
        Person with Rank THREE
```

/* Note that since *RankControl()* takes an argument of type *Position*, only the values defined by *Position* can be passed to the method, e.g,.

r.RankControl(5);

shall result in a compile-time *error*! This is because there is no pre-defined conversion from *int* to *Position*. Thus, this code prevents the passing of invalid commands/ arguments to *RankControl()*. Of course, you could forciblly cast a conversion, but this would not be accidental misuse; rather, it would be a well planned premeditated act. Furthermore, since commands/arguments are specified by name rather than by any number, the chances of inadvertently passing a wrong value to *RankControl()* are considerably reduced.

*/

We would like to state just one more point before rounding off this section and chapter. And, that is, *Example 105* uses an *enum* type to control the *switch-case* construct. This is perfectly in accordance with our previous observation that being integer types, enumerations can be used to control *for* loops (as illustrated in *Examples 103* and *104*) or *switch-case* constructs as illustrated in this particular example program.

PRACTICAL SESSION

#1 What are the major advantages of interfaces?

#2 At a function to commemorate the beginning of a new retail chain, invitations are sent to fifty distinguished persons. It is expected that each invitee shall buy goods worth *minimum* of rupees two hundred and *maximum* eight hundred only. Based on the concept of ***structures/enumerations*** and data input by the user, design a *C# program* to output the number of actual persons who attended the function and the total sales made in rupees.

#3 Given that:

music.cassettes.songs = 70;

Which of the following statements is true in your opinion ? (Support your answer logically).

1. Structure songs is nested within structure music.
2. Structure songs is nested within structure cassettes.
3. Structure cassettes is nested within structure songs.
4. Structure music is nested within structure songs.

#4 State True (T) or False (F):

(i) The default type of an enumeration is byte.
(ii) By default, the first identifier in the enumeration list gets the value 0.
(iii) An interface just like a class cannot inherit more than one interface.
(iv) Structures exhibit inheritance.
(v) Structures cannot be nested.

#5 Given that:

struct time { int hours; int minutes; int seconds} t;
struct time tt;
tt = t;

Which of the following refers to seconds correctly?

1. *tt.seconds
2. time.t
3. tt.seconds
4. tt->seconds

#6 What is the main difference between C# structures and classes?
How is it different from the one in C++?
Explain giving suitable example(s), wherever necessary.

#7 Identify the error(s), if any, in each of the following code fragments:

(i)
```
interface X { }
class Y { }
class Z : X, Y
{
        ..........
        ..........
}
```

(ii)
```
interface X
{
        void show( );
}
interface Y : X
{
        void show( );
}
```

#8 What is an interface? Elaborate in detail giving a suitable example.

#9 Point out at least three differences between classes and interfaces. Also, point out two similarities between them.

#10 Why do we need structures? Elaborate and elucidate.

#11 Suppose we need to indicate that class CLASSX derives from base class CLASSB and implements the interfaces INTERFACEA and INTERFACEB.
How do we do it?

#12 Design a structure data type using a suitable name for an inventory record consisting of item code, item name, item cost, item quantity available, and item quantity reorder level. Write a C# program that uses five records of this type and displays them in the tabular format shown below:

Item Name	Item Cost	Item Quantity	Reorder Level
....	....	....	....
....	....	....	....
....	....	....	....
Total			

#13 Pick out the correct alternative(s) in each of the following multiple choice problems:

(i) Which of the following statements about interfaces are correct?

(a) All interfaces are derived from the **object** class.
(b) Intefaces can be inherited.
(c) Interfaces can contain only method declaration.
(d) All interfaces are derived from the **object** interface.
(e) None of the above

(ii) Which of the following statements are correct about interfaces in C#?

(a) A class can implement multiple interfaces.
(b) In C#, : is used to specify that a class inherits a specific interface.
(c) An interface can implement multiple classes.
(d) The *static* attribute can be used with a method that implements an interface declaration.
(e) None of the above

(iii) Consider the following C# code fragment:

```
interface ij
{
        void fa( );
        void fb( );
}
class z : ij
{
        private int k;
        void ij.fa( )
        {
                ............
                ............
        }
}
```

In the light of this code fragment, which of the following statements are true?

(a) Class z fully implements interface ij.
(b) The compiler will report an error since the interface ij is only partially implemented.
(c) Class z is an abstract class.
(d) Class z cannot contain instance data.
(e) None of the above

(iv) Which of the following can implement an interface?
   (a) Data
   (b) Class and Structure
   (c) Namespace
   (d) Enumeration
   (e) None of the above

#14 What role do enumerations play in C# programming? Elucidate giving suitable example(s), wherever necessary.

#15 Find errors, if any, in the following code segments:

(i) *enum abc {a, b, c = -78 };*

(ii) *enum paint {p, a, i, n, t }*

CHAPTER 7

EXCEPTION HANDLING

7.0 INTRODUCTION

It's a fact of life that bad things sometimes happen. Tyres get punctured, batteries run down, screwdriivers are never found where you left them, and users of your applications behave in an unpredictable manner. In the world of computers, disks fail, other applications running on the same computer as your program run amok and use up alll the available memory, and networks go awry and disconnect at the most awkward and critical moment. Errors can occur at almost any stage when a program runs; so how do you detect them and try to recover? Over the years, numerous mechanisms have evolved. A typical approach adopted by older systems such as UNIX involved arranging for the operating system to set a special global variable whenever a method failed. Then, after each call to a method, you would check the gobal variable to see if the method succeeded. C# and most other object-oriented programming languages do not handle errors this way. It's just too error-prone, clumsy and painful. Rather, they use exceptions; if you want to write robust C# programs, you need to know about exceptions and exception handling.

In simple terms, an exception is an error that occurs at run-time. Exception handling streamlines the process of error-handling by allowing the program to specify a special code block, known as exception handler, that is invoked and executed automatically when an error occurs. Thus, there is no need to check the success/failure of each method call or a specific operation. In the event of an error occurring, the error shall be processed by the provided exception handler.

The main advantage of C#'s exception handling mechanism is that it allows us to handle run-time logical errors in an automated orderly fashion. Using exception handling, we can automatically call the specific error-handling routine in the event of a particular error occurring. Exception handling is especially useful for exiting from a deeply nested set of routines when a catastrophic error occurs. Anyway, the main point to note is that exception handling provides a means to an efficient and orderly way/method of handling errors, particulary the run-time ones. This includes rectifying the situation, if somehow possible. Thus, exception handling is designed to provide a structured means to handle or take care of abnormal outputs/events/situations. Exception handling is also important since C# defines standard exceptions for common programming errors such as divide-by-zero or index-out-of-range. To successfully take care of these errors, the C# program must watch out for and handle these exceptions.

7.1 THE EXCEPTION CLASS

In C#, exceptions are represented by classes. And, all exception classes are derived from the built-in exception class *Exception*, which is, in turn, part of the *System* namespace. In this way, all exceptions are sublasses of *Exception*. One of the important subclasses of *Exception* is *SystemException* from which all exceptions generated by the C# run-time system, viz., CLR, are derived. The .Net Framework specifies several built-in exceptions which are derived from *SystemException*, e,g., when a divide-by-zero is attempted, a *DivideByZeroException* is generated. You can also create your own exception classes derived from *Exception*, as we shall see later in this chapter.

7.2 EXCEPTION HANDLING: FUNDAMENTALS & BASICS

The four keywords, viz., try, catch, and throw, and finally are the foundation on which the whole exception handling mechanism of C# is built on. All program statements that we wish to check for exceptions are contained within the 'try' block. If an error./exception occurs within that try block, it is "thrown". We can monitor this exception using 'catch'. While system-generated exceptions like divide-by-zero and index-out-of-range are "thrown" by the C# run-time system automatically, we can use the keyword 'throw' to manually "throw" an exception. Finally, if we want to make it absolutely mandatory for any code to be executed upon exiting from a 'try' block, it can be put in a 'finally' block.

The most general forms of *try* and *catch* blocks are:

```
try
{
        // body of try block containing statement(s) to monitor
}
catch(Excptype1 ExcpObj)
{
        // body of catch(Excptype1) block
}
catch(Excptype2 ExcpObj)
{
        // body of catch(Excptype2) block
}
...............................................
...............................................
...............................................
catch(ExcptypeN  ExcpObj)                    // N  is a whole number
{
        // body of catch(Excptype N) block
}
```

where, *Excptype* indicates the type of exception and *ExcpObj* receives its value when an exception is actually caught.

Here is our first simple exception handling example for you (*Example 106*).

Example 106

```
/* Illustrates a simple exception */
/* Author: Arunesh; Date: 27/03/2011 */
using System;
class Demo_Excp1
{
	static void Main()
	{
		int j = 10;

		Console.WriteLine("begin");

		try
		{
			Console.WriteLine("try BLOCK");
			for (int i = 5; j = j / i; i -= 5)
				Console.WriteLine(j);
			Console.WriteLine("this line shall never print");
		}

		catch(DivideByZeroException)
		{
			Console.WriteLine("Attempting to Divide by Zero!");
		}

		Console.WriteLine("end");
	}
}
```

Output:

```
begin
try BLOCK
2
Attempting to Divide by Zero!
end
```

/* In the second iteration of the *for* loop, the value of *i* becomes zero, giving rise to the *DivideByZeroException* which is caught by the catch statement.
*/

If the type of exception thrown doesn't match the type mentioned in the catch statement, the exception shall not be caught and instead, abnornmal program termination shall take place. *Example 107* is a case in point.

Example 107

```
/*Illustrates Mismatch in Type of Exception */
/* Author: Arunesh; Date: 27/03/2011 */
using System;
class Demo_Excp2
{
        static void Main()
        {
                int j = 10;

                Console.WriteLine("begin");
                try
                {
                        Console.WriteLine("try BLOCK");
                        for (int i = 5; j = j / i; i -= 5)
                                Console.WriteLine(j);
                        Console.WriteLine("this line shall never print");
                }

                catch(IndexOutOfRangeException)
                {
                        Console.WriteLine("Attempting to Divide by Zero!");
                }

                Console.WriteLine("end");
        }
}
```

Output:

```
begin
try BLOCK
2
Abnormal program termination
```

/* The above example also illustrates a case of an *uncaught exception*. And, since the exception is not caught due to *mismatch* in exception type, it results in abnormal program termination, as confirmed by the output.
*/

We must also note that the code associated with a catch statement shall be executed only if it catches an exception. *Otherwise. the catch statement is bypassed altogether.*
Example 108 is a case in point.

Example 108

```
/* Illustrates bypassing of code associated with an Exception */
/* Author: Arunesh; Date: 27/03/2011 */
using System;
class Demo_Excp3
{
        static void Main()
        {
                Console.WriteLine("begin");

                try
                {
                        Console.WriteLine("try BLOCK");
                }

                catch(DivideByZeroException)
                {
                        Console .WriteLine("CAUGHT divide-by-zero exception" );
                }

                Console.WriteLine("end");
        }
}
```

Output:

```
begin
try BLOCK
end
```

/* Thus, the catch statement is bypassed and ignored altogether as no exception is caught in this instance.
*/

Also, we can have nested try blocks. In such a case, if we have an exception that is not caught by the inner try block, it is transfered to the outer try block.
Example 109 is a case in point.

Example 109

```
/* Illustrates Nested try blocks */
/* Author: Arunesh; Date: 27/03/2011 */
using System;
class Demo_Excp4
{
        static void  Main()
        {
                int j = 10;
                Console.WriteLine("begin");
                try             // outer try block
                {
                        try     // inner try block
                        {
                                Console.WriteLine("inner try BLOCK");
                                for (int i = 5; j = j / i; i -= 5)
                                        Console.WriteLine(j);
                        }
                        catch(IndexOutOfRangeException)
                        {
                                Console.WriteLine("No Matching Element FOUND");
                        }
                Console.Writeline("outer try BLOCK");
                catch(DivideByZeroException)
                {
                        Console.WriteLine("Attempting to Divide by Zero!");
                }
                Console.Writeline("end");
                }
        }
}
```

Output:

```
begin
inner try BLOCK
2
outer try BLOCK
Attempting to Divide byZero!
end
```

/* Here, the *DivideByZeroException* is not caught by the inner try block but by the outer try block, as confirmed by the output. */

7.3 MULTIPLE CATCH STATEMENTS

We can have *more than one catch statements* associated with one try block. However, each such statement must associate with a *different type of exception*.

Example 110 is a case in point. It handles both array boundary and divide-by-zero exceptions.

<u>*Example 110*</u>

```
/* Multiple Catch statements */
/* Author: Arunesh; Date: 27/03/2011*/
using System;
class Demo_Excp5
{
    static void Main()
    {
        int [ ] numerators = {2, 4, 8, 16, 32, 64, 128, 128, 256};

        int [ ] denominators = {2, 0, 4, 8, 0, 4};
            // numerators is longer than denominators

        for (int x = 0; x < numerators.Length; x++)
        {
            try
            {
                Console.WriteLine("numerators[x] + " / " + denominators[x]
                    + " = " + numerators[x]/denominators[x]);
            }

            catch (DivideByZeroException)
            {
                Console.WriteLine("Division by zero not allowed");
            }

            catch(IndexOutOfRangeException)
            {
                Console..WriteLine("No Matching Element FOUND"):
            }
        }
    }
}
```

<u>Output</u>:

2 / 2 = 1
Division by zero not allowed
8 / 4 = 2
16 / 8 = 2
Division by zero not allowed
64 / 4 = 16
No matching element FOUND
No matching element FOUND
No matching element FOUND

/* Thus, each catch statement associates only with its corresponding type. In general, catch expressions are checked in the order in which they occur in a program. Only the first matching statement is executed; and, all other catch statements are bypassed/ignored. */

7.4 CATCHING ALL EXCEPTIONS

If we want an *exception handler to cater to all exceptions instead of just a certain type,* we can use the following form of <u>catch</u>:

```
catch
        // note the parameterless catch that match any type of data
{
        // all exceptions processed
}
```

For instance, the following program (*Example 111*) <u>explicitly</u> catches character exceptions but uses *catch* to catch all other exceptions, i.e., it uses *catch* as a <u>default</u>.

<u>*Example 111*</u>

```
/*  Catching  all Exceptions */
/* Author: Arunesh; Date: 27/03/2011 */
using System;
class Demo_Excp6
{
        static void Main()
        {
                int [ ] numerators = {2, 4, 8, 16, 32, 64, 128, 128, 256};

                int [ ] denominators = {2, 0, 4, 8, 0, 4};

                        // numerators is longer than denominators
```

```
            for (int x = 0; x < numerators.Length; x++)
            {
                try
                {
                    Console.WriteLine("numerators[x] + " / " + denominators[x]
                            + " = " + numerators[x]/denominators[x]);
                }
                catch   // catch all exceptions
                {
                    Console..WriteLine("An exception Occurred"):
                }
            }
        }
}
```

Output:

```
    2 / 2 = 1
    An exception Occurred
    8 / 4 = 2
    16 / 8 = 2
    An exception Occurred
    64 / 4 = 16
    An exception Occurred
    An exception Occurred
    An exception Occured
```

/* Thus, using catch as a default is a nice way to catch *all exceptions* that we don't want to catch explicitly. Also, since all exceptions are caught, an unhandled exception is prevented from causing an *abnormal program termination.*

We would like to mention just one more point about this catch-all catch. IT MUST BE THE LAST CATCH CLAUSE IN THE CATCH SEQUENCE.*/

7.5 THROWING AN EXCEPTION

So far, we have been catching exceptions generated automatically by C#'s run-time system. But, it is also possible to throw an exception manually by the use of *throw* statement, whose general form is:

throw exceptionObj;

where throw generates the exception specified by *exceptionObj* (which must be an object of an exception class derived from *Exception*). *Example 112* illustrates the *throw* statement by manually throwing a *DivideByzeroException*.

Example 112

```
/* Illustrates throwing an  exception manually */
/* Author: Arunesh; Date: 27/03/2011 */
using System;
class Demo_Excp7
{
        static void  Main()
        {
                Console.WriteLine("begin");

                try
                {
                        Console.WriteLine("try BLOCK");
                        throw new DivideByZeroException();
                                        // Manually throwing an exception
                        Console.WriteLine("this line shall never print");
                }

                catch(DivideByZeroException)
                {
                        Console.WriteLine("Caught Exception");
                }

                Console.WriteLine("end");
        }
}
```

Output:

```
begin
try BLOCK
Caught Exception
end
```

/* Carefully note how the *DivideByZeroException* was generated using *new* in the *throw* statement. */

7.6 RETHROWING AN EXCEPTION

An exception caught by one *catch* can be *rethrown* allowing it to be caught by an outer *catch*. Rethrowing an exception allows multiple handlers access to the exception. One handler can take care of one aspect of an exception while a second handler takes care of another. To *rethrow* an exception, simply specify throw without any expression as follows:

throw;

Example 113 is a case in point. It rethrows an *IndexOutOfRangeException*.

<u>*Example 113*</u>

```
/* Rethrowing an Exception */
/* Author: Arunesh; Date: 27/03/2011 */
using System;
class RethrowHandle
{
        public static void Exception_Generate()
        {
                int [ ] numerators = {2, 4, 8, 16, 32, 64, 128};
                int [ ] denominators = {2, 0, 4, 8, 0, 4};
                                // numerators is longer than denominators
                for (int x = 0; x < numerators.Length; x++)
                {
                        try
                        {
                                Console.WriteLine("numerators[x] + " / " + denominators[x]
                                                + " = " + numerators[x]/denominators[x]);
                        }
                        catch (DivideByZeroException)
                        {
                                Console.WriteLine("Division by zero not allowed");
                        }
                        catch(IndexOutOfRangeException)
                        {
                                Console.WriteLine("No Matching Element FOUND"):
                                throw;          // retrowing the exception
                        }
                }
        }
}

class Demo_Excp8
{
        static void Main()
        {
                try
                {
                        RethrowHandle.Exception_Generate();
                }
```

```
        catch(IndexOutOfRangeException)
        {
                Console.WriteLine("Fatal ERROR -- Abnormal Program
                                                        Termination");
        }
    }
}
```

Output:

2 / 2 = 1
Division by zero not allowed
8 / 4 = 2
16 / 8 = 2
Division by zero not allowed
64 / 4 = 16
No matching element FOUND
Fatal ERROR -- Abnormal Program Termination

/* In *Example 113*, divide-by-zero errors are handled locally by *Exception_Generate()*, but an array boundary error is rethrown. Herein, the *IndexOutOfRangeException* is handled by *Main()*.
*/

7.7 HOW TO USE "finally"?

If we want certain code to be executed when a try/catch block is exited, we can include a finally block at the end of this try/catch block. The most general form of such a block is:

```
try
{
        // monitoring errors code
}
catch(Excptype1 ExcpObj)
{
        // handling Excptype1 Excp
}
catch(Excptype2 ExcpObj)
{
        // handling Excptype2Excp
}
..................
..................
..................
..................
```

```
..................
..................
catch(ExcptypeN ExcpObj)
{
        // handling ExcptypeN Excp; N is a whole number
}
finally
{
        // code for finally
}
```

The finally block shall necessarily be executed whenever execution leaves a *try/catch* block, irrespective of the conditions responsible for it. The finally block will also get executed if any code within the *try* block or any of its *catch* blocks returns from the method. For instance, the following program (*Example 114*) uses finally.

Example 114

```
/* Using "finally" */
/* Author: Arunesh; Date: 27/03/2011 */
using System;
class Demo_Excp9
{
        static void Main()
        {
                int j = 4;
                int [ ] i = {1, 0, 2};

                Console.WriteLine("begin");

                for (k = 0; k < 3; k++)
                        try
                        {
                                Console.WriteLine("try BLOCK");
                                if (k == 2)
                                        i[-1] = k;
                                else
                                        {
                                                j = j / i[k];
                                                Console.WriteLine(j);
                                                return; // back from try
                                        }
                        }
```

```
        catch(IndexOutOfRangeException)
        {
                Console.WriteLine("Index is Out of Range!");

                return;  // back from catch
        }
        catch(DivideByZeroException)
        {
                Console.WriteLine("Attempting to Divide by Zero!");
        }
        finally
        {
                Console.WriteLine("finally);
        }
    }
}
```

Output:

```
begin
try BLOCK
4
finally
try  BLOCK
Attempting to Divide byZero!
finally
try BLOCK
Index is Out of Range!
finally
```

/* Thus, in every case, the finally code is executed irrespective of the fact how the try block is exited.
*/

There is one more point we would like to make about using "finally".

And, that is, when a finally block follows a *try* block, no *catch* statements are technically required. In such cases, the finally block is executed after exiting *try*, but exceptions are not handled.

7.8 HOW TO HANDLE ERRORS CONVENIENTLY/GRACEFULLY?

(Allowing the program to continue running smoothly in case of run-time errors)

In the introductory section to this chapter, we had remarked that exception handling is a tool to prevent the occurrence of abnormal events during the normal execution flow of a program. This means that the error handler must do something rational to manage such a critical situation.

Take, for example, the following simple program (*Example 115*) that manages a divide-by-zero error. In particular, it divides the elements of one array by the elements of another. If a division-by-zero error occurs, a *DivideByZeroException* is generated; in the example, this exception is handled by reporting the error and then continuing with further execution of the program. In this orderly manner, an attempt to divide by zero does not result in a catastrophic abnormal termination of the program but, is handled gracefully, by not hindering program execution.

Example 115

```
/* An Application of Exception Handling:  Managing Divide-by-Zero Situation */
/* Author: Arunesh; Date: 27/03/2011 */
using System;
class Demo_Excp10
{
        static void Main()
        {
                int [ ] numerators = {2, 4, 8, 16, 32, 64};
                int [ ] denominators = {2, 0, 4, 0, 0, 4};

                for (int x = 0; x < numerators.Length; x++)
                {
                        try
                        {
                                Console.WriteLine("numerators[x] + " / " + denominators[x]
                                                + " = " + numerators[x]/denominators[x]);
                        }

                        catch (DivideByZeroException)
                        {
                                Console.WriteLine("Division by zero not allowed");
                        }
                }
        }

}
```

Output:

2 / 2 = 1
Division by zero not allowed
8 / 4 = 2
Division by zero not allowed
Division by zero not allowed
64 / 4 = 16

/* *Example 115* reveals another remarkable point. And that is, once an exception has been handled, it is removed from the system. Thus, in the program, each pass through the *for* loop enters the *try* block afresh and anew; any prior exceptions have already been handled; this, in turn, allows the program to handle repeated errors and exceptions.
*/

7.9 THE EXCEPTION CLASS (Revisited)

So far, we have caught exceptions but have not done with the exception object itself. As you know, a catch statement allows one to specify a exception type and a variable. This variable receives a reference to the exception object. As already explained, since all exceptions are derived from *Exception*, all exceptions support the members defined by *Exception*. We shall now describe some of these members and constructors.

Exception specifies some interesting properties such as *Message*, *StackTrace*, and *TargetSite*. All of these are read-only with *Message* containing a string describing the nature of the error, *StackTrace* containing a string about the stack of calls which actually led to the exception, and *TargetSite* obtaining an object which specifies the method that generated the exception. *Exception* defines some methods as well. One of the most frequently used is *ToString()*, which returns a string describing the exception. This method is invoked by itself, when an exception is display through *WriteLine()*. *Exception* defines the following four constructors:

(1) public Exception()
(2) public Exception(string Message)
(3) public Exception(string Message, Exception inner Exception)
(4) protected Exception(System.Runtime.SerializationInfo info,
System.Runtime.Serialization.StreamingContext context)

The first of these four is the default constructor. The second defines the string associated with the *Message* property of the exception. The third one defines an inner exception which is used when one exception evokes another. In such a case, *innerException* specifies the first exception (which will be null if no inner exception exists; if the inner exception exists, it can be obtained through the *InnerException* property specified by *Exception*). The last and fourth constructor handles exceptions occurring remotely and requiring deserialization. In this particular constructor, the types *System.Runtime.SerializationInfo* and *System.Runtime.Serialization.StreamingContext* are contained in the *System.Runtime.Serialization* namespace.

7.9.1 Exceptions Commonly Used

The System namespace specifies numerous standard built-in exceptions. All are derived directly/ indirectly from SystemException since they are generated by the CLR when run-time errors occur. Some of the frequently used standard exceptions are shown in Table 7.1.

Table 7.1 Common Exceptions Defined within the **System** namespace

Exception	Meaning
ArrayTypeMismatchException	*Type of value being stored is incompatible with the type of the array.*
DivideByZeroException	*Division by zero attempted*
IndexOutOfRangeException	*Array index is out-of-bounds*
InvalidcastException	*A run-time cast is invalid*
OutOfMemoryException	*Insufficient free memory exists for program continuation, e.g., in case there is not sufficient free memory to create an object through new, this exception will be thrown.*
OverflowException	*An arithmetic overflow occurred.*
NullReferenceException	*An attempt was made to operate on a null reference, that is, a reference thast does not refer to an object*

Most of the exceptions in Table 7.1 are more or less, self-explanatory. A notable exception could be *NullReferenceException*. This exception is invoked if there is an attempt to use a null reference to an object, e.g., if you try to call a method on a null reference. A *null reference* is a reference that doesn't point to any object. One of the possible ways to create a null reference is by assigning explicitly to it the value null using the keyword null. But, be careful. Null references can also happen in other less obvious ways.

7.10 HOW TO DERIVE EXCEPTION CLASSES?

C#'s built-in exceptions are able to handle most of the errors. Yet, its exception handling mechanism is not limited to merely these errors. You can create customized exceptions of your own as well. To create an exception, simply define a class derived from *Exception*. The exception classes you create will have all of the properties and methods specified by *Exception* available to them. You may like to override one or more of these members, though. While creating your own exception class, you will, in general, want your class to support all of the four constructors specified by *Exception*. This is not difficult as you can just pass along the arguments of the constructor to the corresponding *Exception* constructor through *base*. Technically, of course, you need to provide for only those constructors which are actually used by your program.

Example 116 uses a custom exception type. In the case study at the end of chapter 4, we had developed an array class called *ArbitraryIndexedArray*. You *may* recall that this array class allowed users to create an arbitrarily specified indexes array (indexing can begin at values other than 0; in fact, the array is created starting from the specified beginning index and ending at the specified ending index; allows specified indexes to be negative as well; thus, you can create arrays that index/run from -2 to 2, 1 to 5, or, 25 to 30, both indexes inclusive, for example). In this particular case, we had used a special error variable (called *Error*) which had to be checked after each and every operation. Quite clearly, such an approach is not only tedious but clumsy and error-prone as well. A much better way is to use a custom exception as is done in *Example 116*.

<u>*Example 116*</u>

```
/* Use custom exception for ArbitraryIndexedArray errors */
/* Author: Arunesh; Date: 23/03/2011*/
using System;
// create a custom exception for ArbitraryIndexedArray
class ArbitraryIndexedArrayException : Exception
{
        /* implement all of the four Exception constructors; you may note that the constructors
simply execute the base class constructor; this is because ArbitraryIndexedarray adds nothing
to Exception; whence, eliminating the need for any more actions. */
        public ArbitraryIndexedArrayException() : base { }

        public ArbitraryIndexedArrayException(string Message) : base(message) { }

        public ArbitraryIndexedArrayException(string Message,
                Exception inner Exception) :     base(message, inner exception) { }

        protected ArbitraryIndexedArrayException(System.Runtime.SerializationInfo info,
                        System.Runtime.Serialization.StreamingContext context) :
                                        base (info, context) { }

        /* override ToString() for ArbitraryIndexedArrayException */
        public override string ToString()
        {
                return Message;
        }
}
```

```
// an improved version of ArbitraryIndexedArray that uses a custom exception

class ArbitraryIndexedArray
{
        // Private data
        int [,] i;          /* reference to underlying array */
        int lb, ub;; // lower and upper bounds indicating smallest and largest indexes respectively

        /* Auto-implemented Read-only Length and Error Properties follow */
        public int Length { get; private set; }

        /* construct array given its size */
        public ArbitraryIndexedArray(int lo, int hi)
        {
                hi++;
                if (hi <= lo)
                {
                        throw new ArbitraeryIndexedArrayException
                                        ("Low index not less than high index)";
                }
                i = new int [hi - lo];
                Length = hi - lo;
                lb = lo;
                ub = --hi;
        }

        /* indexer for ArbitraryIndexedArray follows */
        public int this[int index]
        {
                // get accessor
                get
                {
                        if (okay(index))
                        {
                                return i[index - lb];
                        }
                        else
                        {
                                throw new ArbitraryIndexedArrayException("Index error");
                        }
                }
```

```
                // set accessor
                set
                {
                        if (okay(index))
                        {
                                i[index - lb] = value;
                        }
                        else
                                throw new ArbitraryIndexedArrayException("Index error");
                }
        }

        // CHECKING BOUNDS
        private bool okay(int index)
        {
                if (index >= lb  & index <= ub)
                        return true;
                else
                        return false;
        }
}

//      Demonstrate the arbitrary-indexed array
class ArbitraryIndexedArray_Demo
{
        static void Main( )
        {
                ArbitraryIndexedArray aia1 = new ArbitraryIndexedArray( -2, 3);
                ArbitraryIndexedArray aia2 = new ArbitraryIndexedArray( 1, 4);
                ArbitraryIndexedArray aia1 = new ArbitraryIndexedArray( -5, -1);

                // demonstrate aia1
                Console.WriteLine("Length of aia1 = " + aia1.Length);
                for (int x = -2; x <=3; x++)
                        aia1[x] = x;
                Console.Write("Contents of aia1: ");
                for (int x = -2; x <=3; x++)
                        Console.Write(aia1[x] + "\t");
                Console.WriteLine('\n");

                // demonstrate aia2
                Console.WriteLine("Length of aia2 = " + aia2.Length);
                for (int x = 1; x <=4; x++)
                        aia1[x] = x;
```

```
        Console.Write("Contents of aia2: ");
        for (int x = 1; x <=4; x++)
                Console.Write(aia2[x] + "\t");
        Console.WriteLine("\n");

        // demonstrate aia3
        Console.WriteLine("Length of aia3 = " + aia3.Length);
        for (int x = -5; x <=-1; x++)
                aia3[x] = x;
        Console.Write("Contents of aia3: ");
        for (int x = -5; x <=-1; x++)
                Console.Write(aia3[x] + "\t");
        Console.WriteLine("\n");

        // Now, demonstrate some errors
        Console.WriteLine("Now, generate some index errors");

        // use an invalid constructor
        try
        {
                ArbitraryIndexedArray aia4 = new ArbitraryindexedArray(10, -5);
        }
        catch(arbitraryIndexedArrayException excep)
        {
                Console.WriteLine(excep);
        }

        // use an invalid index
        try
        {
                ArbitraryIndexedArray aia4 = new ArbitraryindexedArray(-1, 1);

                for (int x = -1; x <=1; x++)
                        aia4[x] = x;
                Console.Write("Contents of aia4: ");
                for (int x = -1; x <=5; x++)    // generate index error
                        Console.Write(aia1[x] + "\t");
        }
        catch(arbitraryIndexedArrayException excep)
        {
                Console.WriteLine(excep);
        }
    }
}
```

Output:

Length of aia1 = 6
Contents of aia1: -2 -1 0 1 2 3

Length of aia2 = 4
Contents of aia2: 1 2 3 4

Length of aia3 = 5
Contents of aia3: -5 -4 -3 -2 -1

Now, generate some index errors
Low index not less than high index
Contents of aia4: -1 0 1 Index error

/* As you can see for yourself, when an index error occurs, *ArbitraryIndexedArray* throws an object of type *ArbitraryIndexedArrayException.* There are three places where this might occur:

(1) in the *get* indexer accessor
(2) in the *set* indexer accessor
(3) in the *ArbitraryIndexedArray* constructor

To catch these exceptions, *ArbitraryRangeArray* objects must be constructed and accessed from within a *try* block, as illustrated by the program.

Further, by using an exception to report errors, *ArbitraryIndexedArray* now acts and behaves like one of C#'s built-in types and whence, can be fully integrated into a the exception handling mechanism of a program.

*/

7.11 HOW TO CATCH DERIVED CLASS EXCEPTIONS?

The order of catch clauses is of extreme importance when trying to catch exception types involving both base and derived classes. This is because a catch clause for a base class shall also match any of its derived classes, e.g., the base class of all exceptions is *Exception* and whence, catching *Exception* catches all possible exceptions. Using a catch clause without any expression type might offer a cleaner way to catch all exceptions, as already explained. But, the issue of catching derived class exceptions is of extreme importance in other contexts, especially in situations where you create your own exceptions.

If you need to catch exceptions of both a base class type and a derived class type, you must put the derived class first in the catch sequence. This is because a base class catch will also catch all derived classes. Moreover, if you put the base class first, it shall lead to a compile-time error.

The following program (*Example 117*) creates two exception classes named *Excpt1* and *Excpt2*. *Excpt1* is derived from *Exception*. *Excpt2* is derived from *Excpt1*. The program then throws an exception of each type. For the sake of brevity, the custom exceptions supply only one constructor (that takes a string describing the exception). However, in commercial code, you would need to provide all the four constructors defined by *Exception*.

<u>*Example 117*</u>

```
/* Derived class Exceptions must come before Base class Exceptions */
/* Author: Arunesh; Date: 27/03/2011 */
using System;
class Excpt1 : Exception          // create an exception
{
        public Except1(string message) : base(message) { }

        public override string ToString()
        {
                return Message;
        }
}

class Excpt2 : Except1  // create an exception derived from Except1
{
        public Except2(string message) : base(message) { }

        public override string ToString()
        {
                return Message;
        }
}

class Demo_Excp11
{
        static void Main()
        {
                for (int i = 0; i < 3; i++)
                {
                        try
                        {
                                if (i ==0)
                                        throw new Except1("Except1 exception caught");
                                else if (i == 1)
                                        throw new Except2("Except2 exception caught);
                                else
                                        throw new Exception();
                        }
```

```
                catch (Except2 excep)
                {
                        Console.WriteLine(excep);
                }
                catch (Except1 excep)
                {
                        Console.WriteLine(excep);
                }
                catch (Exception excep)
                {
                        Console.WriteLine(excep);
                }
            }
        }
}
```

Output:

```
Except1 exception caught
Ecept2 exception caught
System.Exception: exception of type 'System.Exception' was thrown .
        at Demo_Excp11.Main()
```

/* In *Example 117*, carefully note the order and type of catch clauses. In fact, this is the only order in which they can occur; since *Except2* is derived from *Except1*, the catch for *Except2* must come before the one for *Except1*. On the same lines, the catch for *Exception* (which is the base class for all exceptions) must come last.
*/

7.12 USING THE KEYWORDS - checked AND unchecked

A special featue of C# is related to the generation of overflow exceptions in arithmetic computations. If an arithmetic result exceeds the range of data type involved in the computation, the result is said to overflow, e.g., consider the following:

```
byte x;
byte y;

byte r;

x = 127;
y = 127;

r = (byte) (x * y);
```

Herein, the product of *x* and *y* exceeds the range of a byte value and whence, *r* overflows its type.

C# makes it possible for you to specify whether your code will cause an exception when such overflow occurs by the use of the keywords - checked and unchecked. You can use checked to indicate that an expression be checked for overflow; similarly, you can use unchecked to indicate that overflow should be ignored, in which case, the result would be truncated to fit into the target type of the expression.

Both the checked and unchecked keywords have two general forms. One checks a particular expression and is known as the *operator form* while the other checks a block of statements and is referred to as the *statement form*. These are given as follows:

```
checked(expr)  // expr is the expression for which overflow is checked
               // in case of overflow, an OverflowException is thrown

checked
{
        // statements to be checked
}

unchecked(expr)        // expr is the expression for which overflow is ignored
                       // in case of oveflow, truncation will occur

unchecked
{
        // statements for which overflow is ignored
}
```

The following two examples (*Examples 118 and 119*) demonstrate both checked and unchecked for a single expression and a block of statements, respectively.

Example 118

```
/* Illustrates checked and unchecked for a single expression */
/* Author: Arunesh; Date: 27/03/2011 */
using System;
class Demo_Excp12
{
        static void Main()
        {
                byte x;
                byte y;

                byte r;

                x = 127;
                y = 127;
```

```
            try
            {
                        r = unchecked ((byte) (x * y));
                        Console.WriteLine("Unchecked Result = " + r);

                        r = checked((byte)(x * y));        // this raises OverflowException
                        Console.WriteLine("Checked Result =" + r); // this won't be executed
            }
            catch(OverflowException excep)
            {
                        Console.WriteLine(excep);
            }
      }
}
```

Output:

```
      Unchecked Result = 1
      System.OverflowException: Arithmetic operation resulted in an overflow.
            at Demo_Excp12.Main()
```

/* As the output confirms, the unchecked expression caused a truncation while the checked expression raised an exception.
*/

Example 119

```
/* Illustrates checked and unchecked for a single expression */
/* Author: Arunesh; Date: 27/03/2011 */
using System;
class Demo_Excp13
{
      static void Main()
      {
            byte x;
            byte y;

            byte r;

            try
            {
                        unchecked
                        {
```

```
                x = 127;
                y = 127;
                r = unchecked ((byte) (x * y));
                Console.WriteLine("Unchecked Result = " + r);

                x = 125;
                y = 5;
                r = unchecked ((byte) (x * y));
                Console.WriteLine("Unchecked Result = " + r);
            }
            checked
            {
                x = 3;
                y = 4;
                r = checked((byte)(x * y));       // this is fine
                Console.WriteLine("Checked Result =" + r);

                x = 127;
                y = 127;
                r = checked ((byte) (x * y)); // this raises OverflowException
                Console.WriteLine("Checked Result = " + r);
                                                   // this won't be executed
            }
        }
        catch(OverflowException excep)
        {
            Console.WriteLine(excep);
        }
    }
}
```

Output:

```
Unchecked Result = 1
Unchecked result = 113
Checked result = 12
System.OverflowException: Arithmetic operation resulted in an  overflow.
        at Demo_Excp13.Main()
```

/* As the output confirms, the unchecked block caused the overflow to be truncated while the checked block raised an exception, when an overflow occurred in it.
*/

PRACTICAL SESSION

#1 What do you mean by an 'exception'?
How is it "handled" in C#?

#2 When should a program 'throw' an exception?
What are the advantages of using the exception handling mechanism in a C# program?

#3 What is placed inside the 'try' block? What in the 'catch' block?
When do we need to use multiple catch handlers?

#4 Explain the circumstances/situations under which the following statements would be needed:

(i) *catch*
(ii) *throw;*
(iii) *void method_M(int i) throw()*

#5 State what shall <u>happen</u> *when/if*:
(i) An exception is rethrown within a catch block.
(ii) *throw()* is placed in a method header line.
(iii) *catch* is the first of a cluster of catch handlers.
(iv) A method throws an unspecified exception.
(v) A catch handler throws an exception.
(vi) Several handlers match the type of exception thrown.
(vii) No catch handler matches the type of exception thrown.
(viii) An exception is thrown outside a try block.

#6 Point out the error(s), if any, in the following C# statements/code:

(i)
```
try
{
    throw;
};
```

(ii)
```
throw;
```

(iii)
```
try
{
    throw;
}
```

(iv)
```
catch(DivideByZeroException exc)
{
        throw exc;
}
```

(v)
```
try
{
        if (!i) throw new DivideByZeroException();
}
catch(DivideByZeroException)
(
        i = 0;
}
```

#7 You have written a very long and complex program that compiles and executes, but provides an incorrect solution. You have tried to locate the error, but without success so far. What would you do to fix the program bug(s)?

#8 The following code fragment generates a compile-time error:

```
private int TestCode()
{
        int j;
        int x;
        j = 4;
        (if j == 4)
                x = 5;
        return x;
}
```

What is the problem with the code?

#9 Attempt the following (*programming exercises*):

(i) Write a *program* containing a possible exception. Use a try/catch sequence to *handle* it appropriately..

(ii) Write a *program* that:

(a) *Demonstrates the concept of* rethrowing *an exception;*
(b) *Uses the catch (*ALL exceptions*) handler;*
(c) *Shows the application of* multiple catch statements.

(iii) Write a *Main() program* that calls a series of deeply nested try sequences. Insert suitable *exception handling* mechanism into your program.
{ *Tip:* You may make suitable assumptions wherever appropriate. }

#10 Identify the error(s), if any, in the following C# program:

```
using System;
void compute(int z)
{
        if (z)
            throw new DivideByZeroException();
        else
            throw new IndexOutOfRangeException();
}
void compute(string s)
{
        try
        {
            if (s)
                throw new DivideByZeroException();
            else
                throw new IndexOutOfRangeException();
        catch(DivideByZeroException exc)
        {
            Console.WriteLine(exc);
        }
}
class Generate_Excp
{
        static void Main()
        {
            try
            {
                compute("ALL");
                compute(1);
                compute(0);
            }
            catch(DivideByZeroException exc)
            {
                Console.WriteLine(exc);
            }
            catch(IndexOutOfRangeException exc)
            {
                Console.WriteLine(exc);
            }
        }
}
```

CHAPTER 8

I/O, STRINGS AND FORMATTING

8.0 INTRODUCTION

We have already used I/O earlier such as *Console.WriteLine()* but without formal explanation. It was important first to discuss classes, inheritance, and exceptions in detail. Now, we seek to describe C#'s approach to I/O and it is pertinent to mention here that since C# uses the I/O system and classes defined by the .NET Framework, a description of I/O under C# is also a description of the generalized .NET I/O system. We shall study both console I/O and file I/O in this chapter.

This chapter also examines the *String* class, which underlies C#'s *string* type. The *String* class defines an extensive range of methods, properties, and fields, giving the user a good control over the construction and manipulation of strings.

Now, a word about formatting under C#. Whenever we need a human readable form of a built-in C# data type such as int or float, a string representation is required. Again, C# does supply a default format for this representation, but we can also create a customized format of our own accord.

This chapter seeks to describe both I/O and string handling followed by formatting.

8.1 STREAMS & STREAM CLASSES

C# performs I/O through streams. Now, what exactly is a stream? A stream is an abstraction that produces/consumes information. At the lowest level, all C# I/O operates on bytes. Three predefined streams, which are exposed by the properties called *Console.In*, *Console.Out*, and *Console.Error*, are available for all C# programs that use the *System* namespace. *Console.Out* is the standard output stream, which is the console, by default. *Console.In* is the standard input stream, which is the keyboard, by default. Again, *Console.Error* is the standard error stream, which is once more the console, by default.

The .Net Framework defines both byte and character stream classes. However, the character stream classes are actually just wrappers that convert an underlying byte stream to a character stream, taking care of any conversion automatically. In this way, the character streams are logically separate but still based and built upon byte streams. The core stream class is *System.IO.Stream. Stream* represents a byte stream and acts as a base class for all other streams. At the top of the character stream hierarchy are the two abstract classes, *TextReader* and *TextWriter*; *TextReader* handles input while *TextWriter* takes care of output. The methods defined by these two abstract classes are available to all their subclasses and these methods can throw an *IOException* on error, in general. Apart from the byte and character streams, there are two binary stream classes, viz., *BinaryReader* and *BinaryWriter*, that can be used to directly read and write binary data, respectively.

8.2 CONSOLE I/O

C# achieves console I/O through the three standard streams, viz., *Console.in*, *Console.Out*, and *Console.Error*, respectively.

8.2.1 Console.In

Console.In is an instance of *TextReader* and we can, in general, use the methods and properties defined by it to access it. But, we usually use the methods provided by *Console* that automatically read from *Console.In*. *Console* defines three input methods:

(i) *Read()*
(ii) *ReadLine()*
(iii) *ReadKey()*

The first two methods, viz., *Read()* and *ReadLine()* have been available since the .NET Framework 1.0 while third one, viz., *ReadKey()* was added by the .NET Framework 2.0.

8.2.1.1 Read()

To read a single character, C# uses the *Read()* method:

static int Read()

Read() returns the next character read from the console. It waits until the user presses a key and then returns the result. The characte is returned as an *int* and must be cast to *char*. On error, *Read()* returns -1 and throws an *IOException* on failure. When using *Read(),* console input is line-buffered; so, ENTER must be pressed before any character will be sent to the concerned program. Take *Example 120* as a case in point.

<u>*Example 120*</u>

```
/* Illustrates Read() */
/* Author: Arunesh; Date: 23/03/2011 */

using System;

class ReadCh
{
        static void Main()
        {
                char ch;
```

```
            Console.WriteLine("begin");
            Console.Write("Enter a character:\t");
            ch = (char) Console.Read(); // get a character
            Console.WriteLine("The character entered by you is:\t" + ch);
            Console.WriteLine("end");
      }
}
```

Output (A sample run):

begin
Enter a character: t
The character entered by you is: t
end

/* It must be noted that *Read()* is line-buffered and this can be irritating at times. To overcome this problem, the *ReadKey()* method can be used, as we shall see later on. */

8.2.1.2 *ReadLine()*

To read a string of characters, C# uses the *ReadLine()* method:

static string ReadLine()

ReadLine() reads a string of characters from the console until ENTER is pressed. It also throws *IOException* on failure. Take *Example 121* as a case in point.

Example 121

```
/* Illustrates ReadLine() */
/* Author: Arunesh; Date: 23/03/2011 */

using System;

class ReadLn
{
      static void Main()
      {
            string s;
            Console.WriteLine("begin");
            Console.Write("Enter a string of characters:\t");
            s = Console.ReadLine(); // get a string of characters
            Console.WriteLine("The string entered by you is:\t" + s);
            Console.WriteLine("end");
      }
}
```

Output (A sample run):

begin
Enter a string of characters: take your own test.
The string entered by you is: take your own test.
end

Console methods are an easy way to read from *Console.In*, but we can also call methods on the underlying *TextReader. Example 121* is rewritten as *Example 122* as an illustration of this fact.

Example 122

```
/* Illustrates TextReader's ReadLine() */
/* Author: Arunesh; Date: 23/03/2011 */

using System;

class ReadLn2
{
        static void Main()
        {
                string s;
                Console.WriteLine("begin");
                Console.Write("Enter a string of characters:\t");
                s = Console.In.ReadLine(); // Textreader's ReadLine() method
                Console.WriteLine("The string entered by you is:\t" + s);
                Console.WriteLine("end");
        }
}
```

Output (A sample run):

```
begin
Enter a string of characters:      take your own test.
The string entered by you is:              take your own test.
end
```

/* It must be noted that *ReadLine()* is now directly invoked on *Console.In*. Also, observe that the output hasn't changed.
*/

8.2.1.3 ReadKey()

Starting with the C# 2.0 version, we can read individual keystrokes directly from the keyboard in a non-line-buffered way using the method *ReadKey()*:

static ConsoleKeyInfo ReadKey() *// first form*

/* waits for a key to be pressed. When that happens, it returns the key and also displays the key on the screen. */

static ConsoleKeyInfo ReadKey(bool intercept) *// second form*

/* also waits and returns a keypress. But, if *intercept* is true, then the key is not displayed on the screen. If *intercept* is false, the key is not displayed. */

ReadKey() returns nformation about the keypress in an object of type *ConsoleKeyInfo,* which is a structure. It contains the following read-only properties:

char KeyChar
ConsoleKey Key
ConsoleModifiers Modifiers

where, *KeyChar* contains the *char* equivalent of the keypress, *Key* contains a value from the *ConsoleKey* enumeration that is an enumeration of all the keys on the keyboard, and *Modifiers* describes which, if any, of the keyboard modifiers: ALT, CTRL, or SHIFT were pressed when the keypress was generated (These modifiers are represented by the *ConsoleModifiers* enumeration that has these values:*Control*, *Shift*, and *Alt*. Note that more than one modifier value may be present in *Modifiers*).

ReadKey() is especially useful in achieving interactive keyboard input as it is not line-buffered. Take *Example 123* as a case in point.

Example 123

```
/* Illustrates ReadKey() */
/* Author: Arunesh; Date: 23/03/2011 */

using System;

class ReadKy
{
    static void Main()
    {
        ConsoleKeyInfo keyprs;

        Console.WriteLine("begin");

        Console.WriteLine("Enter keystrokes;   'q' to quit.");

        do
        {
            keyprs = Console.ReadKey(); // Read Keystrokes

            Console.WriteLine("The Key presed by you is:\t" + keyprs.KeyChar);

            /* check for modifier keys */
            if ((ConsoleModifiers.Control & keyprs.Modifiers) != 0)
                Console.WriteLine("Control Key pressed!");
            if ((ConsoleModifiers.Shift & keyprs.Modifiers) != 0)
                Console.WriteLine("Shift Key pressed!");
            if ((ConsoleModifiers.Alt & keyprs.Modifiers) != 0)
                Console.WriteLine("Alt Key pressed!");
        }
        while (keyprs.KeyChar != 'q');

        Console.WriteLine("end");
    }
}
```

Output (A sample run):

```
begin
Enter keystrokes;          'q' to quit.
D The Key pressed by you is:          D
e The Key pressed by you is:          e
Alt Key pressed!
a The Key pressed by you is:          a
B The Key pressed by you is:          B
Shift Key pressed!
g The Key pressed by you is:          g
Control Key pressed!
L The Key pressed by you is:          L
q The Key pressed by you is:          q
Shift Key pressed!
end
```

/* It must be noted that while *Read()* and *ReadLine()* are line-buffered, *ReadKey()* immediately returns the keypress and is thus, non-line-buffered and whence, can be used for interactive input/responses.
*/

8.2.2 Console.Out & Console.Error

Console.Out and *Console.Error* are objects of type *TextWriter*. Console output is best achieved through *Write()* & *WriteLine()* with which you are already familiar. Versions of these methods exist that output each of the built-in types. *Console* specifies its own versions of *Write()* and *WriteLine()* so that they can be directly called on *Console*, as you have been doing throughout this book. But, you can choose to call these and (other methods) on the *TextWriter*, which underlies *Write()* and *WriteLine()*. The following program (*Example 124*) illustrates writing to *Console.Out* and *Console.Error*. As already explained, both write to the console, by default.

Example 124

```
/* Illustrates Console.Out & Console.Error */
/* Author: Arunesh; Date: 23/03/2011 */

using System;

class WrtErrOut
{
        static void Main()
        {
                int i =1, j = 0, r;

                Console..Out.WriteLine("begin"); // Console.Out
                Console..Out.WriteLine("Generating Divide by Zero Exception");
```

```
            try
            {
                    r = i / j;          // Divide by zero
            }
            catch(DivideByZeroException excep)
            {
                    Console.Error.WriteLine(excep.Message); // Console.Error
            }
            Console..Out.WriteLine("end");
        }
}
```

Output:

```
        begin
        Generating Divide by Zero Exception
        Attempted to divide by zero.
```

/* It must be noted that 'end' is not a part of the above output. */

At times, there is a lot of confusion about when to use *Console.Error*. Further, as both *Console.Out* and *Console.Error* write to the console (by default), what is the need for two different streams? The solution to this query is that standard streams can be redirected to other devices, e.g., *Console.Error* can be redirected to write to a disk file instead of the screen so that it becomes possible to direct error output to a log file, say, without affecting console output. Moreover, if console output is redirected and error output is not redirected, then error messages shall be displayed on the screen.

8.3 BYTE-BASED FILE I/O (Using FileStream)

The .NET Framework provides classes enabling you to read and write files. The most common types of files are the disk files. But, at the operating system level, all files are byte-oriented. To create a byte-oriented stream attached to a file, you will use the *FileStream* class. *FileStream* is derived from *Stream* and contains all its functionality. The stream classes, including *FileStream*, are defined in *System.IO* so that you will usually include

using System.IO;

near the top of any program using them.

8.3.1 Opening and Closing a File

To create a byte stream linked to a file, just create a *FileStream* object. *FileStream* defines several constructors, of which the most common one is:

FileStream(string path, FileMode mode)

where, *path* specifies the name of the file to open, which can be a full path specification, while the *mode* parameter specifies how the file shall be opened; it must be one of the values defined by *FileMode* enumeration, which are shown in Table 8.1.

Table 8.1 Values of the *FileMode* Enumeration

Value	Description
FileMode.Append	*Output is appended to end of file..*
FileMode.Create	*Creates a new output file. Any preexisting file by the same name is destroyed.*
FileMode.CcreateNew	*Creates a new output file. The file must not exist already.*
FileMode.Open	*Opens a preexisting file.*
FileMode.OpenOrCreate	*Opens a file if it exists, or creates the file if it does not exist already.*
Filemode.Truncate	*Opens a preexisting file but truncates its length to zero.*

In general, this constructor opens a file for read/write access. The only exception is when the file is opened using *FileMode.Append*, in which case, the file is write-only. If a failure occurs while attempting to open a file, an exception will be thrown. If a failure occurs because the file does not exist, *FileNotFoundException* will be thrown. In case of some I/O error while opening a file, *IOException* will be thrown. Of course, there are other possible exceptions which can be thrown such as *ArgumentNullException* (filename is null), *PathTooLongException* (filename/path is too long), and so on.

<u>Remark</u>: To keep the code simple, the examples in this chapter catch only *IOException*, but your own code may need to handle other possible exceptions or each type of I/O exception individually.

There are many ways to handle the process of opening a file. *Example 125* shows one of the ways. It opens a file named *myfile.dat* for input.

<u>Example 125</u>

```
/* Opening a file myfile.dat for input */
/* Author: Arunesh; Date: 23/03/2011 */

FileStream finp = null;

try
{
        finp = new FileStream("myfile", FileMode.Open);
}
```

```
catch (IOException excep)        // catch all I/O exceptions
{
        Console.WriteLine(excep.Message);
                // Handle the error
}
catch (Exception excep)          // catch any other exception
{
        Console.WriteLine(Excep.Message);
                // If possible, handle the error
                // Rethrow all those exceptions that you do not handle
}
```

When you are done with a file, you must close it, which can be done using *Close()*. Its most general form is:

void Close()

Closing a file releases the system resources allocated to the file [by calling a method named *Dispose()*], allowing them to be used by another file.

Remark: There is a form of the *using* statement which offers a more convenient way to automatically close a file when it is no longer required. But, to highlight the fundamentals of file handling, we shall explicitly invoke *Close()* in this chapter. We are not going to discuss this form of the *using* statement anyway.

8.3.2 Reading Bytes from a File

FileStream defines two methods that read bytes from a file, viz., *ReadByte()* and *Read()*. *ReadByte()* is used to read a single byte from a file. Its general form is:

int ReadByte()

Each time it is called, it reads a single byte from the file and returns it as an integer value. When end of file is encountered, it returns -1.

Read() is used to read a block of bytes. Its general form is:

int Read(byte[] array, int offset, int count)

Read() tries to read up to *count* bytes into *array* starting at *array[offset]*. It returns the number of bytes successfully read.

Example 126 uses *ReadByte()* to input and display the contents of a text file whose name is specified as a command-line argument. You may note that the program first checks that a filename has been specified before trying to open the file.

Example 126

```
/* Display a Text file */
/* Author: Arunesh; Date: 23/03/2011 */
/* To use this program, specify the name of the file you want to see, e.g., to see a file called
myfile.cs, use the following command line:
        DisplayFile myfile.cs
*/
```

```
using System;
using System.IO;

class DisplayFile
{
        static void Main(string[] args)
        {
                int k;
                FileStream finp;

                if (args.Length != 1)
                {
                        Console.WriteLine("Usage: DisplayFile filename");
                        return;
                }

                try
                {
                        finp = new FileStream(args[0], FileMode.Open);
                }
                catch (IOException excep)        // catch all I/O exceptions
                {
                        Console.WriteLine("Cannot open file");
                        Console.WriteLine(excep.Message);
                        return;  // stop the program since file cannot be opened
                }

                // Read bytes untl EOF is encountered
                try
                {
                        do
                        {
                                k = finp.ReadByte();
                                if (k ! = -1)
                                        Console.Write((char) k);
                        } while (k != -1);
                }
                catch (IOException excep)        // catch all I/O exceptions
                {
                        Console.WriteLine("Error reading file");
                        Console.WriteLine(excep.Message);
                }
```

```
                finally
                {
                        finp.Close();
                }
        }
}
```

/* *Example 126* uses two *try* blocks. The first one catches any I/O exceptions that might prevent the file from being opened. If an I/O error occurs, the program terminates. Otherwise, the second *try* block monitors the read operation for I/O exceptions. In this way, the second *try* block is executed only when *finp* refers to an open file.

Further, note that the file is closed in the *finally* block associated with the second *try* block. This implies that irrespective of how the *do* loop ends (normally or abnormally due to an error), the file will be closed in all cases.
*/

In some cases, it may be easier to wrap the portions of *Example 126* that open the file and access the file within a single *try* block (instead of separating the two). *Example 127* does exactly this.

<u>*Example 127*</u>

```
/* Display a Text file: Compact Version */
/* Author: Arunesh; Date: 23/03/2011 */
/* To use this program, specify the name of the file you want to see, e.g., to see a file called
myfile.cs, use the following command line:
        DisplayFile myfile.cs
*/

using System;
using System.IO;

class DisplayFile
{
        static void Main(string[] args)
        {
                int k;
                FileStream finp = null;

                if (args.Length != 1)
                {
                        Console.WriteLine("Usage: DisplayFile filename");
                        return;
                }
```

```
        // Use a single try block to open the file
        // and then read bytes from it untl EOF is encountered
        try
        {
                finp = new FileStream(args[0], FileMode.Open);

                do
                {
                        k = finp.ReadByte();
                        if (k ! = -1)
                                Console.Write((char) k);
                } while (k != -1);
        }
        catch (IOException excep)        // catch all I/O exceptions
        {
                Console.WriteLine("I/O error:");
                Console.WriteLine(excep.Message);
        }
        finally
        {
                if (finp != null)
                        finp.Close();
        }
    }
}
```

/* *Example 127* initializes the *FileStream* reference *finp* to null. If the file can be opened by the *FileStream* constructor, *finp* will be non-null. On the other hand, if the constructor fails, *finp* will remain null. This is important since inside the *finally* block, *Close()* is invoked only if *finp* is not null. Such a mechanism prevents an attempt to invoke *Close()* on *finp* when it does not refer to an open file.
*/

8.3.3 Writing Bytes to a File

Use the *WriteByte()* method to write a single byte to a file. Its simplest form is:

void WriteByte(byte value)

WriteByte() writes the byte specified by *value* to the file.

An array of bytes can be written to a file using *Write()*, which is shown as follows:

void Write(byte[] array, int offset, int count)

Write() writes *count* bytes from *array* beginning at *array[offset]* to the file.

Once you are done with an output file, you must close it by calling *Close()*.

Example 128 uses *WriteByte()* to write to a text file called "*myfile.txt*".

Example 128

```
/* Write to a Text file */
/* Author: Arunesh; Date: 23/03/2011 */

using System;
using System.IO;

class WriteFile
{
        static void Main()
        {
                char ch;
                FileStream fout = null;

                try
                {
                        fout = new FileStream("myfile.txt", FileMode.CreateNew);
                                                // open output file
                        for (ch = 'z'; ch <= 'a'; ch--)
                                fout.WriteByte((byte) ch);
                                                // write to file characters from z to a
                }
                catch (IOException excep)       // catch all I/O exceptions
                {
                        Console.WriteLine("I/O error:");
                        Console.WriteLine(excep.Message);
                }
                finally
                {
                        if (fout != null)
                                fout.Close();
                }
        }
}
```

/* *Example 128* first creates a text file called *myfile.txt* for output by using *FileMode.CreateNew* (which means that the file must not exist already; if it does, an *IOException* will be thrown). Once the file is opened for output, the lowercase alphabet is written to the file in the reverse order so that upon execution of this program, *myfile.txt* will contain the following output:

zyxwvutsrqponmlkjihgfedcba

*/

8.3.4 Copying a File

One of the advantages of the byte-based I/O used by *FileStream* is that you might use it on any type of file, and not just those containing text, e.g., *Example 129* copies any type of file, inclusive of executable ones, the names of the source and target files being specified on the command line.

Example 129

```
/* Copy a file one byte at a time */
/* Author: Arunesh; Date: 23/03/2011 */
/* To use this program, specify the names of the source file and target file, e.g., to copy a file
called myfile1.cs to a file called myfile2.cs, use the following command line:
        Copy myfile1.cs myfile2.cs
*/

using System;
using System.IO;

class Copy
{
        static void Main(string[] args)
        {
                int k;
                FileStream finp = null;
                FileStream fout = null;

                if (args.Length != 2)
                {
                        Console.WriteLine("Usage: CopyFile SourceFile TargetFile");
                        return;
                }

                try
                {
                        // open files
                        finp = new FileStream(args[0], FileMode.Open);
                        fout = new FileStream(args[1], Filemode.Create);

                        // copy file
                        do
                        {
                                k = finp.ReadByte();
                                        // read one byte
```

```
                    if (k ! = -1)
                              fout.WriteByte((byte) k);
                                        // write one byte
          } while (k != -1);
     }
     catch (IOException excep)         // catch all I/O exceptions
     {
          Console.WriteLine("I/O error:");
          Console.WriteLine(excep.Message);
     }
     finally
     {
          // close files
          if (finp != null)
                    finp.Close();
          if (finp != null)
                    finp.Close();
     }
  }
}
```

8.4 CHARACTER-ORIENTED FILE I/O

Even though byte-based file I/O is quite common, it is possible to use character-oriented streams for this purpose. The main advantage of character streams is that they operate on Unicode characters directly. Thus, for handling unicode text, character streams are the best option. To perform character-based file handling, *FileStream* is wrapped inside a *StreamReader* or a *StreamWriter*, which convert a byte stream into a character stream and vice versa automatically. *StreamReader* is derived from *TextReader* while *StreamWriter* is derived from *TextWriter* so that *StreamReader* and *StreamWriter* have access to all the properties and methods defined by their base classes, *TextReader* and *TextWriter*, respectively.

8.4.1 Character-Based Output (Using StreamWriter)

For creating a character-based output stream, just wrap a *Stream* object (such as *FileStream*) inside a *StreamWriter*, whiich defines several constructors, of which one of the most popular ones is:

StreamWriter(Stream stream)

where, *stream* is the name of an open stream.

Example 130 is a simple key-to-disk utility that reads line of text entered at the keyboard and writes them to a text file named "*myfile.txt*". Text is read until the user enters the word "STOP". This example uses a *FileStream* wrappped in a *StreamWriter* to output to the file "*myfile.txt*".

Example 130

```
/* Demonstrates a simple key-to-disk Utility that uses a StreamWriter */
/* Author: Arunesh; Date: 23/03/2011 */

using System;
using System.IO;

class KeyToDisk
{
        static void Main()
        {
                string s;
                FileStream fout;

                try     // open the file stream first
                {
                        fout = new FileStream("myfile.txt", FileMode.Create);
                }
                catch (IOException excep)       // catch all I/O exceptions
                {
                        Console.WriteLine("Error opening file:");
                        Console.WriteLine(excep.Message);
                        return; // stop the program since file cannot be opened
                }

                StreamWriter fsw = new StreamWriter(fout); // wrap the file in a StreamWriter

                try     // write from key to disk
                {
                        Console.WriteLine("Enter text ('STOP' to quit)");

                        do
                        {
                                Console.Write(": ");
                                s = Console.ReadLine();

                                if (s ! = "STOP")
                                {
                                        s = s + "\r\n"; // add carriage return and newline
                                        fsw.Write(s);
                                }
                                        ;
                        } while (s != "STOP");
                }
```

```
            catch (IOException excep)        // catch all I/O exceptions
            {
                    Console.WriteLine("I/OError:");
                    Console.WriteLine(excep.Message);
            }
            finally
            {
                    fsw.Close();
            }
    }
}
```

Sometimes, it might just be more convenient to open a file directly using *StreamWriter*. For this, one of the these two constructors are often used:

StreamWriter(string path)

StreamWriter(string path, bool append)

where, *path* specifies the name of the file to open, which can, of course, be a full path specification. In the second constructor, if *append* is true, then output is appended to the end of an existing file; otherwise, output overwrites the specified file. In both the constructors, if the file does not exist, it is created.

Example 131 rewrites *Example 130* so as to use *StreamWriter* directly to open the output file "*myfile.txt*".

<u>Example 131</u>

```
/* Demonstrates a simple key-to-disk Utility that opens a file directly using StreamWriter */
/* Author: Arunesh; Date: 23/03/2011 */

using System;
using System.IO;

class KeyToDisk
{
        static void Main()
        {
                string s;
                StreamWriter fsw = null;

                try
                {
                        fsw = new StreamWriter("myfile.txt");
                                // open the file directly wrappped in a StreamWriter

                        Console.WriteLine("Enter text ('STOP' to quit)");
```

```
                do
                {
                        Console.Write(": ");
                        s = Console.ReadLine();

                        if (s ! = "STOP")
                        {
                                s = s + "\r\n"; // add carriage return and newline
                                fsw.Write(s);
                        }
                                ;
                } while (s != "STOP");
        }
        catch (IOException excep)       // catch all I/O exceptions
        {
                Console.WriteLine("I/OError:");
                Console.WriteLine(excep.Message);
        }
        finally
        {       if (fsw != null)
                        fsw.Close();
        }
    }
}
```

8.4.2 Character-Based Input (Using StreamReader)

For creating a character-basaed input stream, just wrap a byte stream inside a *StreamReader,* which derfines several constructors, of which, one of the commonly used ones is:

StreamReader(Stream stream)

where, *stream* is the name of an open stream.

Example 132 is a simple disk-to-screen utility that reads a text file named "*myfile.txt*" and displays its contents on the screen so that it is just the complement of the key-to disk utility as shown in *Example 130.*

<u>*Example 132*</u>

```
/* Demonstrates a simple disk-to-screen Utility that uses a StreamReader */
/* Author: Arunesh; Date: 23/03/2011 */

using System;
using System.IO;
```

```
class DiskToScreen
{
        static void Main()
        {
                string s;
                FileStream finp;

                try        // open the file stream first
                {
                        finp = new FileStream("myfile.txt", FileMode.Open);
                }
                catch (IOException excep)        // catch all I/O exceptions
                {
                        Console.WriteLine("Error opening file:");
                        Console.WriteLine(excep.Message);
                        return; // stop the program since file cannot be opened
                }

                StreamReader fsr = new StreamReader(finp); // wrap the file in a StreamReader

                try        // read from file and display its contents on the screen
                {
                        while (!fsr.EndOfStream);
                        {
                                Console.Write(": ");
                                s = fsr.ReadLine();
                                Console.WriteLine(s);
                        }
                }
                catch (IOException excep)        // catch all I/O exceptions
                {
                        Console.WriteLine("I/OError:");
                        Console.WriteLine(excep.Message);
                }
                finally
                {
                        fsr.Close();
                }
        }
}
```

/* Notice, how the *EOF (End-Of-File)* is determined in the program using the read-only property of *StreamReader*, viz.*EndOfStream* . This property is true when the end of the stream has been reached and false otherwise. Whence, it can be used to detect the *EOF* as shown in the program. */

At imes, it might just be more convenient to open a file directly using *StreamReader*. For this, use the constructor:

StreamReader(string path)

where, *path* specifies the name of the file to open, which can, of course, be a full path specification. The file must exist, otherwise an exception will be thrown.

8.5 BINARY I/O

Uptil now, we have been reading/writing bytes or characters but it is possible (and quite common) to read/write binary values of the C# built-in types such as *int, double, short* etc. For this, we shall use *BinaryReader* and *BinaryWriter*. While using these streams, what is important is to understand the fact that this data is read/written using its internal binary form, and not its human-readable text format.

8.5.1 Binary Output (Using BinaryWriter)

A *BinaryWriter* is a wrapper around a byte stream that manages the writing of binary data. One of its most commonly used constructors is:

BinaryWriter(Stream output)

where, *output* is the stream to which data is written. To write output to a file, you can use the object created by *FileStream* for this parameter. Various exceptions are thrown in case of invalid *output*. You must close *BinaryWriter* when you are done with it. Closing it closes the underlying stream as well.

BinaryWriter defines methods that can write all of C#'s built-in types. Several of these commonly used methods are shown in Table 8.2. All can throw an *IOException* (other exceptions are also possible). You may note that a string is written using its internal format, which includes a length specifier. *BinaryWriter* also defines the standard *Close()* method, which works as elaborated earlier.

8.5.2 Binary Input (Using BinaryReader)

A *BinaryReader* is a wrapper around a byte stream that manages and handles the reading of binary data. One of its most commonly used constructors is:

BinaryReader(Stream input)

where, *input* is the stream from which data is written. To read input from a file, you can use the object created by *FileStream* for this parameter. Various exceptions are thrown in case of invalid *input*. You must close *BinaryReader* when you are done with it. Closing it closes the underlying stream as well.

BinaryReader defines methods that can read all of C#'s built-in types. Several of these commonly used methods are shown in Table 8.3. All can throw an *IOException* (other exceptions are also possible). You may note that *ReadString()* reads a string that is stored using its internal format, which includes a length specifier as well. Furher, this method should only be used to read a string that has been written using *BinaryWriter*. *BimaryReader* also defines the standard *Close()* method, just like the *BinaryWriter*.

Table 8.2 Comonly used Output Methods Defined by *BinaryWriter*

Method	Description
void Write(sbyte value)	*Writes a sbyte*
void Write(byte value)	*Writes a byte*
void Write(short value)	*Writes a short*
void Write(int value)	*Writes an int*
void Write(long value)	*Writes a long*
void Write(float value)	*Writes a float*
void Write(double value)	*Writes a double*
void Write(decimal value)	*Writes a decimal*
void Write(char value)	*Writes a char*
void Write(char[] value)	*Writes an array of characters*
void Write(string value)	*Writes a string using its internal binary representation/form, inclusive of a length specifier*

Table 8.3 Comonly used Input Methods Defined by *BinaryReader*

Method	Description
bool ReadBoolean()	*Reads a bool*
byte ReadByte()	*Reads a byte*
sbyte ReadSByte()	*Reads a sbyte*
char ReadChar()	*Reads a char*
decimal ReadDecimal()	*Reads a decimal*
double ReadDouble()	*Reads a double*
float ReadSingle()	*Reads a float*
short ReadInt16()	*Reads a short*
int ReadInt32()	*Reads an int*
long Readint64()	*Reads a long*
string ReadString()	*Reads a string represented in its internal binary form, including a length specifier; should be used only to read a string written using BinaryWriter*

Binary I/O - A CASE STUDY

In this case study, we take up *Example 133, which* is demonstrative of both *BinaryReader* and *BinaryWriter*. It writes and then reads back various types of data to and from a file called "*myfile*".

Example 133

```
/* Write and then Read back Binary data using BinaryWriter and
BinaryReader, respectively */
/* Author: Arunesh; Date: 23/03/2011 */

using System;
using System.IO;

class DataWrtRd
{
	static void Main()
	{
		BinaryWriter datawrt;
		BinaryReader datard;

		int k = 100;
		double d = 2345.67;
		bool b = false;
		string s = "Testing it OUT!";
		float f;

		try	// open file for writing
		{
			datawrt = new BinaryWriter(newFileStream("myfile",
									Filemode.Create);
		}
		catch (IOException excep)  // catch all I/O exceptions
		{
			Console.WriteLine("Error opening file:");
			Console.WriteLine(excep.Message);
			return;
			// stop the program since file cannot be opened
		}
```

```
try     // write data to file: "myfile"
{
        Console.WriteLine("Writing to myfile:\t" + k);
        datawrt.Write(k);

        Console.WriteLine("Writing to myfile:\t" + d);
        datawrt.Write(d);

        Console.WriteLine("Writing to myfile:\t" + b);
        datawrt.Write(b);

        Console.WriteLine("Writing to myfile:\t" + s);
        datawrt.Write(s);

        Console.WriteLine("Writing to myfile:\t" + (9.1 * 11.3));
        datawrt.Write(9.1 * 11.3)
}
catch (IOException excep)  // catch all I/O exceptions
{
        Console.WriteLine("I/OError:");
        Console.WriteLine(excep.Message);
}
finally
{
        datawrt.Close();        // close file: myfile
}

Console.WriteLine();

try     // Now, open file for reading
{
        datard = new BinaryReader(newFileStream("myfile",
                                        Filemode.Open);
}
catch (IOException excep)  // catch all I/O exceptions
{
        Console.WriteLine("Error opening file:");
        Console.WriteLine(excep.Message);
        return;
        // stop the program since file cannot be opened
}
```

```
        try     // read data from file: "myfile"
        {
                k = datard.ReadInt32();
                Console.WriteLine("Reading from myfile:\t" + k);

                d = datard.ReadDouble();
                Console.WriteLine("Reading from myfile:\t" + d);

                b = datard.ReadBoolean();
                Console.WriteLine("Reading from myfile:\t" + b);

                s = datard.ReadString();
                Console.WriteLine("Reading from myfile:\t" + s);

                f = datard.ReadSingle();
                Console.WriteLine("Reading from myfile:\t" + f);
        }
        catch (IOException excep)  // catch all I/O exceptions
        {
                Console.WriteLine("I/OError:");
                Console.WriteLine(excep.Message);
        }
        finally
        {
                datard.Close();         // close file: myfile
        }
    }
}
```

Output:

Writing to myfile: 100
Writing to myfile: 2345.67
Writing to myfile: False
Writing to myfile: Testing it OUT!
Writing to myfile: 102.83

Reading from myfile: 100
Reading from myfile: 2345.67;
Reading from myfile: False
Reading from myfile: Testing ot OUT!
Reading from myfile: 102.83

/* Upon examination of the file: "*myfile*", produced by this program, you will find that it contains binary data, and not human-readable text.
***/**

8.6 USING RANDOM ACCESS FILES

Uptil now, we have only used *sequential files* - files accessed in a stricly linear fashion, one byte after another. But, the contents of a file can be accessed in a *random order* also. One way of doing this is with the help of the *Seek()* method as defined by *FileStream*. The *Seek()* method allows the *file position indicator* (*file pointer* or *current position*) to be set to any point within a file. *Seek()* has the following form:

long Seek(long offset, SeekOrigin origin)

where, *offset* specifies the new position (in bytes) of the *file pointer* from the location specified by *origin*. The *origin* will be one of the values (defined by the *SeekOrigin* enumeration) in Table 8.4.

Table 8.4 Values of the *SeekOrigin* Enumeration

Value	Meaning
SeekOrigin.Begin	*Seek from the beginning of the file.*
SeekOrigin.Current	*Seek from the current location.*
SeekOrigin.End	*Seek from the end of the file.*

After a call to *Seek()*, the next read/write operation will occur at the new file position. The new position is returned. If an error occurs while seeking, an *IOException* is thrown (other exceptions are possible).

Example 134 is illustrative of *random access* I/O. It writes the lowercase alphabet in reverse order to a file and then reads it back in non-sequential order.

<u>*Example 134*</u>

```
/* Demonstrates Random Access I/O */
/* Author: Arunesh; Date: 23/03/2011 */

using System;
using System.IO;

class RandomAccess
{
        static void Main()
        {
                char c;
                FileStream fs = null;
```

```
try
{
        fs = new FileStream("myfile.dat", FileMode.Create);     // open file

        // write alphabet to file
        for (int k = 0; k < 26; k++)
                fs.WriteByte((byte) ('z' - k));

        // read back particular values now
        fs.Seek(0, SeekOrigin.Begin);     // seek to 1st byte
        c = (char) fs.ReadByte();
        Console.WriteLine("First value is:\t" + c);

        fs.Seek(0, SeekOrigin.Current); // seek to 2nd byte
        c = (char) fs.ReadByte();
        Console.WriteLine("Second value is:\t" + c);

        fs.Seek(4, SeekOrigin.Begin);     // seek to 5th byte
        c = (char) fs.ReadByte();
        Console.WriteLine("Fifth value is:\t" + c);

        Console.WriteLine();

        // now, read every third value
        Console.WriteLine("Every third value is as follows:);
        for (int k = 0; k < 26; k +=3;)
        {
                fs.Seek(k, SeekOrigin.Begin);     // seek to kth byte
                c = (char) fs.ReadByte();
                Console.Write(c + "\t");
        }
        Console.WriteLine();
}
catch (IOException excep)          // catch all I/O exceptions
{
        Console.WriteLine("I/OError:");
        Console.WriteLine(excep.Message);
}
finally
{
        if (fs != null)
                fs.Close();       // close file
}
```

```
    }
}
```

Output:

First value is: z
Second value is: y
Fifth value is: v

Every third value is as follows:
z w t q n k h e b

8.7 STRINGS IN C#

We have already familiarised you with a bit of string handling in chapter 1, and that discussion need not be repeated here. But, it is good to review how strings are implemented in C# before having a look at the *String* class. A string is a sequence of characters in all computer languages but how such a sequence is implemented varies from one language to the other. In some like C++, a string represents an array of characters but in C#, strings are objects of the built-in *string* data type. In this way, *string* is a reference type. Further, *string* is C#'s name for *System.String*, the standard .NET string type so that a C# string has access to all the methods, properties, fields, and operators defined by *String*. C# strings are immutable, that is to say, that once they are created, their contents cannot be altered (to create a string whose contents can be changed, C# provides a class called *StringBuilder* in the *System.Text* namespace; but you will seldom require it). This constraint allows C# to implement strings more efficiently since unused string objects are automatically garbage-collected. A *string* reference variable may, of course, change the object to which it refers but the character sequence of a particular *string* object cannot be altered after its creation.

String is defined in the *System* namespace. It implements the *IComparable, IComparable<string>, ICloneable, IConvertible, IEnumerable, IEnumerable<char>,* and *IEquatable<string>* interfaces. *String* is sealed, which implies that it is a class that cannot be inherited. It provides string-handling functionality for C#, underlies C#'s built-in *string* type, and is part of the .NET Framework.

8.7.1 String Construction

The *String* class defines several constructors that let you construct a string in a variety of ways. In order to create a string from a character array, use one of the following two constructors:

public String (char[] val)
public String(char[] val, int startIndex, int length)

where, the first form creates a string that contains the characters in *val* while the second form uses *length* characters from *val*, starting at the index given by *startIndex*.

A string containing a particular character repeated a given number of times can be constructed using the following constructor:

public string(char ch, int count)

where, *ch* specifies the character to be repeated *count* number of times.

Another way of string construction is by means of a string literal, which automatically creates a string object. It is, for this reason, that a *string* object is frequently initialized by assigning it a string literal. This is shown as follows:

string s = "string created";

8.7.2 The String Operators

The string class overloads two operators, viz., == and !=. To test two strings for equality, use the == operator. Usually, when the == operator is applied to object references, it checks whether they refer to the same object. But, this differs for objects of type *String*. In this case, the contents of the strings are compared for equality. The same is true of the != operator. But, the other relational operators, such as >= or <, compare the references, just as they do for other types of objects. To check if one string is less than or greater than the other, use the *Compare()* / *CompareTo()* method as defined by *String*.

8.7.3 The String Field, Indexer, and Property

The *String* class defines one field:

public static readonly string Empty

where, *Empty* specifies an empty string (a string with no characters at all). Note that this is different from a null *String* reference, which just refers to no object.

There is one read-only indexer defined for *String*:

```
public char this[int index]
{
        get;
}
```

This indexer lets you get the character at a specified index. Just like arrasys, the indexing for strings starts at zero. Because *String* objects are immutable, it is only logical that *String* provides a read-only indexer.

String defines one read-only property:

```
public int Length
{
        get;
}
```

Length returns the number of characters in the string.

8.7.4 The String Methods

The String class defines numerous methods and many of them have two or more overloaded forms. Therefore, it is not useful or practical to list them all. Rather, some commonly used methods will be presented, along with programming examples illustrating them.

8.7.4.1 String Comparison Methods

The forms of the most commonly used string comparison methods, viz., *Compare()* and *Equals()*, have already been given in chapter 1. So, we do not feel any need to discuss these methods over here again.

8.7.4.2 String Search Methods

The two overloaded forms of each of the two important string comparison methods, viz., *IndexOf()* and *LastIndexOf()*, have already been described in chapter 1. Whence, there is no more need to discuss them again over here.

8.7.4.3 String Case Changing Methods

String offers two simple methods enabling the change of case of letters within a string. Their simplest forms are:

public string ToLower()
public string ToUpper()

ToLower() lowercases all letters within the invoking string while *ToUpper()* uppercases all letters within the invoking string. The resulting string is returned in both cases. You may recall from chapter 1 that both of these methods have already been explained over there.

8.7.4.4 The String Extension Methods

As mentioned in the introductory part to strings, *String* implements *IEnumerable<T>*. This implies that beginning with C# 3.0, a *String* object can invoke the extension methods as defined by *Enumerable* and *Queryable*, both of which are in the *System.Linq* namespace. These extension methods are primarily meant for supporting LINQ, but some of them may be used for other purposes, such as certain types of string handling.

8.7.4.5 The Substring() Method

Part or portion of a string can be obtained using the *Substring()* method, which has two forms:

public string Substring(int startIndex)
public string Substring(int startIndex, int length)

where, the substring starts at *startIndex* and runs to the end of the invoking string in the first form, while in the second form, it starts at *startIndex* and runs for *length* characters. In both the forms, the substring is returned.

Take *Example 135* as a case in point.

Example 135

```
/* Illustrates Substring() */
/* Author: Arunesh; Date: 23/03/2011 */

using System;

class Substr
{
        static void Main()
        {
                string s = "abcdefgh";

                Console.WriteLine("s:\t" + s);
                Console.WriteLine();

                Console.Write("s.Substring(3):\t");
                string subs = s.Substring(3);
                Console.WriteLine(subs);

                Console.Write("s.Substring(0, 3):\t");
                string subs = s.Substring(0, 3);
                Console.WriteLine(subs);
        }
}
```

Output:

```
        s:      abcdefgh

        s.Substring(3):  defgh
        s.Substring(0, 3):      abc
```

8.7.4.6 String Concatenation Methods

There are two ways of concatenating two or more strings. Either you can make use of the + operator, as we have been doing so far or you can make use of the various concatenation methods as defined by *String*. The method that carries out concatenation is called *Concat()*, whose simplest form is:

public static string Concat(string s0, string s1)

This form returns a string that has *s1* concatenated to the end of *s0*. Another form of *Concat()* conctenates three strings:

public static string Concat(string s0, string s1, string s2)

Thiis form returns a string which is the concatenation of *s0*, *s1*, and *s2*. Still another form of *Concat()* concatenates four strings:

public static string Concat(string s0, string s1, string s2, string s3)

This form returns a string which is the concatenation of *s0, s1, s2,* and *s3*. Yet another form of *Concat()* concatenates an arbitrary or variable number of strings:

public static string Concat(params string [ ], val)

where, *val* refers to a variable number of arguments that are concatenated and returned. Take *Example 136* as a case in point.

Example 136

```
/* Illustrates Concat() - variable length argument version */
/* Author: Arunesh; Date: 23/03/2011 */

using System;

class Conct
{
        static void Main()
        {
                string s  = String.Concat("C# ", "is ", "the ", "most ", "versatile ",
                                "object ", "oriented ", "computer ", "language ",
                                "in ", "vogue ", "today!");

                Console.WriteLine("Concatenated string:\t" + s);
        }
}
```

Output:

Concatenated string: C# is the most versatile object orioented computer language in vogue today!

C# 4.0 adds two more forms of *Concat()*:

public static string Concat<T>(IEnumerable<T>, val)
public static string Concat(IEnumerable<string>, val)

where, the first form returns a string which is the concatenation of the string representation of the values in *val*, which can be any type of object that implements *IEnumerable<T>*, while the second form concatenates the strings specified by *val*.

There are also versions of *Concat()* that take object references, instead of string references. These obtain the string representation of the objects with which they are called and return a string which is the concatenation of those strings (the string representations are obtained by invoking *ToString()* on the objects). These forms of *Concat()* are given here as folows:

public static string Concat(object arg0)
public static string Concat(object arg0, object arg1)
public static string Concat(object arg0, object arg1, object arg2)
public static string Concat(object arg0, object arg1, object arg2, object arg3)
public static string Concat(params object[ ] args)

where, the first form just returns the string equivalent of *arg0*, while the other forms reurn a string containing the concatenation of their respective arguments. These object versions of *Concat()* are very convenient since they allow you to avoid manually obtaining string representations before concatenation.

8.7.4.7 String Splitting and Joining Methods

There are two basic string handling operations, viz., *split* and *join.* A *split* splits a string into its constituent parts whereas a *join* joins a set of strings. To split a string, we have *Split()* while for joining a set of strings, we have *Join()*.

There are various forms of *Split()*, out of which two common ones available ever since version 1.0 of C#, are:

public string [ ] Split(params char[ ], separator)
public string [ ] Split(char[ ] separator, int count)

where, the first form splits the invoking string into pieces/parts and returns an array that contains the substrings. The characters that delimit each substring are specified by *separator.* (if *separator* is null or refers to an empty string, then whitespace is used as the *separator*)..The second form returns no more than *count* substrings.

There are various forms of *Join()*, out of which two common ones available ever since version 2.0 of C#, are:

public static string Join(string separator, params string[ ] val)
public static string Join(string separator, string[ ] val, int startIndex, int count)

where, the first form returns a string which is the join of the strings in *val*, while the second form returns a string which is the join of *count* strings in val, starting at *startIndex.* In both the cases, each string is separated from the next by the string specified by *separator.*

Take *Example 137* as a case in point.

<u>Example 137</u>

```
/* Illustrates Split() and Join() */
/* Author: Arunesh; Date: 23/03/2011 */

using System;

class SpltJoin
{
        static void Main()
        {
                string s  =  "One in hand, two in the bush!";
                char[ ] sps = { ' ', ',', '!' };

                string [ ] pieces = s.Split(sps);  // split s into pieces
                Console.WriteLine("Split up pieces:");
                for (int k = 0; k < pieces.Length; k++)
                        Console.Writeline(pieces[k]);
```

```
            string sjoin = String.Join(" # ", pieces);          // now, join the split up pieces
            Console.Write("Join of the split up pieces:\t");
            Console.WriteLine(sjoin);
      }
}
```

Output:

```
      Split up pieces:
      One
      in
      hand
      two
      in
      the
      bush

      Join of the split up pieces:      One # in # hand #  # two # in # the # bush #
```

/* Note the empty string occurring between "*hand*" and "*two*" in this output. This is due to the fact that in the original string *s*, the word "*hand*", is followed by a comma and a space, viz., "*hand, two*". Now, we have specified both the comma and the space as separator characters. Whence, when *s* is split, the empty string that lies between the two separator characters, viz., the comma and the space, is returned.
*/

There are also versions of *Split()* that take a parameter of type StringSplitOptions, which controls whether empty strings shall be a part of the resulting split. These forms of *Split()* are given here as folows:

```
public string [ ] Split(char[ ] separator, StringSplitOptions options)
public string [ ] Split(string[ ] separator, StringSplitOptions options)
public string [ ] Split(char[ ] separator, int count, StringSplitOptions options)
public string [ ] Split(string[ ] separator, int count, StringSplitOptions options)
```

where, the first two forms split the invoking string into piecces/parts and return an array that contains the substrings. The characters that delimit each substring are specified by *separator*. (if *separator* is null or refers to an empty string, then whitespace is used as the *separator*)..The third and fourth forms return no more than *count* substrings. In all the four cases, the value of *options* decides handling of empty strings which result when two separators are next to each other. The *StringSplitOptions* enumeration defines only two values as enumerated in Table 8.5.

Table 8.5 Values of the *StringSplitOptions* Enumeration

Value	Meaning
None	*Empty strings are included in the result..*
RemoveEmptyEntries	*Empty strings are removed from the result.*

To fully appreciate the effects of excluding empty entries, replace this line in the preceding example program (*Example* 137):

string [ ] pieces = s.Split(sps); // split s into pieces

with the following line:

string [ ] pieces = s.Split(sps, StringSplitOptions.RemoveemptyEntries);
// split s into pieces removing any empty substrings

On executing the program now, the resulting outcome will be as shown:

Output:

Split up pieces:
One
in
hand
two
in
the
bush
Join of the split up pieces: One # in # hand # two # in # the # bush

C# 4.0 adds three more forms of *Join()*:

public static string Join(string separator, params object [ ] val)
public static string Join(string separator, IEnumerable<string>[ ] val)
public static string Join<T>(string separator, IEnumerable<string>[ ] val)

where, the first form returns a string which is the concatenation of the string representation of the objects in *val*, the second form returns a string which is the concatenation of the collection of strings referred to by *val,* and the third form returns a string which is the concatenation of the string representation of the collection of objects in *val.* In all three cases, each string is separated from the next by the string specified by *separator*.

8.7.4.8 String Padding and Trimming Methods

At times, there is a need to remove trailing and leading spaces from a string. This type of operation, referred to as *trimming*, is quite often required by command processors. For *trimming*, use one of the following two *Trim()* methods:

```
public string Trim()
public string Trim(params char[] trimChars)
```

where, the first form removes leading and trailing whitespace from the invoking string, while the second form removes leading and trailing occurrences of the characters specified by *trimChars*. The resulting string is returned in both the cases.

A string can be padded to either its left or right.

For *padding* on the left, use one of the following two methods:

```
public string PadLeft(int totalWidth)
public string PadLeft(int totalWidth, char paddingChar)
```

where, the first form adds spaces to the left of the invoking string so that its total length equals *totalWidth*, while the second form adds the character specified by *paddingChar* to the left of the invoking string so that its total length equals *totalWidth.* The resulting string is returned in both the cases. In case, *totalWidth* is less than the length of the invoking string, a copy of the invoking string is returned without any alteration.

For *padding* on the right, use one of the following two methods:

```
public string PadRight(int totalWidth)
public string PadRight(int totalWidth, char paddingChar)
```

where, the first form adds spaces to the left of the invoking string so that its total length equals *totalWidth*, while the second form adds the character specified by *paddingChar* to the left of the invoking string so that its total length equals *totalWidth.* The resulting string is returned in both the cases. In case, *totalWidth* is less than the length of the invoking string, a copy of the invoking string is returned without any alteration.

Take *Example 138* as a case in point.

Example 138

```
/* Illustrates Trimming and Padding */
/* Author: Arunesh; Date: 23/03/2011 */

using System;

class TrmPad
{
        static void Main()
        {
                string s = "OVER";

                Console.WriteLine("Original string:\t" + s);
                Console.WriteLine();
```

```
        s = s.PadLeft(10);        // pad on left with spaces
        Console.WriteLine("|" + s + "|");

        s = s.PadRight(20);       // pad on right with spaces
        Console.WriteLine("|" + s + "|");

        s = s.Trim();     // trim spaces
        Console.Writeline("|" + s + "|");

        s = s.PadLeft(10, '$');  // pad on left with $s
        Console.WriteLine("|" + s + "|");

        s = s.PadRight(20, '$');// pad on right with $s
        Console.WriteLine("|" + s + "|");

        s = s.Trim('$'); // trim $s
        Console.Writeline("|" + s + "|");
    }
}
```

<u>Output</u>:

```
Original string:        OVER

|      OVER|
|      OVER          |
|OVER|
|$$$$$$OVER|
|$$$$$$OVER$$$$$$$$$$|
|OVER|
```

8.7.4.9 String Inserting, Removing and Replacing Methods

A string can be inserted intio another string using the *Insert()* method, shown as follows:

public string Insert(int startIndex, string val)

where, the string referred to by *val* is inserted into the invoking string at the index specified by *startIndex*. The resulting string is returned.

A portion of a string can be removed using the *Remove()* method, shown as follows:

public string Remove(int startIndex)
public string Remove(int startIndex, int count)

where, the first form starts at the index specified by *startIndex* and removes all remaining characters in the string, while the second form starts at *startIndex* and removes *count* number of characters. The resulting string is returned in both the cases.

A portion of a string can be replaced using the *Replace()* method, shown as follows:

public string Replace(char oldChar, char newChar)
public string Replace(string oldVal, string newVal)

where, the first form replaces all occurrences of *oldChar* in the invoking string with *newChar*, while the second form replaces all occurrences of the string referred to by *oldVal* in the invoking string with the string referred to by *newVal*. The resulting string is returned in both the cases.

Take *Example 139* as a case in point.

Example 139

```
/* Illustrates Insert(), Remove(), and Replace() */
/* Author: Arunesh; Date: 23/03/2011 */

using System;

class InsRemRep
{
    static void Main()
    {
        string s = "Testing OUT!";
        Console.WriteLine("Original string:\t" + s);
        Console.WriteLine();

        s = s.Insert(8, "it ");    // insert
        Console.WriteLine(s);

        s = s.Replace("OUT", "OVER");        // replace string
        Console.WriteLine(s);

        s = s.Replace('i', 'z');  // replace character
        Console.Writeline(s);

        s = s.Remove(7, 3);       // remove 3 chars beginning with index 7
        Console.WriteLine(s);

        s = s.Remove(7);          // remove all chars beginning with index 7
        Console.WriteLine(s);
    }
}
```

Output:

```
Original string:        Testing OUT!

Testing it OUT!
Testing it OVER!
Testzng zt OVER!
Testing OVER!
Testing
```

8.8 FORMATTING

We have already mentioned in the introductory part of this chapter that human-readable form of the data is dictated by a string representation. This string is the format specifier/string. For instance, to format data using *WriteLine()*, we use:

WriteLine("format specifier", arg0, arg1, ..., argN);

where, the arguments to *WriteLine()* are separated by commas and not the '+' signs. In general, format commands take the form as outlined below:

{argnum, width : fmt}

where, argnum specifies the number of arguments (starting with 0) to display, the minimum width of the field is given by *width* while the format specifier is represented by *fmt*. Note that both *width* and *fmt* are optional so that in its simplest form, a format command only indicates which arguments are to be displayed, e.g. {0} specifies arg0, {1} specifies arg1, ..., {N} specifies argN. During execution, when a format command is found in the format specifier, the corresponding argument indicated by argnum is substituted and displayed. If fmt is present, the data is displayed using the given format specifier otherwise the default formatting is used. If *width* is present, the output is padded up with adequate spaces in order to ensure that the minimum width is achieved. If this *width* is positive, the output is right-justified and in the event of its being negative, the output is left-justified.

8.8.1 Using Numeric Format Specifiers

Table 8.6 shows all the format specifiers for numeric data. Each format specifier can contain an additional precision specifier. For instance, to specify a fixed point value with 4 decimal places, we can use F4. Consider the following example program (*Example 140*) demonstrating several of the numeric format specifiers given in Table 8.6.

<u>Example 140</u>

```
/* Illustrates format specifiers */
/* Author: Arunesh; Date: 23/03/2011 */

using System;

class DemoFormat1
{
        static void Main()
        {
                double a = 88176.75849;
                double b = 0.25;
                int c = 19;

                Console.WriteLine("{0 : F2}", a);

                Console.WriteLine("{0 : N5}", a);
```

Table 8.6 Numeric Format Specifiers

Specifier	Format	Meaning
C or c	*Currency*	*Specifes the no. of decimal places*
D or d	*Whole no. numeric data*	*Minimum no. of digits*
E	*Scientific Notation (uses uppercase E)*	*No. of decimal places. Default is 6*
e	*Scientific Notation (uses uppercase e)*	*No. of decimal places. Default is 6*
F or f	*Fixed point notation*	*No. of decimal places*
G	*Uses E or F format (whichever is shorter)*	*Refer E and F*
g	*Uses e or f format (whichever is shorter)*	*Refer e and f*
N or n	*Fixed point notation with comma separators*	*No. of decimal places*
P or p	*Percentage*	*No. of decimal places*
X	*Hexadecimal (uppercase letters A through F)*	*Minimum no. of digits*
x	*Hexadecimal (loercase letters a through f)*	*Minimum no. of digits*

```
            Console.WriteLine("{0 : e}", a);

            Console.WriteLine("{0 : p}", b);

            Console.WriteLine("{0 : X}", 15);

            Console.WriteLine("{0 : d10}",c);

            Console.WriteLine("{0 : c}", 18.18);
        }
}
```

<u>Output</u>:

88176.76
88,176.75849
8.817676e+004
25.00 %
F
0000000019
$18.18

8.8.2 Understanding Argument Numbers

There is an important thing to understand about argument numbers, viz., the argument number associated with a format specifier is determined by the argument number and not by the argument's position in the argument list. Thus, the arguments can be displayed in a sequence that is different than how they are specified in the argument list. Moreover, the same argument can be ouput more than once within the same call to *WriteLine()*. For instance, in the following example program (*Example 141*), the three arguments are displayed in non-sequential order. This is made possible by the fact that that there is no hard rule that the format specifiers must the arguments only in sequential order and any format specifier can refer to any argument. Also, in this example, the same argument 100.01234 is formatted in two different ways in the second *WriteLine()* statement. This is made possible by the fact that each format specifier refers to the one and only argument.

<u>*Example 141*</u>

```
/* Illustrates argument numbers */
/* Author: Arunesh; Date: 23/03/2011 */

using System;

class DemoFormat2
{
        static void Main()
        {
                double a = 88176.75849;

                Console.WriteLine("{1 : D} {2 : D} {0 : D}", 1, 2, 3);
                                        // displaying arguments non-sequetially

                Console.WriteLine("{0 : N5} {0 : e}", a);
                                        // formatting the same argument in two different ways

        }
}
```

<u>Output</u>:

```
        2       3       1
        88,176.75849            8.817676e+004
```

8.8.3 Customizing Numeric Format

For customizing numeric format, we need certain placeholder characters as enumerated in Table 8.7. In the previous two sections, we have seen the utility of the predefined numeric format specifiers. In this section, we shall see the additional ability to define our own custom format using a feature called <u>picture format</u> (it is called <u>picture formatting</u> as we create the custom format by specifying an example/picture of what we want our output to look like). For

Table 8.7 Placeholder Characters

Character/Placeholder	Meaning
#	*Digit*
.	*Decimal point*
,	*Thousands separator*
%	*Percentage (value being formatted multiplied by 100)*
0	*Pads with leading/traing zeros*
;	*Separates sections desribing the format for positive, negative, and zero values*
E0 e0 E+0 e+0 E-0 e-0	*Scientific notation*

this type of formatting we need the characters shown in Table 8.7 as placeholders. Let us now take a brief look at each of these placeholder characters.

The period specifies the decimal digit position. The # placeholder character signifies a digit position. It can occur either by itself or on the left/right side of the decimal point. When they occur on the right side of the decimal point, they define the number of decimal digits to display with the value being rounded, if necessary. And, when they occur on the left of the decimal point, they define the whole-number part of the value with leading zeros added, if necessary. In case of no decimal point, the value shall be rounded to its integer value.

The 0 placeholder can be used on the right/left side of the decimal point to ensure that a minimum number of digits shall always be present, e.g.

Console.WriteLine("{0 : 0## . #000}", 19.8);

gives the output:

019.8000

Values containing more digits shall be displayed in full on the left hand side and rounded on the right side of the decimal point. We can insert commas into large numbers by defining a pattern that sandwiches a comma within a sequence of #'s, e.g.

Console.WriteLine("{0 : #,### . #}", 1998.8);

gives the output:

1,998.8

Further, it is not necessary to signify a comma for each position. Specifying one comma causes it to be inserted into the number every third digit from the left, e.g.

Console.WriteLine(" {0 : #,# ##. #}", 1998123 .8);

gives the output:

1,998,123.8

Commas also have second meaning, viz. if they occur on the immediate left of the decimal point, they act as a scaling factor (the value is scaled in terms of thousands.), e.g.

Console.WriteLine("Scaled value in thousands: {0 : #,###, . #}", 1998123.8);

gives the output:

Scaled value in thousands: 1,998.1

A custom format specifier can contain other characters besides placeholders. Such characters are simply passed through, e.g.

Console.WriteLine("Length of cloth is {0 : ## . # m}", 19.8);

gives the output:

Length of cloth is 19.8 m

The E or e placeholders cause the value to be displayed in scientific notation (note that escape sequences such as \t, \n etc. can also be used in case they are required). At least one 0, and optionally more, must follow the E or e. The 0's indicate the number of decimal digits that shall be displayed. To make sure that the sign character preceds the exponent, we use the E+ or e+. And, to display sign in case of negative values only, we use E, E-, e or e-. The ';' placeholder is a separator that enables us to specify different formats for positive, negative, and zero values. The most general format of such a separator is:

positive-format; negative-fornmat; zero-format ,

e.g.,

Console.WriteLine("{0 : #.# ; (#.#) ; 0.0}", number);

/ If number is positive, the value is displayed with one decimal place; if number is negative, the value is displayed with one decimal place and is within a set of parentheses; if number is zero, the string 0.0 is displayed. */*

It would be pertinent to mention one more point here. When we use separators, we don't really need to supply all the parts, e.g. if we wish to specify how positive and negative values shall look, we omit the zero part, and so on and so forth (note that if we want to omit the negative part, the postive and zero formats shall be separated by two semi-colons.).

The following example program (*Example 142*) illustrates some of the possible custom numeric formats.

Example 142

```
/* Illustrates custom formatting */
/* Author: Arunesh; Date: 23/03/2011 */

using System;

class DemoFormat3
{
        static void Main()
        {

                double a = 88176.7584;

                Console.WriteLine("Default format: " + a);

                Console.WriteLine( "With two decimal places:{0 : # . ##}", a);
                                // 2 decimal places
```

```
        Console.WriteLine("Adding commas: {0 : #,### . ##}", a);
                        // Commas and 2 decimal places

        Console.WriteLine("Value scaled by 1000: {0 : # 0,}", a);
                        // Scaling by 1000

        Console.WriteLine("Using scientific notation: {0 : #.###E+00}", a);
                        // Scientific notation

        /* Displaying positive, negative, and zero values differently */
        Console.WriteLine("Positive, negative, and zero values differently:");
        Console.WriteLine("{0 : #.# ;(#.##);0.00}", a);
        a *= -1;
        Console.WriteLine("{0 : #.# ;(#.##);0.00}", a);
        a = 0.0;
        Console.WriteLine("{0 : #.# ;(#.##);0.00}", a);

        // display a percentage
        a = 0.20;
        Console.WriteLine("Displaying a percentage: {0 : # %} ", a);
    }
}
```

<u>Output</u>:

```
Default format:              88176.7584
With two decimal places:          88176.76
Adding commas:               88,176.76
Value scaled by 1000:   88
Using scientific notation:        8.818E+04
Positive, negative, and zero values differently:
88176.5
(88176.76)
0.00
Displaying a percentage:          20 %
```

PRACTICAL SESSION

#1 Distinguish between *Write()* and *WriteLine()* methods.

#2 What is a format string?

#3 Give some examples of numeric formatting.

#4 What is the need for custom formatting?
Elucidate using suitable example(s) wherever necessary.

#5 How does the percent character work in a format string?

#6 Suppose you write a long line and store it in a string named *message*. Now, you have a nagging feeling that you misspelled *Friday* as *Frday* somewhere in the string. Write down the statement(s) that would be able to find and correct the misspelling.

#7 If you are designing a program that must persist a specific set of information, how would you decide whether to use sequential or random access files.

#8 (a) Write a program with the help of a *for* loop and a String *property* to display the contents of a string object.
(b) Give two methods for concatenating three strings.

#9 Write a program which counts the number of occurrences of a given word in a text document.

#10 Attempt the following (*programming exercises*):

(i) Write a program that stores the numbers *1, 2,* and *3* in an array and displays them as follows without using any looping statements:

1 2 3

(ii) Write a program to print a multiplication table from *1 x 1* to *9 x 9* as shown below using one *Write()* and one *WriteLine()* statement only:

```
1   2   3   4   5   6   7   8   9
2   4   6   8   10  12  14  16  18
.........................................
.........................................
.........................................
.........................................
.........................................
.........................................
9   18  27  36  45  54  63  72  81
```

(iii) Write a program using nested *for* loops and only one *WriteLine()* statement that would produce the following <u>output</u>:

Product of 9 and 9 is 81
Product of 8 and 8 is 64
Product of 7 and 7 is 49
Product of 6 and 6 is 36
Product of 5 and 5 is 25
Product of 4 and 4 is 16
Product of 3 and 3 is 9
Product of 2 and 2 is 4
Product of 1 and 1 is 1

(iv) Write a program to read and display the following table of data:

Item-Code	*Item-Name*	*Item-Cost (Rs.)*
89756	*Cooler*	*2000/-*
12345	*Wasing Machine*	*8000/-*
54321	*Refrigerator*	*6000/-*

In the display, *item-code* and i*tem-name* must be left-justified while *item-cost* must be right-justified.

(v) Write a program to illustrate the use of the following format characters:
(a) Percent character (%)
(b) Period (.)
(c) Semi-colon (;)

(vi) Write a program that print the value *3456* in a column width of *8*:
(a) Left-justified
(b) Right-justified
(c) Right-justified with zeros padded on the left

(vii) Write a program to print the integer *123457* using the following format specifications:
(a) Comma separator
(b) Scientific notation
(c) Zero placeholder
(d) Format character d
(e) Fixed point notation

(viii) Write a prgram to do the following:

(a) Print the value *123.4567* in fixed-point format correct to *5* decimal places

(b) Print the value *24.12345* using the placeholder *E* correct to *3* and *8* decimal places respectively

APPENDIX

A SET OF TYPICAL PROBLEMS

#1 If x and y are floating point numbers with the values 211.12 and 211.21 respectively, evaluate the following:

i. y + 211.12 / x + 211.12
ii. y / 211.21 + x /2 11.12
iii. (x * y) / (y * x) * (x/y) * (y/x)
iv. (x++) + (- - y)
v. (- - x) - (y ++)

#2 Write a C# program to determine the roots of the quadratic equation: $az^2 + bz + c = 0$.

#3 Given the radii of two circles, write a C# program to compare their respective perimeters and areas. Use the concept of classes in your program.

#4 In an examination, there are two subjects viz., Mathematics and Computer Science. If a student obtains more than 80% marks in both of them, he is awarded Grade A. If he obtains more than 80% in either of the two and more than 50% in the other, he is awarded Grade B. If he obtains more than 50% in both, he is awarded Grade C. If he o btains more than 50% in one of them, he is awarded Grade D. Otherwise, he is said to have failed. Write a C# program to receive the marks of 10 students in both the subjects and output their results / grades.

#5 Write C# program in order to demonstrate garbage collection.

#6 Write C# program to illustrate the use of constructors.

#7 Write C# program to demonstrate the use of destructors.

#8 Given a text file, write a C# program to create another text file *replacing* the words "an" with "a" and "the" with a blank, respectively, from the first file. Use the concept of command-line arguments in your program.

#9 Create a structure to store the customer data in a bank. Assume there are 100 customer of the bank. The data to be stored is: Name, Phone No., Account No., Balance in Account. Write a C# program to deal with *customer request* for withdrawal from his account. In case, the amount in the account is not sufficient, the program should output the message – "*Insufficient balance*".

#10 Given two complex numbers (a + ib) and (c + id) write C# functions:

i. To *multiply* them.
ii. To *add* them.

#11 Write a C# program to find the square root, the logarithm to the base 10, and sin, cos, and tan trignometric ratios of a given number input by the user. You may assume the input to be a real number.

#12 Using arrays and strings, write C# programs to:

i. Determine whether a square matrix (2x2, 3x3, 4x4, 5x5, and 6x6) is *symmetric*.
ii. *Swap* the odd and even elements of an array.

#13 Write C# program to copy its input to output *replacing* each string of more than one blanks with a single blank space.

#14 Write a C# program to *check* a text file specified at the command line for unbalanced parentheses, brackets and braces.

#15 Write a C# program to *compare* two files, printing the first line where they differ. Use the concept of command-line arguments in your program.

#16 Write a C# program that reads a file containing integers (file must be specided at the command line) and *appends* at its end the sum of all these integers.

#17 Write a C# program to *replace* a particular word by another given word in a text file, e.g., replacing each occurrence of "in" by "out". The text file must be specified as an argument at the command line.

#18 Define a class called *cricket* that specifies the following:

player_name
team_name
batting_average

Using *cricket*, declare an array player with 100 elements. Then, write a program to read information/data about all the 100 players and print a team-wise list containing names of the players with their batting averages respectively.

#19 Write a C# method that can be called to compute the product of two matrices *m by n* and *n by m.* The main program should provide the values of *m and n* and the *two matrices* (i.e., *their elements*).

#20 Find error(s), if any, in each of the following code fragments:

i.
```
char str[20];
Console.System.Write(char);
```

ii.
```
if ("Arunesh Goyal", "run") == 1)
Console.System.Writeline("substring: 'run' is FOUND.");
```

#21 State True (T) or False (F) against each of the following statements:

i. C# methods can return only one value under their method names.
ii. A method in C# must have at least one argument/parameter.
iii. A method can be declared and defined before the *main program*.
iv. A method can be defined within the *main program*.
v. A user-defined method must be called at least once.
vi. Any name can be used as a method name.
vii. Program execution always begins from *main program* irrespective of its location in the C# program.
viii. A method can call itself.
ix. A method without a *return* statement is illegal/invalid.
x. String variable initialization includes the NULL character as part of the string constant, e.g., "GOOD & BAD\0".

#22 State True (T) or False (F) against each of the following statements:

i. While initializing a multi-dimensional array, there is no need to specify all its dimensions.
ii. String variables cannot be used with the assignment operators.
iii. A character constant/variable can be assigned to an *int* type variable.
iv. It is illegal to mix character and numeric data in C#.
v. As soon as an array is declared, all its elements are initialized to 0 by C#.
vi. A subscript can be an integral expression.
vii. Trying to access an array below its range gives a compile time error.
viii. A *char* type variable cannot be used as the subscript of an array.
ix. An *unsigned long int* type variable can be used as the subscript of an array.
x. In C#, the first subscript of an array variable is not 0, by default.
xi. When we use arithmetic expressions as the subscript of an array, the result of the expression must always be above 0.

xii. We can use more than 6-dimensional arrays in C#.
xiii. The declaration *int a[3] = {1, 4, 5, 9};* is illegal.
xiv. While declaring an array, the array size can both be a constant and a variable.
xv. The *foreach* statement is used in conjunction with *jagged* arrays.

#23 State True (T) or False (F) against each of the following statements:

i. The three loop expressions in a '*for*' loop header must be separated by semicolons.
ii. The initialization, test condition, and the increment parts could be missing in a '*for*' loop.
iii. In a '*for*' loop, the starting value of the control variable can be greater than the ending value.
iv. The number of times a control variable in a loop is updated always equals the number of iterations of the loop.
v. In a pre-test loop, if the body of the loop is executed k times, the test expression is evaluated (k + 1) times.
vi. The *do.....while* statement first checks the loop control expression and then executes its body.
vii. When *if* statements are nested, the last *else* gets associated with the nearest *if* without an *else*.
viii. One *if* can have more than one *else* clause.
ix. A *switch* statement can always be rewritten as a series of *if...else* statements.
x. A *switch* expression can only be of integral type.
xi. As soon as a *break* statement is encountered, the program execution ends.
xii. Each and every expression in the *else if* clause must test the same variable.
xiii. Any expression i.e., arithmetic, relational or logical can be used for an *"if"* condition.
xiv. Each *case label* in a *switch* construct can have only one statement each.
xv. The *default case* statement is necessary in a *switch* construct.

#24 What is the output of the following program segment?

```
using system;
static void Main()
{
        Console.Writeline("Welcome!\n");
        return;
        Console.Write("See you again some day!\n");
        return;
}
```

#25 State True (T) or False (F) against each of the following statements:

i. All arithmetic operators have the same level of *precedence*.
ii. *Modulo division operator' %'* can be used only with integers.
iii. The operators <, >, <=, >=, and = =, all have the same *level of priority*.
iv. In modulo division, the *sign of the result is negative*, if either but not the both operands are of the same sign.
v. In C#, if a data item is 1, it is considered to be *true* and *vice versa*.
vi. The *EXPRESSION: (! (a > b))* is the same as the *PRED ICATE (a <= b)*.
vii. A *unary expression* has only one operand with no operators.
viii. A *binary expression* has two operators with a single operand.
ix. The *associativity of operators* is used to decide which of the several different operations at the same precedence level is to be carried out first.
x. An *expression statement* is always terminated with a period.
xi. In the evaluation of mixed expressions, an *implicit cast* is generated by itself.
xii. An *explicit cast* can be employed to change any expression.
xiii. *Parentheses* can be employed to change the order of evaluation in expressions.
xiv. *Character constants* are written using double quotes.
xv. Just like variables, constants also have a *type*.
xvi. *String constants* are written using single quotes.
xvii. In C#, the keyword *void* is a data type.
xviii. The *underscore* can be used anywhere in an identifier.
xix. *C# declarations* can be made ANYWHERE IN THE PROGRAM.
xx. When the *variables* are declared, they must be assigned some *data type*.

#26 State True (T) or False (F) against each of the following statements:

i. Use of comments *reduces* the speed of execution of the program.
ii. Comments serve as *internal documentation* for the programmers.
iii. In C#, we can have *nested comments*.
iv. There are three types of comments that are allowed to be used in C#.
v. *Comments* cause the computer to print the text enclosed between /*.............. */ when the program is executed.
vi. The *logical end* of the C# program is the *closing brace* of the *Main() method*.
vii. Every line in a C# program must *end* with a *semicolon*.
viii. In C#, *lowercase letters are significant* and treated to be *different from uppercase letters*.
ix. *Only one method*can be named *Main()* in any C# program.
x. Every C# program must have at least *one user-defined method*.
xi. Each and every *syntax error* is detected by the *C# compiler*.
xii. Every logical error is detected by the C# runtime system.
xiii. To avoid abnormal termination, we can use the concept of *exceptions* in C#.

xiv. *Dynamic method dispatch* is not necessary for rin-time polymorphism.
xv. *Polymorphism* is necessary for an OOP language like C#.

#27 Write a method called *prev_month()* that returns the previous month. Start with the code:

enum months {jan, feb, mar, apr, ..., nov, dec};

If *jan* is passed as an argument to the method, then, *dec* should be returned. More explicitly, if the enumerator *jan* is passed as an argument, then, *dec* should be printed.

Write a *Main() program* such that it calls the relevant methods and produces a table of all the 12 months with its predecessor listed next to it.

#28 Pick out the correct alternative(s) from the following multiple choice problem:

Which of the following cannot belong to a C# namespace?
(a) class
(b) struct
(c) interface
(d) enum
(e) data

#29 Pick out the correct alternative(s) from each of the following multiple choice problems:

i. Which of the following statements about a string are correct?
(a) A string is created on a heap.
(b) A string is created on a stack.
(c) A string is a C# built-in type.
(d) A string can be created as: string s = new string;
(e) Length of the string determines whether it is created on the heap or the stack.

ii. Consider the following code fragment:
using System;
string s1 = "GOD Has Created Us in His own image!";
string s2 = s1.Substring((8, 17);
Console.WriteLine(s2);
What will be its output?
(a) Us
(b) Created Us in His
(c) Has Created
(d) image
(e) GOD

iii. Which of the following statements about a string are correct?

(a) We can cocatenate two strings by using an expression of the form:
str3 = str2 + str1;

(b) We can cocatenate two strings by using an expression of the form:
str3 = str2 & str1;

(c) We can cocatenate two strings by using an expression of the form:
str3 = *String.Concat(str2, str1);*

(d) A string built using String class is immutable.

(e) A string built using StringBuilder class is mutable.

iv. If str1 and str2 are two references to strings then which of the following is/are the correct way(s) to determine whether their contents are equal?

(a) if (str1 == str2)

(b) if (str1 = str2)

(c) if (str1 is str2)

(d) if (strcmp(str1, str2))

(e) int i = str1.CompareTo(str2);

v. Given the following code fragment:

using System;
string str1 = "STAR";
string str2 = "star";
int i = str1.CompareTo(str1);
Console.WriteLine(i);

What will be its output?

(a) 1

(b) 0

(c) -1

(d) -2

(e) 2

vi. Given the following code fragment:

using System;
string str1 = "STAR";
string str2 = "star";
str2 = str1.Insert(4, str2);
Console.WriteLine(str2);

What will be its output?

(a) starSTAR

(b) star

(c) STAR

(d) STARstar

(e) STAR star

vii. Given the following code fragment:

using System;
string str = "STAR";
int i = str..IndexOf('R');
int j = str.Length;
Console.WriteLine(i + "\t", + j);

What will be its output?

(a) 4 4
(b) 4 3
(c) 3 4
(d) 3 3
(e) 4 5

viii. Given the following code fragment:

using System;
string str1 = "STAR";
string str2 = "STAR";

Which of the following statements are true?

(a) Two object will be created, one referred to by str1, and the other by str2.
(b) str1 and str2 are references to the same object.
(c) Only one object will get created.
(d) Objects of type string cannot be created without using new.
(e) Both str1 and str2 will refer to the same object.

ix. Which of the following are true about strings?

(a) String objects can be modified after creation.
(b) The equality operators are defined to comapare the values of the string objects as well as references.
(c) Strings are value types.
(d) String literals can contain any character literal including escape sequences.
(e) Trying to acccess a character outside the bounds of a string causes an IndexOutOfRangeException.

x. If str1 and str2 are references to two strings, then which of the following is/are the correct way(s) to compare them:

(a) str1 is str2
(b) str1 = str2
(c) str1 == str2
(d) str1.Equals(str2)
(e) strcmp(str1, str2)

#30 Pick out the correct alternative(s) from the following multiple choice problem:

Given the code fragment:
using System;
int[, ,] arr = new int[2, 3, 3];
int i = arr.Length;
Console.WriteLine(i);
Write its output from amongst the following:
(a) 3
(b) 8
(c) 20
(d) 10
(e) 18

#31 Can static methods access instance data?
If not, why not? Elaborate.

#32 Pick out the correct alternative(s) from each of the following multiple choice problems:

i. Which of the following statements about a string are correct?
(a) Constructors cannot be overloaded.
(b) Constructors allocate space for the object in memory.
(c) Constructors are never called explicitly.
(d) Constructors never return any value.
(e) Constructors always have the same name as the name of their class.

ii. To be treated as overloaded methods, in which of the following should the methods of a class differ?
(a) Order of arguments
(b) Type of arguments
(c) Names of methods
(d) Return type of methods
(e) Number of arguments

iii. Which of the following statements are true?
(a) C# allows a method to have arguments with default values.
(b) C# allows a method to have variable number of arguments.
(c) Omitting the return type in a method definition causes an exception.
(d) params is used to specify the syntax for a method with variable number of arguments.
(e) Redfining a method parameter in the body of the method causes an exception.

#33 Pick out the correct alternative(s) from each of the following multiple choice problems:

i. Which of the following is/are not assignment operators in C#?

(a) /=
(b) \=
(c) *=
(d) +=
(e) %=

ii. Which of the following is/are not relational operators in C#?

(a) >=
(b) !=
(c) <=
(d) <>=
(e) Not

iii. Which of the following is/are not arithmetic operators in C#?

(a) **
(b) /
(c) +
(d) %
(e) *

iv. Given the code fragment:
using System;
Console.WriteLine(15 / 2 + "\t" + 15 % 2);
What is its output?

(a) 7 0
(b) 7 1
(c) 7.5 0
(d) 7.5 1
(e) 7.5 7.5

v. Which of the following is/are the correct way(s) to increment the value of a variable k by 1?

(a) ++k++-;
(b) k += 1;
(c) k = k + 1;
(d) k ++ 1;
(e) k =+ 1;

#34 Pick out the correct alternative(s) from each of the following multiple choice problems:

i. Which of the following statements about JIT are correct?
   (a) The instructions compiled by JIT compilers are written in Intermediate Language code.
   (b) The instructions compiled by JIT compilers are written in native code.
   (c) A method is compiled by the JIT compiler even if it is not called.
   (d) The code compiled by the JIT compiler runs under CLR.
   (e) The JIT compiler compiles instructions into machine code at run-time.

ii. Code that targets the CLR is known as:
   (a) Native Code
   (b) Distributed Code
   (c) Legacy Code
   (d) Unmanaged Code
   (e) Managed Code

iii. Which of the following is the root of the C# type hierarchy?
   (a) System.Root
   (b) System.Parent
   (c) System.Object
   (d) System.Base
   (e) System.Type

iv. Which of the following is the correct default value of a Boolean type?
   (a) True
   (b) 0
   (c) 1
   (d) False
   (e) -1

v. Which of the following are reference types?
   (a) Integer
   (b) Array
   (c) Double
   (d) String
   (e) Byte

vi. Which of the following statements are true?
   (a) A switch statement can act on numerivcal as well as Boolean types.
   (b) A switch statement can act on characters, strings, and enumeration types.

(c) All of the expressions in the for loop are optional.
(d) The foreach statement is uised to iterate through a collection such as an array, arraylist, stack, queue, and so on.
(e) break or goto can be used to terminate a while loop and transfer control outside it.

vii. Given: if (A > 20 && B < 30) C = 25;
Which of the following statements are true?
(a) && is known as short-circuit AND logiical operator.
(b) The statement C = 25 wiil be executed if any one condition is True.
(c) The condition B < 30 will be evaluated only if A > 20 evaluates to True.
(d) The condition B < 30 will be evaluated only if A > 20 evaluates to False.
(e) The statement C = 25 wiil be executed if both the conditions are True.

viii. Given: if (A > 20 | | B < 30) C = 25;
Which of the following statements are true?
(a) | | is known as short-circuit OR logiical operator.
(b) The statement C = 25 wiil be executed if any one condition is True.
(c) The condition B < 30 will be evaluated if A > 20 evaluates to True.
(d) The condition B < 30 will be evaluated only if A > 20 evaluates to False.
(e) The statement C = 25 wiil be executed only if both the conditions are True.

ix. Which of the following is/are the correct way(s) to set a value 3.14 in a variable PI such that it can't be modifed?
(a) float PI = 3.14F;
(b) #define PI 3.14F;
(c) PI = 3.14F;
(d) const float PI;   PI = 3.14F;
(e) const float PI = 3.14F;

x. Which of the following is/are the correct way(s) to initialize the variables m and n to a value 5 each?
(a) int m = n = 5;
(b) int i, j = 5;
(c) int m = 5, n = 5;
(d) int m = 5; int n = 5;
(e) int m, n; m = 5: n = 5;

#35 State True (T) or False (F) for each of the following statements:

i. Variables cannot be used as values of the case statements in a switch construct.
ii. The switch statement can include any number of case instances with two cases having the same value.
iii. We can assign values of any type to variables of type **object.**
iv. When a variable of a value type is converted to object, it is said to be boxed.
v. All value types are derived implicitly from *System.ValueType* class.
vi. Decimal data type has a size of 16 bytes.
vii. Long is an 8-byte integer.
viii. Widening conversions occur automatically.
ix. Information is never lost during a narrowing conversion.
x. The byte data type does not store a sign.
xi. Garbage collector can be used to remove unused references from the managed heap.
xii. CLR provides core services such as memory management, thread management, and remoting.
xiii. CLR enforces strict type safety.
xiv. CLR provides garbage collection services.
xv. The .Net Framework provides a code-execution environment that minimizes software deployment and versioning conflicts.

GLOSSARY

Abstract Class — It acts as the basis or foundation for creating new classes; its instances cannot be created; it is usually the root for the class hierarchy. An *abstract class* contains a *virtual method,* and whence, cannot be instantiated.

Base Class — Also *Super Class*; new classes can be created from it.

CLR — *Common Language Runtime*. CLR is the s ystem that manages the execution of C# programs. It is part of the *.NET Framework* that enables programs to be portable, supports mixed-language programming as well as provides for secure execution besides other benefits.

CLS — *Common Language Specification*. CLS describes a set of characteristics that different *.NET* compatible languages have in common. If C# code is to be used by other programs written in different languages, then, it must conform to CLS for maximum usability.

Class — It unites data and the code/methods acting upon the data; it is the basic language construct in C# for creating user-defined data types.

Constructor — It is a method with the same name as its class. It is invoked automatically , by dcfault, when an instance of a class i.e., an object is created. However, the user can define his own constructors as well to instantiate an object of the class.

CTS — *Common Type System*. CTS defines the rules concerning data types. CLS includes a subset of CTS. C# supports both CLS and CTS.

Data Hiding It means that the implementation details are hidden from the user by providing a suitable interface.

Data Member A variable declared in its class definition.

Default Parameter A parameter whose value is already provided for at the time of method declaration and this value is used by default if the corresponding actual parameter is missing at the time of the method call.

Derived Class A class that inherits properties/attributes from a base class.

Destructor In C#, it is possible to define a method that shall get invoked just before the object's final *destruction* by the *garbage collector*. This method is known as the *destructor* and it can be used to ensure that an *object* gets destroyed cleanly. A *destructor* in C#, as in C++, is declarted exactly like a *constructor* but is prefixed by the tilde ~ character. It has no return type and takes no arguments. However, unlike *destructors* in C++, which are called when an *object* goes out of scope, a *destructor* in C# is called just before *garbage collection*. This implies that we can never know when exactly/precisely a *destructor* will get executed or it may not even be invoked at all in case the program terminates before *garbage collection* takes place.

Dynamic Allocation In C#, objects are *dynamically allocated* from a pool of free memory using the *new* operator.

Dynamic Binding Also known as *run-time or late binding* as it postpones the binding of the method call till run-time.

Early Binding Also known as *static or compile-time binding* as in this case, the method call is bound at compile-time.

Encapsulation It means binding of the code and the data into a single unit free from external interference. This concept is achieved by means of the *class* mechanism.

Exception An unusual but predictable abnormal condition in a program used to notify the error to the user and avoid disruption of the running program.

Exception Handling It is the means by which the actual notification is done to make the user aware of the *exception* and avoid abnormal program termination.

Extensibility Through *abstract classes* and *inheritance*, we can extend the *functionality* of the existing software; this is often referred to as *extensibility*.

Garbage Collection In C#, memory is dynamically allocated using the *new* operator. However, *new* can fail as there might not be sufficient memory to allocate/create the desired object. For this reason, there is a need to recover free memory from unused objects. In languages like C++, recovery of \previously allocated memory is handled manually using the d*elete* operator. But, C# uses a more sophisticated approach, viz. *Garbage Collection.* C#'s *garbage collection* system reclaims memory automatically without any programmer interference. When no references to an object exist, the memory occupied by that object is eventually released and collected, and it becomesavailable for subsequent reallocation. However, there is a caveat; that is, it is not known exactly when *garbage collection* shall take place.

Generics It is a technique for defining software components that have more than one interpretation depending on the parameters' data type. It allows the declaration of data items without specifying their exact data type. These data types are resolved at the time of their actual usage at run-time.

Inheritance It involves derivation of new classes from existing ones thus, enabling the creation of an hierarchy of classes *simulating* the real world. This phenomenon enables *reuse* of existing code and elimination of tedious repetitive work.

Instance A variable or an object of a class is referred to as an *instance* of that class.

JIT *Just-In-Time*. MSIL is translated into executable code by the JIT compiler. When a C# program is executed, the CLR activates the JIT compiler, which, in turn, converts MSIL into native code on demand as each part of the program is required. In this way, the C# program, in essence, executes as native code although it is initially complied into MSIL.

Member Data and methods defined within a class are called its *members*. Also, *see* Private/Protected/Public Members.

Message Passing A *message* is a request sent to an object; *message passing* is the process of invoking an operation on an object.

Method Overloading Methods having the same name but differing in the number of parameters or their data types.

MSIL *Microsoft Intermediate Language*. MSIL provides a portable assembly language. When a C# program is compiled by the compiler, the output is not executable code; it is, instead, a file containing a special kind of pseudocode called MSIL. Thus, MSIL defines a set of portable instructions that are independent of any particular CPU. CLR converts this intermediate code into executable code when the program is actually run.

Namespace In C#, a *namespace* defines a declarative region. Through the use of namespaces, one set of names can be kept separate from another. Thus, names declared in one *namespace* will not come into conflict with names declared in a different *namespace*. The default *namespace* used by all C# programs is *System*. This feature is especially useful when a group of programmers is working on the same project as in such a case, each programmer can have his own *namespace*.

.NET Class Library The *.NET class library* gives the C# program access to the *.NET Framework* run-time environment. The C# environment as a totality is a combination of the C# language itself, plus the *.NET standard classes*. In fact, the C# environment relies on the *.NET Framework class library* to provide support for such varied items/things such as Input/Output, String handling, Networking, GUI's, and so on.

.NET Framework C# has a special relationship with its run-time environment, viz. the *.NET Framework*. The *.NET Framework* defines an environment that supports the development and execution of highly distributed, component-based applications. As it relates to C#, the *.NET Framework* defines two extremely important entities, first of which is the CLR while the second is the *.NET class library*. Since C#, by itself, uses the *.NET Framework class library*, all C# programs are, by itself, portable to all *.NET* environments.

new The *new* operator allocates memory at run-time (this is referred to as *dynamic allocation* of memory) for an object and returns a reference to it. This reference is then stored in a variable. Thus, in C#, all *class objects* must be *dynamically allocated* and *new* can be used to create an object of any *class type*. In case *new* fails to allocate memory for an object due to lack of sufficient available space/memory, a run-time *exception* occurs. As a point of interest, in C#, *new* can be used with *value types* as well.

Object An *instance* of a class is called an *object* or a variable of that class. This is much nearer the real-world entity than the *abstract* concept of a *class*.

OO *Object-Oriented.*

OOD *Object-Oriented Design.*

OOP *Object-Oriented Programming.*

Operator Overloading The same *operator* can be used for carrying out different operations.

Pass by Reference In this case, the *address* of an actual parameter is *implicitly* passed to a method.

Pass by Value A *copy* of the actual parameter is passed to the method in this case.

Polymorphism It allows for one name/*interface*, many operations/*methods*. In C#, it is achieved by means of *method overloading*, *operator overloading* and *dynamic method dispatch* including *virtual methods* and *overriding*..

Private/Protected/Public Members A class member accessible only to other members of the class is called a *private member*; a class member with the same access characteristics as the *private* member except that it is inheritable is called a *protected member*; finally, a class member accessible both within and outside its class is called a *public member.*

Reusability In C#, *reuse* of code is achieved by the concept of *class* hierarchy/*mechanism.*

Scope The part of code where a variable is visible is called its *scope*.

Static Member A *static member* of a class is shared by all the instances of that class.

Stream C# programs perform *Input/Output* through streams. A *stream* is an abstraction that either produces or consumes information. For example, there are byte, character, and binary *streams*. In C#, there are three pre-defined *streams* as well called *Console.In*, *Console.Out*, and *Console.Error*, respectively, which are available to all programs using the *System* namespace.

Structured Programming A top-down software development and programming technique that employs *modular* procedural decomposition into *subtasks*. This is the traditional style of *programming* just in contrast to *Object-Oriented Programming*.

Subclass *See* Derived Class.

Super Class *See* Base Class.

System *System* is the *namespace* used by all C# programs; *System* is the *namespace* reserved for items associated with the *.NET Framework class library*, which is, infact, the library used by C#.

this When a method is invoked, it is implicitly passed an argument which is a reference to the calling *object* and this reference is referred to as "*this*".

Virtual Base Class A base class that gets inherited to a derived class more than once.

Virtual Method It is actually a member method of a base class prefixed with the keyword virtual and is redefined in one or more derived classes. Each derived class can have its own version of the *virtual method.* When a *virtual method* is called through a base class reference, C# decides at run-time as to which version of the *virtual method* to call depending upon the type of the *object* referred to by the reference.

INDEX

Learning ASP.Net 4.0

Ramesh Bangia

CONTENTS OF THE BOOK

- **Introduction to ASP.NET 4.0**
- **Understanding the Standard Controls**
- **Using the Navigation Controls**
- **Using Validation Controls**
- **Designing Web Sites with Themes**
- **Overview of Data Access**
- **Questions & Answers**

Pages- 232 **ISBN- 978-93-81068-45-8** **Price- INR 160.00**